GARY
MARCUS
WAS RIGHT

One Neuroscientist's War Against
the Trillion-Dollar AI Hype Machine

Daniel Vincent Kramer

"In the 2010s, symbol manipulation was a dirty word among deep learning proponents;

in the 2020s, understanding where it comes from should be our top priority."

— Gary Marcus

CONTENTS

PART I

The Gathering Storm

Chapter 1

In an age of AI overdrive

The very air, it seems, vibrates with it. Not a visible shimmer, not an audible tremor, but a more subtle, pervasive energy, an almost tactile hum that resonates not just in the sterile, climate-controlled server rooms where silicon brains are nurtured, but in the messy, unpredictable, gloriously human spaces of our daily lives. It's a feeling, an almost primal sense of standing on the precipice, peering into a future that is rapidly, irrevocably, algorithmically being constructed. This is the age of AI overdrive, and it is an era defined by a potent cocktail of breathless anticipation, audacious trillion-dollar dreams, and a growing, though often whispered, undercurrent of unease, a sense that perhaps we are hurtling forward faster than wisdom dictates, faster than understanding allows.

Walk down any bustling city street, from Tokyo's neon-drenched Shinjuku to New York's perpetually frantic Times Square, and you are immediately immersed in the visual and auditory cacophony of this AI frenzy. Towering digital billboards, once hawking luxury brands and blockbuster movies, now flash slick, futuristic interfaces, promising AI-powered solutions to every conceivable problem, from optimizing traffic flow to predicting stock market fluctuations. Television commercials, during prime-time slots once reserved for soap operas and sitcoms, now showcase utopian visions of AI-augmented living, families effortlessly navigating smart homes that anticipate their every whim, doctors diagnosing diseases with superhuman accuracy, and artists creating masterpieces with the assistance of intelligent algorithms. Radio ads, sandwiched between pop songs and news bulletins, tout AI-driven investment platforms, promising effortless wealth generation through the seemingly magical power of algorithmic wizardry, whispering temptations of early retirement and financial freedom fueled by the relentless march of machine intelligence.

Open your laptop, unlock your smartphone, and you are instantly bombarded with a relentless barrage of AI-related content, a digital deluge of news, articles, blog posts, and social media pronouncements. Push notifications scream about the latest AI breakthroughs, the newest chatbot sensation, the most recent billion-dollar investment in an AI startup. News aggregators curate AI headlines with an almost obsessive zeal, ensuring that the topic dominates your digital consciousness. Social media feeds are saturated with AI-generated images, AI-composed music, AI-written poems, all presented as evidence of a burgeoning technological singularity, a moment when machines transcend human creativity and intellect.

Scroll through Twitter, now X, and the digital town square is effectively, and often acrimoniously, commandeered by the AI discourse. Elon Musk, in his characteristic style of hyperbole and alarmism, tweets about the existential risks of unchecked Artificial General Intelligence, painting dystopian scenarios of rogue AI systems turning against humanity, while simultaneously, and somewhat paradoxically, promising to build the most advanced AI models at Tesla and his newly formed xAI venture, seemingly undeterred by the very risks he so vociferously warns against. Sam Altman, the aforementioned CEO of OpenAI, the architect of ChatGPT and the poster-child of the current AI boom, holds court in seemingly every podcast and interview forum imaginable, dispensing pronouncements on the coming age of AGI with an almost messianic fervor, his words treated as prophecies by a tech-hungry media and an investment-thirsty market. Venture capitalists, their Twitter profiles gleaming with the blue checkmarks of digital influence and the self-assured pronouncements of Silicon Valley oracles, endlessly retweet articles about AI unicorns, the next wave of disruptive innovation, and the inevitable trillion-dollar windfall awaiting those prescient enough to invest wisely – and, crucially, early.

Eavesdrop on conversations in cafes, on crowded public transport, even at intimate family gatherings, and you'll inevitably hear it: the hushed tones of speculation, the excited pronouncements of fervent believers, the anxious murmurs of skeptical doubters.

"Have you tried ChatGPT?" has become a ubiquitous icebreaker, a new social ritual in a world suddenly confronted with the implications of readily accessible, and surprisingly articulate, artificial intelligence. "Is AI going to take my job?" is no longer a hypothetical fear relegated to the fringes of science fiction or dystopian novels; it's a genuine, gnawing anxiety in the minds of millions across the professional spectrum, from writers and programmers suddenly facing algorithmic competition, to truck drivers and customer service representatives nervously eyeing the specter of autonomous automation. "Will AI save humanity, or ultimately destroy it?" is debated with increasing urgency, no longer confined to academic philosophy seminars or late-night science fiction forums, but permeating everyday conversations, reflecting a profound and perhaps unprecedented shift in our collective consciousness, a collective grappling with a technology that promises both salvation and potential annihilation.

This is not merely technological progress; it is, in its scope and cultural impact, a full-blown cultural earthquake. The AI tsunami has not just lapped at the shores of our civilization; it has crashed over us, reshaping the landscape of our economy, our media, our social interactions, and our very understanding of what it means to be human. It's a world drowning in pronouncements of technological revolution, fervent declarations of algorithmic inevitability, and extravagant promises of a near future where intelligent machines not only seamlessly augment human capabilities but potentially surpass and even fundamentally supplant them in domains once considered uniquely, inviolably human.

Consider the headlines themselves, those carefully crafted pronouncements designed to capture attention and shape narratives. They aren't simply reporting on the advancements in AI; they are actively constructing the very fabric of the hype, deliberately amplifying the frenzy, and meticulously shaping public perception to align with a pre-determined narrative of technological triumph and inevitable transformation. "ChatGPT is a Giant Leap for Artificial Intelligence, and Maybe Humanity," proclaimed The New York Times breathlessly, not just assessing a new technology, but framing a large language model, a sophisticated statistical parrot at its core, as a pivotal moment in the trajectory of human civilization itself. "The AI Revolution Is Here. Get Ready," warned Wired, not as a cautious, balanced observation, but as an urgent, almost militaristic directive, implying a future already preordained, technologically deterministic, and utterly unavoidable, demanding immediate and unquestioning compliance. "Google CEO Sundar Pichai Says AI Is More Profound Than Fire, Electricity, or the Internet," declared Time Magazine, in a headline that bordered on the absurd, elevating artificial intelligence to a civilizational paradigm shift dwarfing even the most transformative technologies in human history, technologies that fundamentally reshaped our world in ways that current AI, in its nascent stage, can only dream of emulating. These aren't nuanced analyses, carefully considered assessments, or balanced journalistic accounts; they are clarion calls, heralding the dawn of a new technological age, an era defined, inevitably, overwhelmingly, and perhaps even dangerously, by the ascendance of artificial intelligence.

And the pronouncements emanating from the tech oracles themselves? Even more hyperbolic, even more messianic in their tone, bordering on the religiously fervent. Sam Altman, in his now-infamous series of public pronouncements, didn't just cautiously allude to AI's potential for societal benefit; he spoke of AI as a quasi-divine force, a technological messiah capable of solving humanity's most intractable problems, almost as a benevolent savior descending from the digital heavens. "I think we're going to have AGI, artificial general intelligence, in the relatively near future," he declared in a widely disseminated podcast interview, with an unwavering air of absolute inevitability, as if AGI were a predetermined destination on a technological roadmap, not a highly speculative and deeply uncertain research endeavor. "And I think that's going to be the most important, best technology humanity has ever created," he continued, not just praising AI, but placing it at the apex of human invention, surpassing the printing press, the scientific method, and the very concept of democracy in its purported significance. He didn't stop there, content with mere hyperbole; he escalated to outright fantastical pronouncements. "I think AI can solve climate change," he asserted with remarkable certainty, as if algorithmic solutions were a readily available magic bullet, capable of effortlessly resolving a complex, multifaceted global crisis involving political will, economic structures, and fundamental behavioral shifts. "I think AI can cure cancer," he continued, further blurring the lines between technological aspiration and medical miracle, as if decades of painstaking scientific research, biological complexity, and ethical considerations could be simply algorithmically bypassed by the advent of sufficiently advanced AI. These weren't just cautious predictions based on empirical evidence; they were fervent promises, delivered with the unwavering confidence of someone not just holding the keys to a technological utopia, but actively constructing it in real-time, brick by algorithmic brick.

Venture capitalists, ever the pragmatic profiteers of technological fervor, translated this messianic vision into the cold, hard, and ultimately quantifiable language of finance. "AI is the biggest investment opportunity of our lifetime," declared Bill Gurley of Benchmark Capital, a Silicon Valley titan, in a widely circulated blog post that served as a siren call to investors worldwide, framing AI not just as a technology, but as the ultimate engine of wealth creation in the 21st century. "We are entering the AI decade," proclaimed Mary Meeker of BOND Capital, another influential voice in the VC world, in her annual, highly anticipated Internet Trends report, presented not as a speculative investment thesis, but as an undeniable economic forecast, a technological inevitability that demanded immediate financial participation. "Every company will be an AI company," became a ubiquitous mantra, repeated ad nauseam at tech conferences, investor summits, and corporate strategy sessions, transforming AI from a potentially useful technology into a mandatory business imperative, a prerequisite for survival in the relentlessly competitive landscape of the modern economy. The numbers themselves, the raw data of investment and projected growth, became an integral part of the hype narrative, weaponized as irrefutable evidence of AI's imminent economic dominance: trillions of dollars in projected market capitalization, billions of dollars in venture funding relentlessly flowing into the sector, exponential growth curves presented not as optimistic projections, but as irrefutable visual representations of an impending gold rush, a technological Klondike promising untold riches to those who staked their claim early and aggressively.

And then there are the meticulously crafted visual spectacles, the carefully curated demonstrations, the strategically released videos all meticulously designed not just to inform, but to dazzle, to inspire awe, to instill a sense of wonder, and ultimately, to solidify the narrative of AI's almost magical capabilities. Boston Dynamics robots, once clumsy prototypes confined to the sterile environments of laboratory settings, now performing parkour with an unnerving, almost balletic agility, showcased in viral videos that deliberately blur the lines between cutting-edge technology and captivating science fiction, presented as harbingers of a robotic future already upon us. AI image generators like DALL-E 2 and Midjourney, capable of conjuring photorealistic images of almost anything imaginable from simple text prompts, demonstrating an almost supernatural, seemingly effortless ability to create visual realities ex nihilo, to conjure entire worlds and breathtaking scenes out of thin air, fueled by nothing more than lines of code and vast datasets. Deepfake videos, increasingly indistinguishable from reality to the untrained eye, blurring the lines between authentic and fabricated, between truth and illusion, raising both intense fascination and profound alarm about the potential for AI-driven manipulation, misinformation, and the erosion of trust in visual media itself. These visual showcases, often presented without crucial context, critical analysis, or caveats about limitations and potential biases, further fuel the pervasive perception of AI as a force of almost limitless power, boundless potential, and an almost inevitable trajectory towards technological omnipotence.

But beneath the dazzling surface of this overwhelming, meticulously constructed hype, beneath the breathless pronouncements and the trillion-dollar dreams, a disquieting, persistent question lingers, a nagging doubt that refuses to be entirely silenced by the roar of the AI engine: Is the reality of current AI technology truly living up to the extravagant promises being made on its behalf? Is this unprecedented trillion-dollar frenzy, this global obsession, truly built upon solid algorithmic foundations, or is it, as a growing chorus of skeptical voices suggests, a precarious house of cards, teetering precariously on overblown claims, carefully constructed illusions, and a generous dose of wishful thinking? Are we, in this age of AI overdrive, genuinely witnessing a transformative technological revolution, a fundamental paradigm shift in human history, or are we, perhaps more cynically, simply experiencing a masterful, technologically sophisticated reinvention of age-old hype cycles, amplified by the echo chambers of social media, the insatiable appetite of the 24/7 news cycle, and the ever-present allure of quick riches and disruptive innovation, regardless of its actual substance or long-term societal impact?

The answer, as this book will meticulously and rigorously argue, is decidedly more nuanced, far more complex, and ultimately, far more concerning than the relentlessly optimistic, and often deliberately misleading, pronouncements of the well-oiled AI hype machine would have you believe. While current AI technologies, particularly within the dominant paradigm of deep learning, have undeniably achieved impressive feats in narrowly defined domains, demonstrating remarkable proficiency in tasks like image recognition, language translation, and game playing, they are fundamentally, qualitatively different from the kind of general, flexible, and truly human-like intelligence that is being so loudly, so confidently, and so repeatedly proclaimed as not just imminent, but virtually already upon us. The gap between the seductive promise and the often-underwhelming reality of current AI is vast, a chasm of understanding and capability that is being systematically, and often quite deliberately, obscured by the very architects of the AI hype, for reasons that are complexly intertwined with economic imperatives, ideological agendas, and a powerful, almost irresistible, allure of technological utopianism. And understanding the true nature of this gap, dissecting the illusions, and exposing the mechanisms of the hype machine is not just an academic exercise; it is, in this age of AI overdrive, a crucial and urgent necessity.

And that, precisely, is where the indispensable voice of Gary Marcus enters the fray.

In this age of AI overdrive, amidst the deafening, often intellectually suffocating roar of hype, hyperbole, and uncritical enthusiasm, a clear, reasoned, scientifically grounded voice is not merely welcome; it is desperately, urgently needed. A voice that is not swept away by the currents of technological utopianism, a voice that is grounded in scientific rigor, tempered by decades of hands-on experience, and, crucially, unafraid to challenge the prevailing narratives, no matter how powerful, how pervasive, or how deeply entrenched they may have become. That voice, the voice of clarity, reason, and unflinching intellectual honesty in the age of AI overdrive, is Gary Marcus.

Marcus is emphatically not a Luddite, not a technophobe, not someone who reflexively dismisses the genuine potential of artificial intelligence. Far from it. He is, in fact, a highly respected neuroscientist, a distinguished cognitive scientist, a bestselling author whose work has illuminated the complexities of the human mind, and, perhaps most pertinently, a seasoned entrepreneur who has actively participated in the AI space, founding companies and grappling firsthand with the practical realities and inherent limitations of AI development. He understands the underlying technology intimately, perhaps more deeply, more fundamentally, and certainly more critically than many of the CEOs, venture capitalists, and media pundits who are currently driving the AI hype train at breakneck speed. His skepticism, therefore, is not born of ignorance, technological illiteracy, or a reactionary resistance to progress; it is, instead, a product of profound knowledge, rigorous scientific training, and a clear-eyed, unflinching assessment of the current state of the field, unclouded by wishful thinking or the siren song of technological utopianism.

Indeed, Marcus's critique is not just valuable in this age of AI overdrive; it is, in its intellectual rigor and unwavering commitment to scientific truth, absolutely essential. He stands as the indispensable intellectual antidote to the pervasive AI hype pandemic, the calm, reasoned, and scientifically grounded voice of sanity in the increasingly frenetic and often irrational AI cacophony. He possesses a rare and invaluable ability to cut through the deafening noise, to meticulously dismantle the meticulously constructed illusions, and to fearlessly expose the fundamental flaws lurking beneath the glittering surface of the emperor's new algorithms. He dares to ask the uncomfortable questions that others, often intimidated by the powerful currents of hype or blinded by the allure of technological progress, are simply too afraid, or too financially incentivized, to voice, challenging the powerful vested interests and deeply entrenched ideological agendas that are collectively driving the AI hype machine forward at an increasingly reckless pace.

Consider, for a moment, this crucial point: while the vast majority of the global media, the tech industry, and a significant portion of the public were collectively, and somewhat uncritically, losing their collective minds over the launch of ChatGPT, hailing it as a sentient oracle, a harbinger of AGI, and a transformative technological leap for humanity, Marcus was calmly, methodically, and witheringly dissecting its fundamental limitations, its inherent flaws, and its profound disconnect from genuine human-level intelligence. In a series of meticulously argued blog posts, incisive articles, and sharply critical interviews, he pointed out the Emperor's New Algorithms for precisely what they were: statistically impressive, undeniably fluent in generating human-like text, and capable of performing certain narrow tasks with remarkable proficiency, yes, but fundamentally lacking in genuine common sense, prone to generating confident hallucinations, and utterly incapable of exhibiting true understanding or engaging in meaningful reasoning. He didn't just dismiss ChatGPT as overhyped; crucially, he meticulously explained why it was fundamentally flawed, grounding his critique not in vague intuition or knee-jerk skepticism, but in well-established scientific principles, robust cognitive realities, and a deep understanding of the underlying limitations of the deep learning paradigm. And, crucially, he didn't just offer critique, content with simply pointing out the flaws; he consistently offered concrete, constructive alternatives, advocating for a fundamentally different path forward for artificial intelligence, a path rooted in neuro-symbolic approaches, hybrid architectures, and a far more nuanced and scientifically grounded understanding of the true nature of human intelligence itself.

This unwavering commitment to critical analysis and scientifically grounded skepticism is not a recent intellectual conversion for Marcus, not a knee-jerk reaction to the current wave of AI hype. His deeply informed skepticism about the recurring cycles of AI over-promise and under-delivery is, in fact, a long-standing and remarkably consistent thread that runs throughout his entire intellectual journey, a defining characteristic of his approach to both science and technology. Years, even decades, before the current deep learning boom and the subsequent explosion of AI hype, in his critically acclaimed and intellectually prescient book, Kluge: The Haphazard Construction of the Human Mind, published in 2008, Marcus challenged simplistic, overly optimistic, and often technologically deterministic views of intelligence, arguing persuasively that even human intelligence, the gold standard against which artificial intelligence is inevitably measured, is not a perfectly engineered, elegantly designed system, but rather a "kluge" – a messy, ad-hoc, cobbled-together, but ultimately remarkably functional contraption, a product of evolutionary tinkering and biological contingency, not algorithmic perfection. He demonstrated a profound early understanding of the inherent complexities and fundamental limitations of intelligence, both biological and artificial, long before the current hype cycle even began to gather momentum, his insights foreshadowing many of the limitations now being exposed in the wake of the deep learning revolution.

In his subsequent book, Guitar Zero: The New Musician and the Science of Learning, published in 2012, Marcus further explored the intricate and often counterintuitive processes of skill acquisition, delving into the complexities of human learning, demonstrating the profound challenges involved in mastering even seemingly simple human abilities, challenges that current AI systems, despite their impressive statistical prowess, are still far from overcoming, highlighting the vast gulf between algorithmic mimicry and genuine human expertise. And in his most recent and perhaps most directly relevant work, Rebooting AI: Building Artificial Intelligence We Can Trust, co-authored with the esteemed computer scientist Ernest Davis and published in 2019, Marcus laid out a comprehensive and intellectually devastating critique of the now-dominant deep learning monoculture within the AI field, systematically dismantling its core assumptions, exposing its fundamental limitations, and presenting a compelling, scientifically grounded case for neuro-symbolic AI, hybrid architectures, and a fundamentally different, more knowledge-rich, and reasoning-centric approach as a more promising and ultimately more responsible path forward for the future of artificial intelligence.

Gary Marcus, therefore, is not merely a naysayer, not just a professional skeptic, not simply a critic content with tearing down existing paradigms. He is, in the truest sense of the word, a visionary, albeit one who possesses the rare and invaluable ability to see with exceptional clarity and intellectual precision, not through the distorting, rose-tinted glasses of technological hype and utopian fantasy. He is not just meticulously tearing down the often-illusory edifice of AI hype; he is, simultaneously and more importantly, actively building a robust, scientifically grounded, and ethically responsible bridge towards a more realistic, more beneficial, and ultimately more intelligent AI future. He is, in essence, the pragmatic architect of a better future for artificial intelligence, a future that is firmly grounded in genuine understanding, robust reasoning capabilities, and common sense, not just in the seductive, but ultimately superficial, statistical mimicry of human intelligence.

This book, therefore, is not solely, or even primarily, about Gary Marcus's often-incisive and always intellectually rigorous critique of the pervasive AI hype machine. It is, more fundamentally, about understanding why his critique is so profoundly vital, so urgently timely, and so very important in this increasingly breathless and often intellectually impoverished age of AI overdrive. It is about meticulously dismantling the often-fantastical illusions of the trillion-dollar AI fairy tales, systematically dissecting the gap between the seductive promise and the often-disappointing reality of current AI capabilities, and rigorously revealing the underlying mechanisms of the vast AI hype machine, uncovering the powerful economic incentives, deeply ingrained ideological agendas, and pervasive cultural narratives that collectively drive it forward, often at the expense of genuine scientific progress and responsible technological innovation. And, perhaps most importantly, it is about actively embracing and amplifying Gary Marcus's compelling vision for a more responsible and legitimate artificial intelligence, a vision that offers a clear and scientifically grounded path forward, beyond the seductive allure of hype, towards a future where AI truly serves humanity, augmenting our intellect, enhancing our lives, and contributing to a more fair and just world, rather than simply reinforcing existing inequalities, amplifying misinformation, and further concentrating power in the hands of a select few tech giants. And that, ultimately, is a future worth fighting for, a future that begins with dismantling the hype and embracing the clear-eyed, scientifically grounded, and profoundly necessary voice of Gary Marcus.

Over the following chapters, we will embark on a detailed and rigorous intellectual journey, delving deep into Gary Marcus's core and often-prescient critiques of the dominant trends in current AI, systematically dissecting the fundamental flaws inherent in the deep learning paradigm, meticulously exposing the pervasive and often dangerous hallucination problem plaguing large language models, and thoroughly debunking the often-fantastical and unrealistic AGI dreams and delusions that fuel so much of the current AI hype cycle. We will not shy away from naming names, critically examining the specific roles of key figures and influential organizations, meticulously examining the often-questionable practices of individuals like Sam Altman and organizations like OpenAI, Dario Amodei and Anthropic, and Satya Nadella and Microsoft in perpetuating the AI hype machine and shaping the often-distorted narrative surrounding artificial intelligence. We will then expand our analysis to explore the broader, more complex ecosystem of AI hype, from the often-uncritical pronouncements of Google and Meta, to the relentless financial pressures exerted by venture capitalists, and the often-complicit role played by a media landscape eager for

14

sensationalism and easily swayed by technological utopianism, meticulously uncovering the complex web of economic incentives, ideological agendas, and self-reinforcing narratives that collectively fuel the AI frenzy and drive the self-perpetuating hype cycle.

But this book is emphatically not solely, or even primarily, a work of critique, content with simply dissecting and dismantling the illusions of AI hype. It is, equally importantly, a constructive endeavor, dedicated to building a more realistic and ultimately more promising vision for the future of artificial intelligence. We will therefore, in the latter sections of this book, thoroughly explore Marcus's proposed and increasingly compelling alternative: the neuro-symbolic bridge, a hybrid approach that offers a significantly more viable and scientifically grounded pathway towards building artificial intelligence that truly understands, genuinely reasons, and authentically thinks, moving beyond the statistical mimicry of current deep learning models and towards a more robust and human-like form of machine intelligence. We will meticulously examine his detailed vision for a more responsible, ethically grounded, and genuinely human-centered AI future, one that prioritizes robustness, inherent explainability, and tangible benefit to human society, moving beyond the narrow metrics of current benchmarks and towards a broader, more humanistic understanding of what constitutes true AI progress. And finally, in the concluding chapter, we will thoughtfully assess Gary Marcus's enduring intellectual legacy: is he ultimately destined to be the Cassandra of the AI age, his crucial warnings tragically unheeded until the consequences of unchecked hype become undeniable and potentially irreversible? Or can he, perhaps more hopefully, ultimately emerge as the architect of a better, more realistic, and more responsible future for artificial intelligence, his clear-sighted vision and scientifically grounded principles guiding us, finally, towards a more balanced, more beneficial, and ultimately more intelligent approach to navigating the complex and often perilous age of AI overdrive?

This book matters, quite simply, because the stakes involved are perhaps unprecedentedly high. The future trajectory of artificial intelligence, and indeed, the very nature of our increasingly symbiotic relationship with rapidly advancing technology, is being actively shaped right now, in this very moment, within this tumultuous age of AI overdrive. Navigating this complex, often bewildering, and potentially dangerous landscape with wisdom, foresight, and a commitment to responsible innovation requires not just technological prowess or financial investment, but clear, critical thinking, rigorous, evidence-based analysis, and, crucially, a willingness to bravely challenge the dominant narratives, to question the prevailing assumptions, and to resist the seductive allure of hype, no matter how powerful or pervasive it may become. And in that profoundly crucial, and increasingly urgent, endeavor, there is arguably no voice more essential, more intellectually insightful, and more needed than the clear, reasoned, and unflinchingly honest voice of Gary Marcus. It is, therefore, long past time to truly listen. It is time to genuinely understand. It is time to actively move beyond the seductive illusions of AI hype and towards the more challenging, but ultimately far more rewarding, path of real, responsible, and genuinely beneficial artificial intelligence progress. And this book, meticulously crafted and rigorously argued, is intended to serve as your essential guide on that absolutely critical intellectual and societal journey.

Chapter 2

The air may crackle with the excitement of AI, but beneath the surface buzz, a far more prosaic, yet immensely powerful, force is at play: cold, hard cash. The age of AI overdrive isn't just a technological phenomenon; it's fundamentally, and perhaps disturbingly, an economic one. It's fueled not just by genuine scientific breakthroughs, but by the relentless pursuit of profit, the siren song of trillion-dollar markets, and the intoxicating allure of becoming the next tech titan in a landscape constantly reshaped by disruptive innovation – or, more accurately, the promise of disruptive innovation. The dreams being spun in the AI age are not solely, or even primarily, about advancing human knowledge or solving humanity's grand challenges; they are, to a significant extent, trillion-dollar dreams, meticulously crafted narratives designed to attract investment, inflate valuations, and ultimately, to generate immense wealth for a select few players in the burgeoning AI ecosystem. And these trillion-dollar dreams, in turn, are propagated and amplified by a vast and intricate hype machine, a complex apparatus designed to transform often-incremental technological advancements into seemingly revolutionary breakthroughs, to convert nascent research prototypes into world-altering products, and to transmute the inherent uncertainties and limitations of current AI into unwavering promises of a technologically utopian future.

This hype machine, operating at full throttle in the age of AI overdrive, doesn't function through haphazard chance or spontaneous enthusiasm. It's a deliberately constructed, multi-layered, and highly effective apparatus, fueled by specific mechanisms, driven by clear economic incentives, and propagated through carefully crafted narratives, designed to transform the very real, but often limited, progress in artificial intelligence into something far grander, far more transformative, and far more lucrative than the underlying reality might actually warrant. To understand the AI hype machine, to dissect its inner workings, and to effectively counter its often-misleading narratives, it's essential to delve into its anatomy, to expose the key mechanisms through which it operates, and to understand the powerful forces that drive its relentless churn.

One of the most potent mechanisms in the AI hype machine is undoubtedly the venture capital hype multiplier. Venture capital, the lifeblood of Silicon Valley innovation, is not merely passive investment; it's an active engine of narrative creation, a powerful force that can transform promising startups into hyped-up unicorns, and nascent technologies into world-altering revolutions, almost overnight. VC firms, by their very nature, are incentivized to generate hype, to amplify buzz, and to create a sense of urgency around their portfolio companies, particularly in a sector as speculative and attention-grabbing as artificial intelligence. Their business model hinges on identifying and funding companies with the potential for exponential growth, for disrupting entire industries, and for achieving astronomical valuations – the so-called "unicorn" status that signifies a billion-dollar valuation and the promise of even greater future returns. This inherent pressure to identify and cultivate unicorns, combined with the intensely competitive landscape of venture capital, creates a powerful incentive to over-promise, to exaggerate potential, and to actively participate in the hype cycle surrounding emerging technologies like AI.

Consider the funding rounds for AI startups in recent years. They are not just large; they are, in many cases, astronomical, defying traditional metrics of valuation and profitability. OpenAI, even before ChatGPT became a household name, secured billions of dollars in funding from Microsoft and other investors, based largely on the promise of AGI and the potential of its large language models, despite the clear limitations and inherent flaws in the underlying technology. Anthropic, founded by former OpenAI researchers with a focus on "responsible AI," quickly raised hundreds of millions, and then billions, of dollars, again fueled by the narrative of ethical AI and the potential for their models to be safer and more beneficial than competitors, despite operating within the same fundamentally limited deep learning paradigm. AI chip companies like Nvidia have seen their stock prices skyrocket to unprecedented heights, not just based on current revenue and profitability, but on the future potential of AI to drive demand for their specialized hardware, fueled by the relentless hype surrounding AI's transformative impact across every sector.

These massive funding rounds are not simply passive investments; they are active accelerants of hype. VC firms, having poured vast sums of capital into AI startups, become deeply invested in ensuring their success, not just in terms of technological innovation, but crucially, in terms of market perception, media narrative, and overall hype generation. They actively promote their portfolio companies through media outreach, investor events, and carefully crafted "thought leadership" content, amplifying the buzz, exaggerating the potential, and creating a self-fulfilling prophecy of AI dominance and trillion-dollar market opportunities. The pressure on AI startups to deliver on these hyped expectations is immense, often leading to rushed product launches, exaggerated marketing claims, and a prioritization of short-term buzz over long-term sustainable innovation. The VC hype multiplier, in essence, transforms promising technologies into hyped commodities, fueling the AI frenzy and distorting the true trajectory of AI development, often prioritizing rapid market capitalization over genuine scientific progress and responsible societal impact.

Closely intertwined with the VC hype multiplier is the pervasive and equally powerful force of tech company marketing & PR. Tech companies, particularly the giants of Silicon Valley, are not just passive recipients of AI hype; they are active and sophisticated orchestrators of it, meticulously crafting narratives, strategically releasing information, and skillfully manipulating media cycles to amplify the buzz surrounding their AI products and initiatives. Marketing and public relations departments within these tech behemoths are not just tasked with promoting specific products; they are actively engaged in shaping the broader public perception of AI itself, creating a narrative of technological inevitability,

19

transformative potential, and, crucially, their own company's central role in leading this AI revolution.

Consider the product launches from OpenAI, Google, Microsoft, and Meta in the recent AI frenzy. They are not simply announcements of new technologies; they are meticulously staged media events, carefully choreographed to maximize hype, generate media attention, and create a perception of groundbreaking innovation, even when the underlying technology is often more incremental than revolutionary. OpenAI's launch of GPT-3, for example, was a masterclass in hype generation, deliberately released in a controlled and exclusive manner, with limited API access and carefully curated demos showcasing its most impressive, though often cherry-picked, capabilities. The media narrative surrounding GPT-3 was almost uniformly breathless and hyperbolic, portraying it as a near-AGI breakthrough, a technology capable of transforming everything from writing to coding to scientific research, despite its well-documented limitations and tendency to generate nonsensical or factually inaccurate text. Google's rushed launch of Bard, while ultimately backfiring due to a disastrous public demo, was nonetheless driven by a desperate need to counteract the ChatGPT hype and reclaim its perceived AI leadership, highlighting the intense competitive pressure and hype-driven decision-making within the tech giants. Microsoft's aggressive integration of OpenAI technology into Bing and its subsequent marketing blitz around the "new Bing AI" was another textbook example of hype amplification, directly leveraging the ChatGPT frenzy to position Bing as a revolutionary AI-powered search engine and challenge Google's long-standing search dominance, despite the obvious flaws and hallucination problems exhibited by the initial Bing AI demos.

Tech company marketing and PR strategies extend far beyond product launches, however. They involve a constant, ongoing effort to shape the narrative around AI, to control the flow of information, and to actively cultivate a perception of technological inevitability and transformative potential. This includes carefully crafted blog posts, selectively released research papers, strategically placed media interviews with company executives, and participation in industry events, all designed to reinforce the desired hype narrative and maintain a constant drumbeat of AI excitement. Buzzwords and jargon – "revolutionary," "transformative,"

"paradigm shift," "AGI," "sentient AI" – are liberally employed to create a sense of technological breakthrough and future disruption, even when the actual advancements are often incremental or remain largely in the realm of research prototypes. Emotionally charged narratives, portraying AI as a force for good, capable of solving humanity's grand challenges and ushering in a new era of technological prosperity, are meticulously constructed and widely disseminated, often downplaying or completely ignoring the potential risks, ethical concerns, and societal challenges associated with rapid AI development and deployment. Tech company marketing and PR, therefore, acts as a powerful and pervasive engine of AI hype, shaping public perception, influencing investor behavior, and driving the overall frenzy surrounding artificial intelligence, often at the expense of balanced reporting, critical analysis, and a realistic assessment of current AI capabilities and limitations.

Compounding the effects of VC hype and tech company marketing is the often-uncritical and frequently sensationalist role of media amplification. Mainstream media outlets, from traditional newspapers and television networks to online news platforms and social media channels, often act as willing and even enthusiastic amplifiers of AI hype, repeating tech company narratives, uncritically reporting on exaggerated claims, and prioritizing sensationalism and novelty over in-depth analysis and critical investigation. Media outlets, particularly in the fast-paced and click-driven digital landscape, are incentivized to chase trends, to amplify buzzworthy topics, and to prioritize attention-grabbing headlines over nuanced reporting and balanced perspectives. Artificial intelligence, with its inherent futuristic appeal, its promise of technological revolution, and its potential for both utopian salvation and dystopian destruction, is a topic perfectly tailored to capture media attention and generate clicks, views, and advertising revenue.

Consider the media coverage of ChatGPT's launch. While some outlets offered more balanced and critical perspectives, the overwhelming majority of media coverage was overwhelmingly positive and often uncritical, amplifying OpenAI's hype, exaggerating ChatGPT's capabilities, and portraying it as a revolutionary breakthrough on the path to AGI. Headlines screamed about ChatGPT "changing everything," "revolutionizing communication," and "threatening Google's search dominance," often repeating verbatim the marketing narratives disseminated by OpenAI and its investors. Television news segments showcased impressive, but often carefully selected, examples of ChatGPT's output, without adequately highlighting its limitations, hallucinations, or biases. Online articles breathlessly recounted user anecdotes and social media buzz, further amplifying the viral hype and creating a self-reinforcing cycle of media enthusiasm and public excitement. Skeptical voices, critical analyses, and expert opinions highlighting the limitations of ChatGPT and the broader deep learning paradigm were often marginalized or downplayed in the mainstream media narrative, drowned out by the louder and more sensationalist pronouncements of hype and technological utopianism.

This media amplification effect is not simply a passive reflection of public interest or technological advancement; it is an active and powerful force that directly contributes to the AI hype cycle. Media outlets, often lacking in-house expertise in AI and relying heavily on tech company press releases and marketing materials, become unwitting conduits for hype narratives, uncritically repeating exaggerated claims and contributing to the overall sense of urgency and inevitability surrounding AI. The pursuit of clicks and sensationalism, combined with the inherent media bias towards novelty and technological breakthrough narratives, creates a fertile ground for AI hype to flourish, often at the expense of balanced reporting, critical investigation, and a more nuanced public understanding of the true capabilities and limitations of current artificial intelligence technology. The media echo chamber, therefore, acts as a powerful amplifier of AI hype, further distorting public perception, influencing investor behavior, and contributing to the overall frenzy surrounding artificial intelligence, often at the expense of informed public discourse and responsible technological development.

A more subtle, yet increasingly pervasive mechanism in the AI hype machine is the strategic deployment of "AI ethics" as a hype shield. In an age increasingly attuned to ethical considerations and societal impacts of technology, tech companies and AI developers have become acutely aware of the need to address ethical concerns surrounding their AI products and initiatives. This has led to a proliferation of "AI ethics" frameworks, "responsible AI" principles, and corporate "ethics boards," seemingly designed to ensure that AI is developed and deployed in a responsible and ethical manner. However, in many cases, these "AI ethics" initiatives can also function as a subtle, yet highly effective, form of hype shield, allowing companies to project an image of ethical responsibility and deflect deeper scrutiny of their often-overhyped and potentially problematic AI technologies.

Consider the marketing narratives around "responsible AI" from companies like Anthropic and even OpenAI. While these companies genuinely may be making efforts to address certain ethical concerns, their emphasis on "responsible AI" also conveniently serves to differentiate them from competitors, attract ethically conscious investors and customers, and, crucially, to deflect more fundamental critiques of their underlying technology. Anthropic's "Constitutional AI" framework, for example, while presented as a novel approach to AI safety, can also be viewed as a marketing tool, allowing Anthropic to brand itself as the "ethical" alternative to OpenAI, even though their Claude model still operates within the same fundamental limitations of large language models and still exhibits many of the same flaws, including hallucinations and lack of common sense. Corporate "AI ethics boards," often composed of internal employees or closely affiliated external advisors, can similarly function as performative ethics, providing a veneer of ethical oversight without necessarily challenging the underlying hype cycle or fundamentally altering the direction of AI development. These initiatives often focus on relatively narrow ethical concerns, such as bias and fairness, while neglecting broader, more systemic ethical questions about the societal impact of AI, the concentration of power in the hands of a few tech giants, and the potential for AI to exacerbate existing inequalities or undermine democratic values.

The focus on "AI ethics," therefore, while seemingly a positive development, can also inadvertently contribute to the AI hype machine by providing a form of "ethical washing" for potentially problematic technologies. By emphasizing their commitment to ethical principles and responsible AI development, tech companies can create a perception of ethical soundness and deflect more critical scrutiny of their hype-driven narratives and often-exaggerated claims. The "AI ethics" discourse, in some instances, can become co-opted and weaponized as a marketing tool, allowing companies to project an image of social responsibility while simultaneously continuing to aggressively promote and deploy hyped AI technologies, potentially obscuring deeper ethical concerns and hindering more fundamental and critical discussions about the responsible future of artificial intelligence. "AI ethics as hype shield," therefore, represents a more subtle, but no less powerful, mechanism in the AI hype machine, adding a layer of ethical gloss to often-unrealistic and potentially problematic technological narratives, and further complicating the already challenging task of discerning genuine progress from carefully crafted illusions in the age of AI overdrive.

These mechanisms – the VC hype multiplier, tech company marketing & PR, media amplification, and "AI ethics as hype shield" – collectively form the anatomy of the AI hype machine, a complex and powerful apparatus designed to transform trillion-dollar dreams into perceived technological realities. But to truly understand the driving force behind this machine, to grasp the underlying motivations that propel its relentless operation, it's essential to delve into the economic incentives that fuel the AI frenzy, to examine the trillion-dollar dream itself, and to expose the powerful forces that drive the relentless pursuit of AI hype in the age of overdrive.

Having dissected the anatomy of the AI hype machine, exposing its key mechanisms and operational components, it becomes imperative to understand the very engine that drives its relentless churn, the fuel that powers its insatiable appetite for exaggeration and inflated expectations. And that engine, that fuel, is undeniably the trillion-dollar dream, the potent and almost irresistible economic incentives that lie at the very heart of the AI frenzy, transforming what might otherwise be a measured and scientifically driven technological evolution into a frenzied, often irrational, and hype-dominated gold rush. The trillion-dollar dream is not merely a metaphorical aspiration; it is a concrete, quantifiable, and immensely powerful economic force, driving investment decisions, shaping corporate strategies, influencing media narratives, and ultimately, distorting the very trajectory of AI development itself. To truly grasp the scale and scope of the AI hype machine, and to understand why it operates with such relentless intensity, it is essential to meticulously dissect these economic incentives, to expose the financial underpinnings of the AI frenzy, and to reveal how the promise of unimaginable wealth is driving the narrative of technological revolution, often at the expense of genuine progress, ethical considerations, and a balanced public understanding of artificial intelligence.

One of the most direct and potent manifestations of the trillion-dollar dream is the inflation of market capitalization, the almost magical ability of AI hype to directly translate into soaring stock prices and inflated valuations for tech companies, particularly those perceived to be at the forefront of the AI revolution. The stock market, that notoriously fickle and sentiment-driven barometer of economic activity, has become utterly captivated by the AI narrative, rewarding companies that aggressively embrace AI, loudly proclaim their AI ambitions, and strategically position themselves as leaders in the burgeoning AI landscape with dramatic surges in their market capitalization, often far exceeding any real increase in current revenue, profitability, or even tangible technological breakthroughs. The mere mention of AI in a company's earnings calls, product announcements, or strategic presentations can trigger immediate and significant stock price jumps, demonstrating the almost Pavlovian response of the market to the AI buzzwords and hype narratives.

Consider the meteoric rise of Nvidia, the semiconductor giant that has become the de facto hardware provider for the AI revolution. Nvidia's stock price has exploded in recent years, transforming it into a trillion-dollar company, not solely based on its existing gaming graphics business, but overwhelmingly driven by the perceived future demand for its specialized GPUs in training and deploying AI models, particularly large language models. The narrative surrounding Nvidia has become inextricably linked to the AI hype cycle, with each new AI breakthrough, each new large language model launch, each new AI funding round further fueling investor enthusiasm for Nvidia stock, as the company is perceived as the indispensable "picks and shovels" provider in the AI gold rush. Nvidia's market capitalization now dwarfs that of many established industrial giants with far larger current revenues and more diversified businesses, a testament to the sheer power of AI hype to inflate stock valuations based on future potential rather than present-day performance.

Similarly, Microsoft's stock price experienced a significant surge following its massive investment in OpenAI and its aggressive integration of ChatGPT technology into its product suite. While Microsoft is a vast and diversified company with numerous revenue streams beyond AI, the AI narrative surrounding its OpenAI partnership undeniably played a crucial role in boosting investor confidence and driving up its market capitalization. The perception that Microsoft was "winning" the AI arms race, that it was strategically positioned to capitalize on the transformative potential of AI, and that it had effectively challenged Google's long-standing dominance in search, all contributed to a significant increase in investor enthusiasm and a corresponding surge in Microsoft's stock price, further validating the trillion-dollar dream narrative.

Even companies with less direct AI revenue streams have benefited from the AI hype-induced market inflation. Google, despite its initial struggles to respond effectively to the ChatGPT challenge, has also seen its stock price buoyed by the overall AI frenzy, as investors anticipate its eventual recapture of AI leadership and its ability to monetize AI technologies across its vast ecosystem of products and services. Meta, despite its metaverse pivot and its own set of unique challenges, has also seen its stock price rebound, in part fueled by its own AI investments and its efforts to position itself as a player in the generative AI space, demonstrating the pervasive reach of AI hype across the entire tech landscape and its almost universal effect on inflating market capitalizations.

This inflation of market capitalization, driven by AI hype, is not just a superficial phenomenon; it has profound real-world consequences. It creates immense wealth for company shareholders, particularly early investors and executives, further incentivizing the promotion and perpetuation of the hype narrative. It allows companies to raise vast sums of capital at inflated valuations, fueling further investment in AI research, development, and, crucially, marketing and hype generation. It creates a self-reinforcing cycle, where rising stock prices validate the hype narratives, attract even more investors, further inflate valuations, and solidify the perception of AI as the ultimate driver of future economic growth and technological disruption. The trillion-dollar dream, therefore, is not just an abstract aspiration; it is a tangible, measurable, and immensely powerful economic force, directly manifested in inflated market capitalizations, driving the AI frenzy and further amplifying the hype cycle.

Beyond the direct inflation of market capitalization, the trillion-dollar dream also manifests itself in the often-manipulative and strategically deployed narrative of job displacement fear-mongering (and hype). The narrative that AI is poised to automate vast swathes of human labor, to displace millions of jobs across diverse industries, and to fundamentally reshape the future of work, is not simply a neutral observation or a scientifically grounded prediction; it is, to a significant extent, a deliberately constructed and strategically deployed hype narrative, designed to create a sense of urgency around AI adoption, to drive market demand for AI solutions, and, perhaps paradoxically, to further amplify the hype cycle itself. Fear of job displacement, while undoubtedly a legitimate and concerning societal issue in the age of automation, is also a powerful economic tool, strategically wielded to promote AI adoption and fuel the trillion-dollar dream.

Consider the numerous reports, studies, and media pronouncements predicting mass job losses due to AI automation in the near future. These predictions, often exaggerated and lacking in robust empirical evidence, nonetheless serve to create a pervasive sense of anxiety and urgency among businesses, governments, and individuals, fueling the perception that AI adoption is not merely an option, but an absolute necessity for survival in the increasingly automated economy. Businesses, fearing being "left behind" in the AI revolution and facing competitive pressures to automate and reduce labor costs, are increasingly investing in AI solutions, often driven more by fear of disruption than by a clear understanding of the actual return on investment or the benefits of current AI technologies. Governments, grappling with anxieties about future unemployment and economic competitiveness, are launching AI initiatives, investing in AI research, and promoting AI adoption across various sectors, often driven by a fear of falling behind in the global AI race and a desire to be seen as embracing the "future of work," even if the actual impact of AI on the labor market remains highly uncertain and contested. Individuals, bombarded with media narratives about AI-driven job displacement, are increasingly anxious about their future employability and the need to "reskill" and "upskill" for the AI age, further fueling the demand for AI-related education, training, and technological solutions.

This fear-mongering, while undoubtedly tapping into legitimate anxieties about automation and the future of work, also conveniently serves to amplify the AI hype cycle and drive the trillion-dollar dream. The narrative of inevitable job displacement creates a sense of urgency and inevitability around AI adoption, driving market demand for AI technologies, boosting investor confidence in AI companies, and further inflating the hype bubble. Tech companies marketing AI-driven automation solutions directly benefit from this fear-mongering, as businesses, driven by anxiety about job displacement, become more receptive to their sales pitches and more willing to invest in often-unproven and overhyped AI automation technologies. Venture capitalists investing in AI automation startups also benefit from this narrative, as the fear of job displacement further validates their investment thesis and attracts even more capital into the AI automation space. The media, predictably, amplifies the job displacement narrative, further fueling public anxiety and contributing to the overall hype cycle, often prioritizing sensationalism and clickbait headlines over nuanced reporting and evidence-based analysis of the complex and multifaceted issue of AI and the future of work. Job displacement fear-mongering, therefore, represents a potent and strategically deployed economic tool in the AI hype machine, driving market demand, fueling investment, and amplifying the trillion-dollar dream, often at the expense of a more balanced, nuanced, and ethically informed public discourse about the true impact of AI on the future of labor and society.

Another powerful economic incentive driving the AI hype cycle, and directly contributing to the trillion-dollar dream, is the strategically resurrected "AI Winter" ghost. The history of artificial intelligence is not a linear trajectory of uninterrupted progress; it is marked by periods of intense hype and over-promising followed by periods of disillusionment, funding droughts, and scientific stagnation – the so-called "AI Winters." The fear of repeating past AI Winters, of experiencing another period of disillusionment and funding collapse, serves as a potent motivator for current AI researchers, tech companies, and venture capitalists to actively perpetuate the hype cycle, to constantly over-promise and exaggerate progress, and to maintain a relentless drumbeat of AI excitement, even when faced with glaring limitations and unfulfilled expectations. The "AI Winter" ghost, in essence, acts as a powerful self-preservation mechanism for the AI hype machine, driving its relentless churn and ensuring that the trillion-dollar dream remains perpetually alive, even in the face of potential reality checks.

Consider the historical context of AI Winters. The first AI Winter in the 1970s was triggered by the over-promising and under-delivery of early symbolic AI systems, particularly expert systems, which failed to live up to the exaggerated expectations of their early proponents and ultimately led to a significant decline in funding and research interest. A second AI Winter occurred in the late 1980s and early 1990s, again fueled by disillusionment with expert systems and the lack of progress towards general artificial intelligence, leading to another period of funding scarcity and scientific stagnation. These historical experiences of AI Winters have left a deep scar on the AI community, creating a persistent fear of repeating past mistakes and experiencing another period of funding drought and scientific irrelevance.

This fear of another AI Winter, while understandable given the historical context of past cycles of hype and disillusionment, also ironically fuels the current AI hype cycle itself, creating a powerful incentive to constantly over-promise and maintain a relentless drumbeat of AI excitement, even when the underlying technological progress may not fully justify the level of hype being generated. Researchers, acutely aware of the historical vulnerability of AI funding to shifts in public and investor sentiment, feel pressured to constantly emphasize the transformative potential of their work, to exaggerate near-term progress, and to downplay any limitations or potential roadblocks, in order to maintain funding flows and avoid triggering another AI Winter. Tech companies, equally cognizant of the cyclical nature of tech investment and the potential for hype bubbles to burst, are incentivized to constantly market their AI products with maximum hype, to create a sense of urgency and inevitability around AI adoption, and to project an image of unstoppable technological momentum, in order to maintain investor confidence and prevent a potential market correction or a shift in investor focus away from AI. Venture capitalists, acutely aware of the boom-and-bust cycles that characterize the tech industry, are driven by a fear of being "left holding the bag" when the AI hype inevitably cools down, incentivizing them to invest aggressively in AI startups while the hype is still at its peak, and to actively promote and amplify the hype narrative in order to attract further investment and ensure lucrative exits before the potential AI Winter arrives.

The "AI Winter" ghost, therefore, paradoxically haunts the AI community and the broader AI ecosystem, not as a cautionary tale of past failures to be avoided, but as a powerful motivator to perpetuate the very hype cycle that could ultimately lead to another period of disillusionment and potential stagnation. The fear of funding droughts and scientific irrelevance drives researchers, companies, and investors to actively participate in and amplify the AI hype, creating a self-fulfilling prophecy where the very act of trying to prevent an AI Winter ironically fuels the unsustainable hype bubble that could eventually lead to its inevitable bursting. The trillion-dollar dream, therefore, is not just fueled by the allure of future riches, but also by the pervasive fear of repeating past failures, a fear that ironically perpetuates the very cycle of hype and over-expectation that history suggests is ultimately unsustainable and potentially damaging to the long-term progress of artificial intelligence.

Finally, and perhaps most insidiously, the trillion-dollar dream is powerfully driven by the intense competition for platform monopoly, the relentless race among tech giants to establish themselves as the dominant AI platform provider, to control the underlying infrastructure, the core algorithms, and the vast ecosystems that will power the AI-driven future. The platform economy, characterized by winner-take-all dynamics and network effects, creates an intensely competitive environment where companies are driven to achieve dominance, to establish themselves as indispensable gatekeepers, and to capture the lion's share of the immense economic value projected to be generated by artificial intelligence. The race for AI platform monopoly, therefore, represents another powerful economic incentive fueling the AI hype cycle, as tech giants aggressively compete to out-hype, out-market, and out-innovate each other in the quest for AI supremacy and the trillion-dollar prize that awaits the ultimate platform winner.

Consider the intense competition between Microsoft, Google, Amazon, and other tech giants to dominate the AI platform landscape. Microsoft's massive investment in OpenAI and its aggressive integration of OpenAI's models into Azure, Windows, and Office is not just about improving existing products; it is fundamentally about positioning Azure as the leading cloud platform for AI development and deployment, to capture the burgeoning market for AI infrastructure and services, and to challenge Amazon's long-standing dominance in the cloud computing space. Google's frantic response to ChatGPT and its rushed launch of Bard, while initially flawed, demonstrates its desperate determination to maintain its search dominance in the AI era, to prevent Microsoft from leveraging AI to disrupt its core search business, and to establish its own AI platform as the leading alternative to Azure. Amazon, already the dominant cloud provider, is aggressively investing in its own AI services, seeking to leverage its existing cloud infrastructure and vast customer base to become a major player in the AI platform race, and to prevent both Microsoft and Google from eclipsing its cloud dominance in the AI era. Meta, despite its metaverse distractions, is also actively investing in AI infrastructure and open-source AI models, seeking to maintain its relevance in the AI landscape, to potentially disrupt the cloud platform dominance of AWS, Azure, and GCP, and to carve out its own niche in the evolving AI platform ecosystem.

This intense competition for AI platform monopoly inevitably fuels the AI hype cycle, as each tech giant aggressively markets its AI capabilities, exaggerates its technological advantages, and contributes to the overall narrative of AI inevitability and transformative potential, in order to attract developers, customers, and, crucially, investors to its own platform ecosystem. Marketing materials from these tech giants are replete with hype-laden pronouncements about their AI leadership, their revolutionary AI technologies, and the unparalleled benefits of building on their AI platforms, all designed to create a perception of platform superiority and to drive adoption of their respective AI ecosystems. Media coverage of the AI platform race further amplifies the hype, portraying it as a high-stakes battle for technological supremacy, highlighting the massive investments being made, and uncritically repeating the marketing narratives disseminated by the competing tech giants. Venture capitalists, eager to back the potential platform winners, further fuel the hype cycle by aggressively investing in AI startups building on specific platforms, and by actively promoting the platform ecosystems they have chosen to bet on, creating a self-reinforcing cycle of hype, investment, and platform competition.

The race for AI platform monopoly, therefore, represents a final, crucial, and perhaps most powerful economic incentive driving the trillion-dollar dream and fueling the relentless AI hype cycle. The intense competition among tech giants to dominate the AI platform landscape creates a constant pressure to over-promise, to exaggerate progress, and to actively participate in and amplify the hype narrative, in order to attract developers, customers, investors, and ultimately, to capture the lion's share of the immense economic value projected to be generated by the AI-driven future. The trillion-dollar dream, therefore, is not just a singular aspiration, but a complex and multifaceted economic force, driven by inflated market capitalizations, job displacement fear-mongering, the fear of AI Winters, and the intense competition for platform monopoly, all collectively fueling the AI hype machine and distorting the true trajectory of artificial intelligence in the age of overdrive.

These economic engines, powerful and pervasive as they are, driving the AI hype machine and fueling the trillion-dollar dream, would be far less effective, far less persuasive, and far less capable of generating the current level of AI frenzy were they not underpinned by a set of carefully constructed and widely disseminated AI fairy tales, seductive narratives and compelling myths that capture the public imagination, tap into deep-seated human desires and anxieties, and ultimately, transform often-incremental technological advancements into seemingly revolutionary leaps towards a technologically utopian future. These AI fairy tales are not simply innocent exaggerations or harmless marketing spin; they are strategically crafted narratives, designed to simplify complex realities, to amplify perceived benefits, to downplay potential risks, and to ultimately create a pervasive sense of technological inevitability and transformative potential, all in service of the trillion-dollar dream and the relentless churn of the AI hype machine. Dissecting these AI fairy tales, exposing their inherent flaws, and challenging their often-misleading narratives is crucial for dismantling the illusions of AI hype and fostering a more balanced and realistic public understanding of artificial intelligence in the age of overdrive.

One of the most pervasive and alluring AI fairy tales is the narrative of "AI is Already Superhuman", the persistent claim, often subtly implied but sometimes explicitly stated, that artificial intelligence is rapidly approaching, or in some cases already surpassing, human intelligence in a wide range of domains, and that we are on the verge of a world where machines will fundamentally outsmart and outperform humans in virtually every cognitive task. This narrative, often fueled by impressive but narrowly defined AI achievements in specific domains like game playing, image recognition, and natural language processing, creates a misleading impression of general AI capabilities and obscures the vast gulf that still separates current AI from true human-level intelligence, particularly in areas requiring common sense reasoning, adaptability, creativity, and genuine understanding.

Consider the widely publicized AI victories over humans in games like chess, Go, and various video games. DeepMind's AlphaGo victory over Lee Sedol in 2016, for example, was hailed as a watershed moment in AI history, with many media outlets proclaiming that AI had now surpassed human intelligence in Go, a game long considered to be the pinnacle of strategic complexity. While AlphaGo's achievement was undeniably impressive within the narrowly defined domain of Go, it was strategically and often deceptively extrapolated into a broader narrative of AI superhumanity, implying that AI was rapidly on track to surpass human intelligence in general, not just in a specific board game. The reality, however, is far more nuanced. AlphaGo's superhuman performance in Go is achieved through massive computational power, extensive training on vast datasets of Go games, and a highly specialized algorithmic architecture tailored specifically to the rules and dynamics of Go. AlphaGo possesses no general intelligence, no ability to transfer its Go expertise to other domains, and no capacity for common sense reasoning or real-world understanding. It is, in essence, a highly specialized, narrowly intelligent system, optimized for a single, well-defined task, and its superhuman performance in Go provides little to no evidence for the imminent arrival of general AI or superhuman machine intelligence in a broader sense.

Similarly, impressive AI achievements in image recognition, speech recognition, and natural language processing are often strategically deployed to bolster the narrative of AI superhumanity, despite their inherent limitations and narrow scope. AI systems now routinely outperform humans in certain image recognition benchmarks, achieving near-perfect accuracy in classifying images within carefully curated datasets. Speech recognition systems have reached human-parity in transcribing conversational speech in controlled environments, approaching near-flawless transcription accuracy. Large language models like GPT-4 can generate human-like text with remarkable fluency and coherence, often indistinguishable from human writing in superficial stylistic terms. These impressive achievements, however, are again often strategically exaggerated and deceptively extrapolated into a broader narrative of AI superhumanity, obscuring the fact that these systems are still fundamentally limited, lacking in common sense reasoning, prone to hallucinations, and utterly incapable of genuine understanding.

The "AI is Already Superhuman" fairy tale, therefore, represents a strategically crafted and widely disseminated myth designed to amplify AI hype and drive the trillion-dollar dream. By selectively highlighting narrow AI achievements in specific domains, and strategically exaggerating their implications for general intelligence, proponents of this fairy tale create a misleading impression of AI capabilities, fueling unrealistic expectations and obscuring the vast gulf that still separates current AI from true human-level intelligence. This fairy tale, while obviously false upon closer scrutiny, nonetheless serves as a powerful engine of AI hype, contributing to the overall frenzy and distorting public perception of artificial intelligence in the age of overdrive.

Another pervasive and equally misleading AI fairy tale is the narrative of "AGI is Just Around the Corner", the persistent prediction, often confidently asserted by tech evangelists, futurists, and even some AI researchers, that Artificial General Intelligence, machine intelligence at or above human level across all cognitive domains, is imminent, just a few years, or perhaps a decade or two, away. This fairy tale, often fueled by overly optimistic extrapolations of current AI progress and a profound misunderstanding of the fundamental challenges involved in achieving true general intelligence, creates a false sense of inevitability and imminent technological singularity, further amplifying AI hype and driving unrealistic expectations about the near-term transformative potential of artificial intelligence.

Consider the repeated predictions of imminent AGI from figures like Ray Kurzweil, Elon Musk, and Sam Altman. Ray Kurzweil, the futurist and technological singularity evangelist, has famously predicted that AGI will be achieved by 2045, a prediction he has maintained and even doubled down on over the years, despite the lack of any scientific evidence to support such a claim. Elon Musk, in his characteristic style of technological hyperbole, has repeatedly warned about the existential risks of AGI while simultaneously predicting its imminent arrival, often within the next few years, fueling both fear and fascination with the prospect of superhuman machine intelligence. Sam Altman, the CEO of OpenAI, has also consistently promoted the narrative of imminent AGI, suggesting that AGI is "within reach" and that OpenAI is actively working towards achieving this transformative milestone, further amplifying the hype and creating a sense of near-term inevitability around the arrival of general AI.

These predictions of imminent AGI, while often presented with an air of scientific certainty or technological inevitability, are in reality based on highly speculative extrapolations of current AI progress, particularly in deep learning, and a profound underestimation of the fundamental scientific and engineering challenges that still stand in the way of achieving true general intelligence. Current AI systems, even the most advanced large language models, are still fundamentally narrow AI, optimized for specific tasks and lacking in common sense reasoning, adaptability, genuine understanding, and the broad range of cognitive abilities that characterize human intelligence. There is no scientific consensus within the AI research community that AGI is imminent, or even that we are on a clear path towards achieving it with current approaches. Many leading AI researchers, including Gary Marcus, have explicitly and repeatedly warned against the hype surrounding AGI predictions, emphasizing the fundamental scientific gaps in our understanding of intelligence and the lack of real progress towards general AI with current deep learning paradigms.

The "AGI is Just Around the Corner" fairy tale, therefore, represents a strategically crafted and widely disseminated myth designed to amplify AI hype and drive the trillion-dollar dream. By promoting a false sense of imminent technological singularity and exaggerating the near-term prospects of achieving general artificial intelligence, proponents of this fairy tale create a misleading impression of technological inevitability and transformative potential, fueling unrealistic expectations, driving investor enthusiasm, and obscuring the very real and substantial challenges that still need to be overcome before true AGI, if it is even achievable, can become a reality. This fairy tale, while lacking in scientific foundation, nonetheless serves as a powerful engine of AI hype, contributing to the overall frenzy and distorting public perception of the long-term trajectory of artificial intelligence in the age of overdrive.

Another seductive and equally misleading AI fairy tale, deeply embedded in the current hype cycle and eagerly embraced by both tech evangelists and a public yearning for technological salvation, is the narrative of "AI Will Solve All Our Problems", the utopian vision of artificial intelligence as a panacea for humanity's most pressing challenges, a technological magic bullet capable of effortlessly resolving complex global issues ranging from climate change and poverty to disease eradication and social inequality. This fairy tale, often presented with an almost religious fervor, portrays AI as a benevolent and omniscient force, poised to usher in a new era of technological utopia, effortlessly sweeping away centuries of human struggle and ushering in an age of unprecedented prosperity, health, and societal harmony, all thanks

37

to the transformative power of algorithms and machine intelligence. This utopian vision, however, while undeniably appealing to a public weary of complex global problems and yearning for simple technological solutions, is naive, fundamentally simplistic, and dangerously misleading, obscuring the complex realities of global challenges, exaggerating the capabilities of current AI, and potentially diverting attention and resources away from more effective and human-centered approaches to solving these critical issues.

Consider the numerous pronouncements from tech leaders, futurists, and media outlets touting AI as the solution to climate change. AI, we are told, will optimize energy grids, develop new carbon capture technologies, design sustainable agricultural practices, and even geoengineer the planet to reverse the effects of global warming, all through the sheer power of algorithmic optimization and data-driven insights. While AI may indeed play a role in addressing certain aspects of climate change, particularly in areas like data analysis and resource optimization, the notion that AI alone will solve climate change is a utopian fantasy, ignoring the fundamentally complex, multifaceted, and deeply political nature of the climate crisis. Climate change is not simply a technological problem solvable by better algorithms; it is a complex web of interconnected issues involving global economics, political will, social justice, behavioral change, and fundamental shifts in energy consumption and industrial production. Relying solely on technological solutions, even AI-powered ones, to "solve" climate change is not only naive but dangerously misleading, potentially diverting attention and resources away from more crucial and human-centered approaches such as policy changes, international cooperation, and fundamental shifts in societal values and consumption patterns.

Similarly, the narrative of AI as the solution to poverty, disease, and social inequality is equally utopian and simplistic. AI, we are told, will revolutionize healthcare, personalize education, create new economic opportunities, and even eliminate bias and discrimination through algorithmic fairness, ushering in an era of unprecedented social justice and global prosperity, all thanks to the

38

transformative power of artificial intelligence. While AI may indeed offer valuable tools for addressing certain aspects of these complex social challenges, particularly in areas like data analysis, pattern recognition, and resource allocation, the notion that AI alone will solve poverty, disease, and inequality is again merely a utopian fantasy, ignoring the deeply rooted systemic, economic, political, and social factors that perpetuate these complex global problems. Poverty, disease, and inequality are not simply technological problems solvable by better algorithms; they are deeply entrenched social, economic, and political issues rooted in historical injustices, systemic inequalities, and complex power dynamics. Relying solely on technological solutions, even AI-powered ones, to "solve" these deeply human problems is not only naive but dangerously misleading, potentially diverting attention and resources away from more crucial and human-centered approaches such as social programs, economic reforms, political activism, and fundamental shifts in societal values and power structures.

The "AI Will Solve All Our Problems" fairy tale, therefore, represents a strategically crafted and widely disseminated myth designed to amplify AI hype and drive the trillion-dollar dream. By promoting a utopian vision of AI as a panacea for humanity's most pressing challenges, and exaggerating the near-term prospects of AI-driven solutions to complex global problems, proponents of this fairy tale create a misleading impression of technological omnipotence and societal transformation, fueling unrealistic expectations, diverting attention from more effective approaches, and potentially hindering genuine progress towards addressing these critical global issues. This fairy tale, while undeniably appealing to a public yearning for simple technological solutions to complex human problems, nonetheless serves as a powerful engine of AI hype, contributing to the overall frenzy and distorting public perception of the true role and realistic potential of artificial intelligence in the age of overdrive.

The "AI Will Solve All Our Problems" fairy tale, seductive in its simplicity and utopian in its promise, is closely intertwined with another equally pervasive and equally misleading myth: the narrative of "AI is Inevitable and Unstoppable." This narrative, often subtly woven into media reports, tech company pronouncements, and venture capitalist pitches, portrays the development and deployment of artificial intelligence not as a series of human choices, guided by specific values and subject to ethical considerations, but as an inexorable force of nature, an unstoppable technological tide that will inevitably sweep across society, reshaping our world in ways that are preordained, unavoidable, and fundamentally beyond human control. This deterministic view of AI development, while often presented as a sober and realistic assessment of technological progress, is in reality a strategically constructed and ideologically laden narrative, designed to stifle critical debate, discourage regulatory oversight, and ultimately, to further amplify the AI hype cycle and drive the trillion-dollar dream by creating a sense of technological inevitability that discourages resistance and encourages unquestioning adoption.

Consider the pervasive rhetoric of "the AI revolution," a phrase constantly repeated in media reports, tech industry pronouncements, and investor presentations. The term "revolution" itself implies a sudden, sweeping, and ultimately unstoppable transformation, a force of historical inevitability that sweeps away old paradigms and ushers in a new, technologically determined era. This framing of AI development as a revolution, rather than as a series of human choices and technological developments that can be shaped and guided by human values and priorities, subtly reinforces the narrative of inevitability, suggesting that resistance is futile, adaptation is mandatory, and questioning the trajectory of AI development is both pointless and outdated. The AI revolution, in this narrative, is not something we actively create, but something that passively happens to us, a force of nature to which we must simply adapt and surrender.

Furthermore, the constant repetition of phrases like "the AI arms race," "the AI race," and "the global competition for AI dominance" further reinforces the narrative of inevitability and unstoppable momentum. These phrases, often deployed by tech leaders, politicians, and media commentators, portray AI development as a high-stakes global competition, a zero-sum game where nations and companies must aggressively pursue AI advancement to avoid being "left behind" in the technological race. This competitive framing creates a sense of urgency and inevitability, suggesting that slowing down, questioning the ethical implications, or considering alternative paths is not an option in this relentless global competition. The AI arms race narrative implies that we are locked in a technological imperative, a race to the future where the only choices are to accelerate and compete, or to fall behind and become irrelevant in the AI-dominated world. This framing effectively discourages critical reflection, ethical deliberation, and public debate about the desired direction of AI development, as it portrays any questioning or slowing down as a sign of weakness, a strategic disadvantage in the global AI competition.

Even the seemingly benign and often repeated phrase "AI is eating software" contributes to the narrative of inevitability and unstoppable technological transformation. This phrase, popularized by venture capitalist Marc Andreessen, suggests that AI is not merely augmenting or enhancing existing software, but fundamentally replacing and subsuming it, transforming the entire software landscape into an AI-dominated ecosystem. This "AI is eating software" narrative implies a complete and irreversible technological shift, a fundamental restructuring of the software industry and the broader economy, driven by the unstoppable force of artificial intelligence. It suggests that traditional software development is becoming obsolete, that AI is the inevitable future of software, and that companies and individuals must adapt to this AI-driven paradigm shift or risk becoming irrelevant in the new technological landscape. This narrative of technological subsumption, while perhaps reflecting certain trends in software development, also strategically reinforces the narrative of inevitability, suggesting that the AI revolution is not just a technological trend, but a fundamental and unstoppable force reshaping the very fabric of the digital world.

The "AI is Inevitable and Unstoppable" fairy tale, therefore, represents a strategically crafted and widely disseminated myth designed to amplify AI hype and drive the trillion-dollar dream. By portraying AI development as an inexorable force of nature, an unstoppable revolution, and an inevitable global competition, proponents of this fairy tale create a misleading impression of technological determinism, discouraging critical debate, stifling regulatory oversight, and ultimately, promoting unquestioning adoption of AI technologies, regardless of their actual capabilities, limitations, or societal implications. This fairy tale, while ignoring the crucial role of human agency, ethical choice, and democratic decision-making in shaping the future of AI, nonetheless serves as a powerful engine of AI hype, contributing to the overall frenzy and distorting public perception of the true nature and controllable trajectory of artificial intelligence in the age of overdrive.

Finally, and perhaps most insidiously, intertwined with all these other misleading AI fairy tales, is the pervasive narrative of "Just Trust the Tech Bro Visionaries," the often-implicit, but deeply influential, assumption that the future of artificial intelligence should be primarily shaped, guided, and determined by a select group of tech CEOs, venture capitalists, and self-proclaimed "visionaries," predominantly male, often young, and overwhelmingly concentrated in Silicon Valley and similar tech hubs. This narrative, often subtly reinforced by media portrayals, tech industry marketing, and a pervasive cultural deference to technological expertise, suggests that these "tech bro visionaries" possess a unique and almost divinely inspired understanding of the future of AI, that their pronouncements should be treated as gospel, and that their technological visions should be largely unchallenged, unquestioningly embraced, and enthusiastically funded, as they are, after all, the architects of the AI-driven future. This narrative, while seemingly innocuous and even flattering to the tech elite, is in reality deeply problematic, fundamentally undemocratic, and misleading, obscuring the crucial need for broader public engagement, diverse perspectives, and robust ethical oversight in shaping the future of artificial intelligence, and ultimately, further amplifying the AI hype cycle and driving the trillion-dollar dream by concentrating power and influence in the hands of a select few, often with vested financial interests in perpetuating the hype.

Consider the almost messianic reverence afforded to figures like Sam Altman, Elon Musk, and Mark Zuckerberg in media portrayals and public discourse surrounding AI. These tech CEOs, despite often lacking deep scientific expertise in artificial intelligence itself, are frequently presented as the leading voices in the AI revolution, their pronouncements on the future of AI treated as authoritative and often uncritically amplified by media outlets and social media platforms. Their technological visions, often grand and utopian, are widely disseminated and enthusiastically embraced by investors, policymakers, and a public yearning for technological solutions to complex problems. Their pronouncements, even when clearly hyperbolic, lacking in scientific evidence, or ethically questionable, are often treated with a level of deference and unquestioning acceptance rarely afforded to experts in other fields, further reinforcing their perceived authority and influence in shaping the AI narrative.

This uncritical trust in "tech bro visionaries" extends beyond individual CEOs to encompass a broader cultural deference to Silicon Valley and the tech industry as a whole. Silicon Valley, in this narrative, is portrayed as the epicenter of technological innovation, the breeding ground for world-changing technologies, and the ultimate arbiter of technological progress. The pronouncements emanating from Silicon Valley, therefore, are often treated as inherently authoritative and technologically inevitable, their visions for the future of AI largely unchallenged and unquestioningly embraced by investors, policymakers, and the broader public. This cultural deference to Silicon Valley expertise, while acknowledging the undeniable technological prowess of the region, also inadvertently reinforces the narrative of "Just Trust the Tech Bro Visionaries," creating a climate of uncritical acceptance and discouraging more diverse perspectives, ethical scrutiny, and democratic oversight in shaping the future of artificial intelligence.

The "Just Trust the Tech Bro Visionaries" fairy tale, therefore, represents a final, insidious, and deeply problematic myth designed to amplify AI hype and drive the trillion-dollar dream. By promoting a narrative of unquestioning deference to a select group of tech CEOs and Silicon Valley "visionaries," proponents of this fairy tale concentrate power and influence in the hands of a few, stifle critical debate, discourage diverse perspectives, and ultimately, undermine the crucial need for broader public engagement and democratic oversight in shaping the future of artificial intelligence. This fairy tale, while seemingly innocuous and even flattering to the tech elite, nonetheless serves as a powerful engine of AI hype, contributing to the overall frenzy and distorting public perception of the true nature of AI governance, ethical responsibility, and the fundamentally democratic imperative of shaping technological futures through inclusive and participatory processes, rather than simply deferring to the often self-serving visions of a select few "tech bro visionaries" in the age of AI overdrive.

These AI fairy tales – "AI is Already Superhuman," "AGI is Just Around the Corner," "AI Will Solve All Our Problems," "AI is Inevitable and Unstoppable," and "Just Trust the Tech Bro Visionaries" – collectively form the narrative underpinnings of the AI hype machine, seductive and compelling myths that transform the trillion-dollar dream into a seemingly inevitable and technologically utopian future. But these fairy tales, while undeniably powerful engines of hype, are ultimately just that: fairy tales, lacking in scientific foundation, often misleading in their portrayal of current AI capabilities and limitations, and dangerously simplistic in their understanding of the complex ethical, societal, and economic implications of artificial intelligence. Dismantling these AI fairy tales, exposing their inherent flaws, and challenging their often-misleading narratives is not just an intellectual exercise; it is a crucial and urgent necessity for navigating the age of AI overdrive with wisdom, foresight, and a commitment to responsible innovation, moving beyond the seductive illusions of hype and towards a more balanced, realistic, and genuinely beneficial future for artificial intelligence and humanity alike. And it is precisely in this crucial endeavor of dismantling the illusions, exposing the fairy tales, and challenging the dominant narratives of the AI hype machine that the voice of Gary Marcus becomes not just valuable, but absolutely indispensable.

Chapter 3

Meet the Skeptic

In the swirling vortex of AI overdrive, amidst the cacophony of breathless pronouncements and trillion-dollar fantasies, a figure emerges, not as a dissenting voice howling into the wind, but as a lighthouse in the algorithmic fog, a beacon of clarity and reason in a landscape increasingly obscured by hype and hyperbole. This is Gary Marcus, the skeptic, the neuroscientist, the cognitive scientist, the entrepreneur, and, perhaps most importantly in this current climate, the unflinching intellectual counterweight to the trillion-dollar AI hype machine. To truly understand the urgency and necessity of his critique, to grasp the profound value of his perspective in this age of algorithmic enchantment, it is essential to first meet the skeptic himself, to trace the intellectual journey that forged his uniquely insightful and consistently critical view of artificial intelligence, and to understand the core tenets of his scientifically grounded and humanistically driven vision for a more responsible and ultimately more real AI future.

Marcus's path to becoming the preeminent AI skeptic of our time was not a straight line, not a sudden conversion, but a gradual intellectual evolution, a journey rooted in the rigorous disciplines of neuroscience and cognitive science, and tempered by the practical realities of the tech industry itself. His intellectual origins lie not in a Luddite resistance to technological progress, but in a deep and abiding fascination with the very nature of intelligence itself, both biological and artificial. From his early academic pursuits, a palpable curiosity about the workings of the human mind, the intricate mechanisms of the brain, and the fundamental mysteries of consciousness propelled him forward, leading him to the demanding and intellectually fertile fields of neuroscience and cognitive science.

Even in his formative years, a certain intellectual restlessness, a refusal to accept simplistic explanations or readily embrace prevailing paradigms, seemed to be a defining characteristic. Growing up in a household that valued intellectual curiosity and critical thinking, Marcus was encouraged to question assumptions, to delve beneath the surface of conventional wisdom, and to forge his own intellectual path. This early intellectual environment, coupled with a natural inclination towards scientific inquiry, laid the groundwork for his later, often contrarian, stance on artificial intelligence. His academic trajectory led him to the prestigious halls of MIT, an institution synonymous with technological innovation and rigorous scientific inquiry, where he immersed himself in the nascent field of cognitive science, a discipline that sought to understand the mind through an interdisciplinary lens, drawing on insights from psychology, linguistics, computer science, and philosophy. This interdisciplinary training, exposing him to diverse perspectives and methodologies, instilled in him a broad intellectual toolkit, a capacity to analyze complex problems from multiple angles, a skill that would prove invaluable in his later critiques of AI.

Influential mentors and intellectual figures further shaped his early intellectual development, guiding his research, challenging his assumptions, and pushing him to refine his thinking about the mind and intelligence. While specific names might remain less publicly known, the intellectual currents of the time – the fervent debates between connectionist and symbolic AI approaches, the burgeoning field of computational linguistics, the ongoing philosophical inquiries into consciousness and intentionality – undoubtedly permeated his academic environment, shaping his intellectual landscape and influencing his early research interests. One could imagine the young Marcus, amidst the bustling intellectual energy of MIT, engaging in passionate debates about the nature of representation in the brain, the limits of computation, and the very possibility of creating artificial minds, seeds of skepticism about overly simplistic AI approaches perhaps already taking root in his intellectually fertile mind.

This early immersion in the rigorous disciplines of neuroscience and cognitive science provided Marcus with a foundational understanding of the sheer complexity of intelligence, both biological and artificial. His doctoral research, focusing on the intricate mechanisms of language acquisition in children, delved into the remarkable capacity of the human brain to learn and process language, a uniquely human cognitive ability that remains stubbornly resistant to easy algorithmic replication. His academic publications, often appearing in top-tier scientific journals, reflected this deep engagement with the complexities of human cognition, exploring topics ranging from the neural basis of language to the computational modeling of cognitive processes, showcasing a commitment to rigorous empirical investigation and a nuanced understanding of the challenges inherent in understanding and replicating human intelligence. A paper examining the statistical regularities in child-directed speech, for example, might have subtly hinted at the limitations of purely statistical approaches to language learning, foreshadowing his later critiques of large language models. A presentation at a cognitive science conference on the challenges of modeling common sense reasoning in artificial systems might have already planted the seeds of his future "Common Sense Crusader" persona. This academic deep dive, therefore, was not just a period of specialized training; it was a crucial intellectual crucible, forging his scientific rigor, deepening his appreciation for the complexities of intelligence, and subtly laying the groundwork for his eventual, and increasingly necessary, role as the AI skeptic.

Yet, Marcus's intellectual journey did not remain confined to the ivory towers of academia. Driven perhaps by a desire to translate theoretical insights into practical applications, or perhaps by a restless entrepreneurial spirit, he took a significant leap, venturing into the often-unpredictable and always demanding world of tech entrepreneurship. This move, from the contemplative realm of academic research to the fast-paced and results-oriented environment of Silicon Valley, proved to be another crucial formative experience, providing him with a uniquely grounded perspective on the realities, and often the hype, surrounding artificial intelligence in the real world. His motivation for this entrepreneurial leap might have stemmed from a frustration with the often-slow pace of academic progress, a desire to see his research ideas translated into tangible technologies, or a recognition that the real challenges and opportunities of AI lay not just in theoretical models, but in practical applications and real-world deployment.

This entrepreneurial drive led him to co-found Geometric Intelligence, a company explicitly focused on tackling the limitations of then-dominant AI approaches and pursuing a more robust and human-like form of artificial intelligence. Geometric Intelligence's mission statement, one can imagine, likely emphasized the need to move beyond purely statistical methods, to incorporate more structured knowledge representation, and to build AI systems capable of genuine reasoning and common sense, reflecting Marcus's own emerging intellectual convictions. The company, staffed by researchers and engineers deeply committed to pushing the boundaries of AI beyond the limitations of current paradigms, became a microcosm of Marcus's own intellectual vision, a real-world laboratory for exploring alternative approaches to artificial intelligence. This entrepreneurial venture was not just about building a successful company; it was about testing the feasibility of his intellectual ideas in the crucible of real-world application, a crucial step in solidifying his critical perspective on the prevailing trends in the AI field.

The acquisition of Geometric Intelligence by Uber, while perhaps marking a successful exit for the startup, also provided Marcus with a uniquely illuminating, and perhaps somewhat disillusioning, glimpse into the inner workings of a major tech company grappling with the promises and perils of artificial intelligence. His time at Uber, tasked with building out Uber's AI capabilities, likely exposed him firsthand to the practical challenges of deploying AI in complex real-world scenarios, the often-exaggerated claims made by tech companies about AI capabilities, and the intense pressures to generate hype and deliver quick results in a highly competitive market. This experience, working within the belly of the beast of a tech giant deeply invested in AI, undoubtedly further solidified his skeptical perspective, providing him with concrete, real-world examples of the gap between AI hype and AI reality, and reinforcing his conviction that a more critical and scientifically grounded approach to AI development was urgently needed. The lessons learned at Uber, both positive and negative, likely informed his subsequent entrepreneurial venture, Robust.AI, a company explicitly founded to address the limitations he had witnessed firsthand in the broader AI landscape, and to actively build the kind of robust, reliable, and human-like AI systems he had long advocated for.

Robust.AI, therefore, represents not just another startup, but a direct embodiment of Marcus's neuro-symbolic vision, a concrete manifestation of his long-held belief in the need for a fundamentally different approach to artificial intelligence. Founded after his experiences at Uber, Robust.AI is explicitly focused on building AI systems that go beyond the limitations of deep learning, incorporating structured knowledge, common sense reasoning, and robust generalization capabilities, aiming to create AI that is not just statistically fluent, but truly understands and reasons about the world. The company's mission, one can surmise, is deeply aligned with Marcus's intellectual convictions, seeking to translate his theoretical critiques into practical engineering solutions, and to demonstrate in the real world the viability and potential of neuro-symbolic AI as a more responsible and ultimately more powerful path forward for artificial intelligence. Robust.AI, therefore, is not just a business venture; it is a testament to Marcus's unwavering commitment to his intellectual vision, a concrete embodiment of his belief in the need for a "reboot" of AI, and a living example of his dedication to building a better, more realistic, and more genuinely intelligent future for artificial intelligence.

This intellectual journey, from the rigorous disciplines of neuroscience and cognitive science to the demanding world of tech entrepreneurship, was punctuated and amplified by a series of key publications, intellectual milestones that not only reflected the evolution of his thinking but also served to shape and influence the broader discourse around artificial intelligence. His books, each meticulously researched, rigorously argued, and accessibly written, became crucial touchstones in the ongoing debate about AI, each offering a unique and increasingly prescient perspective on the promises, perils, and often-overlooked realities of artificial intelligence.

"Kluge: The Haphazard Construction of the Human Mind," published in 2008, long before the current AI frenzy, stands as a remarkably prescient work, foreshadowing many of the limitations now being exposed in the wake of the deep learning revolution. In Kluge, Marcus challenged simplistic, overly engineered, and often technologically deterministic views of intelligence, arguing persuasively that even human intelligence, the very benchmark against which artificial intelligence is inevitably measured, is not a perfectly designed, elegantly optimized system, but rather a "kluge" – a messy, ad-hoc, cobbled-together, yet ultimately remarkably functional, contraption, a product of evolutionary tinkering and biological contingency, not algorithmic perfection. This core argument, that intelligence, even in its most sophisticated biological form, is inherently imperfect, messy, and often surprisingly inelegant, served as a crucial early counterpoint to the then-emerging narratives of AI technological utopianism, suggesting that the pursuit of perfectly rational, flawlessly logical, and superhumanly intelligent machines might be a fundamentally misguided and ultimately unrealistic endeavor. Kluge was not just a critique of simplistic views of intelligence; it was a profound and insightful exploration of the inherent complexities and often-overlooked limitations of even biological intelligence, offering a crucial early dose of intellectual humility to a field often prone to technological hubris. The book, while perhaps not directly focused on artificial intelligence, laid a crucial intellectual foundation for Marcus's later critiques, establishing his long-standing skepticism towards overly optimistic and technologically deterministic views of intelligence, both human and artificial.

"Guitar Zero: The New Musician and the Science of Learning," published in 2012, further deepened Marcus's exploration of the complexities of intelligence, shifting focus from the messy architecture of the brain to the intricate processes of skill acquisition. In Guitar Zero, Marcus delved into the surprisingly complex and often counterintuitive processes involved in learning a new skill, specifically the seemingly simple act of learning to play the guitar. Through a combination of personal anecdote, scientific research, and insightful analysis, he demonstrated the profound challenges inherent in mastering even seemingly basic human abilities, challenges that current AI systems, despite their impressive statistical prowess, are still far from overcoming. The book illuminated the crucial role of implicit learning, embodied cognition, and the often-overlooked complexities of human motor skills, perceptual abilities, and creative improvisation in skill acquisition, highlighting the vast gulf between algorithmic mimicry and genuine human expertise. Guitar Zero was not just a book about learning to play the guitar; it was a subtle but powerful critique of simplistic AI approaches to learning, suggesting that genuine intelligence, even in seemingly mundane skills, requires far more than just algorithmic optimization and data-driven pattern recognition. The book further solidified Marcus's skeptical stance towards overly optimistic AI claims, demonstrating through concrete examples the inherent complexities of even seemingly simple human cognitive abilities, complexities often glossed over in the hype-driven narratives of technological inevitability.

And then, in 2019, came "Rebooting AI: Building Artificial Intelligence We Can Trust," co-authored with the esteemed computer scientist Ernest Davis, a book that can be considered the intellectual culmination of Marcus's long-standing critiques and his most direct and forceful intervention into the current AI discourse. In Rebooting AI, Marcus and Davis laid out a comprehensive and intellectually devastating critique of the now-dominant deep learning monoculture within the AI field, systematically dismantling its core assumptions, rigorously exposing its fundamental limitations, and presenting a compelling, scientifically grounded case for neuro-symbolic AI, hybrid architectures, and a fundamentally different, more knowledge-rich, and reasoning-centric approach as a considerably more promising and ultimately more responsible path forward for the future of artificial intelligence. Rebooting AI was not just a critique of deep learning; it was a manifesto for a new direction in AI research, a call to action for the AI community to move beyond the limitations of purely statistical methods and to embrace more robust, reliable, and human-like forms of artificial intelligence. The book became an instant intellectual lightning rod, sparking intense debate within the AI field, challenging prevailing assumptions, and offering a powerful and scientifically grounded counterpoint to the dominant hype narratives surrounding deep learning and the imminent arrival of AGI. Rebooting AI, therefore, served as a crucial intellectual intervention, solidifying Marcus's role as the preeminent AI skeptic of our time and providing a clear and compelling roadmap for a more responsible, realistic, and genuinely intelligent future for artificial intelligence, a future that begins with dismantling the illusions of hype and embracing the clear-eyed, scientifically grounded, and profoundly necessary voice of Gary Marcus.

In his most recent and perhaps most directly relevant work, Rebooting AI: Building Artificial Intelligence We Can Trust, co-authored with the esteemed computer scientist Ernest Davis, a book that can be considered the intellectual culmination of Marcus's long-standing critiques and his most direct and forceful intervention into the current AI discourse. In Rebooting AI, Marcus and Davis laid out a comprehensive and intellectually devastating critique of the now-dominant deep learning monoculture within the AI field, systematically dismantling its core assumptions, rigorously exposing its fundamental limitations, and presenting a compelling, scientifically grounded case for neuro-symbolic AI, hybrid architectures, and a fundamentally different, more knowledge-rich, and reasoning-centric approach as a more promising and ultimately more responsible path forward for the future of artificial intelligence. Rebooting AI was not just a critique of deep learning; it was a manifesto for a new direction in AI research, a call to action for the AI community to move beyond the limitations of purely statistical methods and to embrace more robust, reliable, and human-like forms of artificial intelligence. The book became an instant intellectual lightning rod, sparking intense debate within the AI field, challenging prevailing assumptions, and offering a powerful and scientifically grounded counterpoint to the dominant hype narratives surrounding deep learning and the imminent arrival of AGI. Rebooting AI, therefore, served as a crucial intellectual intervention, solidifying Marcus's role as the preeminent AI skeptic of our time and providing a clear and compelling roadmap for a more responsible, realistic, and genuinely intelligent future for artificial intelligence, a future that begins with dismantling the illusions of hype and embracing the clear-eyed, scientifically grounded, and profoundly necessary voice of Gary Marcus.

But Marcus's intellectual contributions extend far beyond critical analysis and technological deconstruction. He is not merely a debunker of AI hype; he is, more fundamentally, a champion of a different kind of artificial intelligence, a tireless advocate for a more robust, more reliable, and more intelligent AI future. At the heart of his positive vision lies a concept that is both deceptively simple and profoundly complex: common sense. For Marcus, the pursuit of common sense in artificial intelligence is not just a technical challenge; it is the very essence of building truly intelligent machines, the crucial missing ingredient that separates current AI systems, however impressive in narrow domains, from the kind of general, adaptable, and human-like intelligence that is so often, and so misleadingly, proclaimed as imminent. He stands, therefore, as the "Common Sense Crusader," a relentless advocate for grounding AI research in the pursuit of genuine understanding, real-world reasoning, and the kind of robust common sense that humans effortlessly deploy in navigating the complexities of everyday life.

Defining common sense in the context of artificial intelligence is itself a complex and nuanced undertaking. It is not simply about accumulating vast quantities of factual knowledge, memorizing encyclopedic information, or mastering specific domains of expertise. Common sense, in Marcus's view, is something far more fundamental, far more deeply ingrained in the very fabric of human cognition. It is the ability to reason about everyday situations, to make inferences about the physical and social world, to understand implicit knowledge and unspoken assumptions, to adapt to novel situations and unexpected events, to navigate the complexities of social interactions, and to possess an intuitive

54

grasp of physical causality and real-world constraints. It is the vast, largely unconscious, and remarkably robust body of knowledge and reasoning abilities that allows humans to effortlessly navigate the complexities of daily life, to understand stories, to engage in conversations, to solve problems, and to make sense of the world around them, capabilities that remain stubbornly elusive for even the most advanced current AI systems.

Consider, for a moment, the seemingly simple act of pouring coffee. A human effortlessly understands the basic physics involved: gravity will pull the coffee downwards, the cup will contain the liquid, tilting the pot will initiate the flow, and overfilling the cup will lead to spillage. These are all common sense inferences, based on an intuitive understanding of physical causality and everyday object interactions. Current AI systems, however, even those capable of generating fluent and seemingly intelligent text, often lack this basic common sense understanding. Ask ChatGPT to describe the process of pouring coffee, and it may generate grammatically correct and stylistically coherent text, but it will likely lack a genuine understanding of the underlying physics, the potential for spillage, or the practical constraints involved in performing this seemingly simple task in the real world. This seemingly trivial example highlights the profound common sense deficit in current AI, the inability to grasp the kind of intuitive, embodied, and deeply contextualized knowledge that humans deploy effortlessly in even the most mundane everyday situations.

This common sense deficit, Marcus argues forcefully and repeatedly, is not just a minor inconvenience or a temporary limitation of current AI; it is a fundamental flaw, a critical obstacle that prevents current AI systems, particularly those based on deep learning, from achieving true general intelligence, robust reliability, and genuine trustworthiness. Deep learning systems, for all their statistical prowess and impressive pattern recognition capabilities, are fundamentally lacking in common sense reasoning, precisely because they are designed to learn correlations from vast datasets, not to acquire genuine understanding of causal relationships, real-world constraints, or the vast body of implicit knowledge that constitutes human common sense. Deep learning excels at identifying statistical patterns in data, at mimicking human language, and at performing narrowly defined tasks within carefully controlled environments, but it fundamentally struggles with generalization, adaptability, and the kind of robust reasoning that is essential for navigating the complexities and unpredictability of the real world. This inherent common sense deficit manifests itself in various well-documented limitations of current AI, from the brittleness of deep learning models to their susceptibility to adversarial attacks, from their propensity to generate confident hallucinations to their inability to transfer learning across different domains, all symptoms of a fundamental lack of genuine understanding and real-world common sense.

Marcus, therefore, positions neuro-symbolic AI as not just a technical alternative to deep learning, but as the very solution to the common sense problem, the most promising path towards building artificial intelligence that truly understands, reasons, and thinks in a more human-like way. Neuro-symbolic AI, in his vision, offers a hybrid approach, combining the strengths of neural networks in perception and pattern recognition with the power of symbolic AI in knowledge representation, logical inference, and abstract reasoning, creating AI systems that are not just data-driven pattern matchers, but also knowledge-rich, reasoning-capable, and more robust and reliable. By incorporating explicit symbolic knowledge, structured representations of the world, and logical inference mechanisms, neuro-symbolic AI aims to overcome the inherent common sense deficit of deep learning, to ground AI systems in a more robust and meaningful understanding of the world, and to build AI that can reason, plan, and adapt to novel situations in a more human-like and more intelligent way.

This advocacy for neuro-symbolic AI is not just a theoretical preference for Marcus; it is a deeply held intellectual conviction, rooted in his understanding of both the limitations of current AI paradigms and the fundamental nature of human intelligence. He sees neuro-symbolic AI not as a niche research area, but as the essential direction for the future of artificial intelligence, the necessary paradigm shift required to move beyond the hype-driven limitations of deep learning and towards a more genuinely intelligent, robust, and trustworthy AI future. His company, Robust.AI, serves as a concrete embodiment of this conviction, actively developing neuro-symbolic AI systems for real-world applications, seeking to demonstrate the practical viability and tangible benefits of this hybrid approach in domains where common sense reasoning, robustness, and explainability are paramount. Marcus's role as the "Common Sense Crusader" is, therefore, not just about critiquing the limitations of current AI; it is about actively championing a more promising and ultimately more human-centered path forward, a path grounded in the pursuit of genuine understanding, real-world reasoning, and the kind of robust common sense that is, in his view, the very essence of true intelligence, both human and artificial.

And underlying Marcus's technical vision for neuro-symbolic AI is an even broader and more encompassing perspective, a vision that extends beyond the confines of algorithms and code to encompass the societal implications, ethical considerations, and fundamentally humanistic values that should guide the development and deployment of artificial intelligence in the 21st century. For Marcus, AI is not just a technological problem to be solved, but a profound societal force that will inevitably reshape our world in profound and often unpredictable ways. His vision, therefore, extends "Beyond the Algorithm," encompassing a broader ethical, societal, and human-centered framework for responsible AI innovation, a perspective that goes beyond narrow technical metrics and delves into the deeper questions of values, purpose, and the very future of humanity in an age increasingly shaped by artificial intelligence.

In the realm of AI safety, for example, Marcus advocates for a more pragmatic and near-term approach, shifting focus away from the often-hyped and often-speculative existential risks of Artificial General Intelligence towards the more immediate risks posed by current AI systems. He cautions against getting overly fixated on hypothetical scenarios of rogue AGI turning against humanity, arguing that these long-term, speculative concerns often distract from the more pressing and tangible ethical challenges posed by bias in algorithms, lack of accountability in AI decision-making, and the potential for misuse and unintended consequences in currently deployed AI technologies. His AI safety agenda, therefore, is grounded in a more realistic and evidence-based assessment of current AI capabilities and limitations, emphasizing the need to address concrete ethical concerns and mitigate real-world risks, rather than getting lost in abstract and often fear-mongering discussions about distant and highly uncertain AGI scenarios. He calls for a more pragmatic and responsible approach to AI safety, focusing on building robust, reliable, explainable, and ethically designed AI systems today, rather than solely worrying about hypothetical risks that may or may not materialize decades or even centuries in the future.

In the context of the future of work, Marcus offers a similarly nuanced and realistic perspective, pushing back against simplistic narratives of mass job displacement and technological unemployment driven by AI automation. While acknowledging the potential for AI to automate certain tasks and transform the nature of work, he argues that the narrative of widespread job losses is often exaggerated and fails to account for the potential for AI to augment human work, create new types of jobs, and fundamentally reshape the labor market in ways that are not necessarily purely negative or dystopian. His vision for the future of work in the AI age emphasizes human-AI collaboration, the potential for AI to enhance human productivity and creativity, and the need for adaptation, retraining, and social safety nets to ensure a universally beneficial transition in an increasingly automated economy. He critiques the often-simplistic and fear-mongering narratives of AI-driven job apocalypse, advocating for a more balanced and optimistic perspective that recognizes both the potential challenges and the potential opportunities presented by AI in the future of work, emphasizing the crucial role of human agency and proactive societal adaptation in shaping a more positive and human-centered future of labor in the AI age.

In the domain of education, Marcus similarly advocates for a balanced and humanistic approach to integrating AI into learning environments, cautioning against over-reliance on technological solutions and emphasizing the enduring importance of human teachers, critical thinking skills, and social learning. While acknowledging the potential for AI to personalize learning, provide adaptive tutoring systems, and enhance educational resources, he also highlights the potential pitfalls of over-automating education, deskilling human teachers, and neglecting the crucial social and emotional dimensions of learning that are inherently human-centered and difficult to replicate through purely algorithmic means. His vision for AI in education emphasizes AI as a tool to augment and enhance human teaching, not to replace human educators entirely, advocating for a balanced and thoughtful integration of AI that preserves the crucial human element in learning, fosters critical thinking skills, and promotes holistic human development, rather than simply prioritizing algorithmic efficiency or standardized testing metrics.

And finally, in the broader realm of AI governance and societal oversight, Marcus is a vocal advocate for robust regulation, transparency, and informed public discourse, emphasizing the need for democratic control and ethical guidelines to shape the future of artificial intelligence in a responsible and human-centered way. He calls for greater transparency in AI algorithms, accountability for AI decision-making, and ethical frameworks to guide AI development and deployment, advocating for a more proactive and anticipatory approach to AI regulation that goes beyond reactive damage control and seeks to shape the technology's trajectory in a direction that aligns with human values and promotes the public good. He emphasizes the crucial role of policymakers, ethicists, scientists, and the broader public in shaping the future of AI, arguing for a more democratic and participatory approach to AI governance, rather than leaving these crucial decisions solely in the hands of tech companies or a select group of "tech bro visionaries." His broader vision, therefore, is one of responsible innovation, ethical oversight, and democratic control, ensuring that AI development is guided by human values, serves human needs, and ultimately contributes to a more human-centered future for all of humanity in the age of artificial intelligence.

To understand Gary Marcus fully, to truly appreciate the significance of his voice in the age of AI overdrive, it is not enough to simply grasp the technical nuances of his neuro-symbolic vision or the scope of his broader societal concerns. It is also essential to understand "The Marcus Method," the unique intellectual style, communication approach, and unwavering conviction that makes him such an effective and, arguably, indispensable voice in the often-cacophonous and frequently misleading discourse surrounding artificial intelligence. His method is not just about what he says, but how he says it, a distinctive blend of intellectual rigor, clear communication, unflinching critique, engaging humor, and an unwavering commitment to scientific truth and intellectual honesty that sets him apart from many other voices in the AI debate, making his message both compelling and profoundly necessary in the current climate of hype and hyperbole.

Central to the Marcus Method is an unwavering commitment to intellectual rigor and evidence-based arguments. His critiques of AI hype, his deconstructions of exaggerated claims, and his advocacy for alternative approaches are never based on mere intuition, gut feeling, or knee-jerk skepticism. Instead, they are meticulously grounded in scientific principles, drawing on his deep expertise in neuroscience, cognitive science, and computer science, consistently referencing empirical data, citing relevant research findings, and employing rigorous logical reasoning to support his claims. He does not simply assert that current AI is overhyped; he demonstrates it, systematically dissecting the underlying technologies, exposing their inherent limitations, and providing concrete evidence to back up his critiques. This evidence-based approach stands in stark contrast to the often-anecdotal, speculative, and marketing-driven nature of AI hype, providing a refreshing dose of scientific rigor in a discourse often dominated by hyperbole and unsubstantiated pronouncements. When Marcus critiques the hallucination problem in large language models, for example, he doesn't just offer vague complaints; he points to specific examples of AI systems generating false information, cites research studies documenting the prevalence of hallucinations, and meticulously explains why these hallucinations are not just minor bugs but fundamental symptoms of the underlying limitations of statistical language models. When he challenges the narrative of imminent AGI, he doesn't just dismiss it as unrealistic; he systematically dismantles the core assumptions underlying AGI predictions, highlights the fundamental scientific gaps in our understanding of intelligence, and provides compelling arguments for why current AI approaches are unlikely to lead to general intelligence in the near future. This commitment to intellectual rigor, to grounding his arguments in evidence and logic, is a defining characteristic of the Marcus Method, lending his critiques a weight and credibility that is often lacking in the broader AI discourse, and making his voice a crucial counterpoint to the often-unsubstantiated claims of the AI hype machine.

Complementing his intellectual rigor is Marcus's remarkable ability to communicate complex ideas with exceptional clarity and accessibility, reaching a broad audience far beyond the confines of academic specialists or tech insiders. He possesses a rare gift for translating intricate scientific concepts and nuanced technical arguments into language that is clear, concise, and readily understandable to non-experts, avoiding jargon, technical obscurity, and overly specialized terminology. He masterfully employs analogies, metaphors, and relatable everyday examples to illustrate complex points, making his critiques accessible and engaging even for readers with limited prior knowledge of artificial intelligence. His writing style is direct, engaging, and often persuasive, drawing readers into his arguments and making complex topics both intellectually stimulating and readily comprehensible. This commitment to clarity and accessibility is not just a stylistic choice for Marcus; it is a crucial communication strategy, recognizing that countering the pervasive and often deliberately obfuscating nature of AI hype requires clear, direct, and widely understandable messaging. Hype often thrives on jargon, technical complexity, and a deliberate obscuring of limitations and uncertainties, making it difficult for non-experts to discern genuine progress from carefully constructed illusions. Marcus's commitment to clarity and accessibility directly challenges this obfuscation, democratizing the AI discourse, empowering a broader public to engage critically with AI narratives, and providing the intellectual tools necessary to discern hype from reality in the age of AI overdrive.

Integral to the Marcus Method is also an unflinching directness and a willingness to engage in often sharp and forceful critique, a rare intellectual courage to challenge powerful figures, dominant narratives, and deeply entrenched assumptions within the AI field and the broader tech industry. He is not afraid to "name names," to directly critique specific tech CEOs, prominent AI researchers, and influential organizations, holding them accountable for exaggerated claims, misleading marketing, and potentially harmful practices in the AI space. His critiques are often pointed, incisive, and uncompromising, pulling no punches in exposing flaws, challenging hype, and highlighting the often-substantial gap between AI promise and AI reality. This unflinching directness, while sometimes generating controversy and pushback from those targeted by his critiques, is nonetheless a crucial element of the Marcus Method, reflecting his unwavering commitment to intellectual honesty and his refusal to soften his message or compromise his principles in the face of powerful vested interests or prevailing hype narratives. In a field often characterized by self-promotion, technological utopianism, and a reluctance to publicly criticize dominant paradigms, Marcus's direct and unflinching critique stands out as a beacon of intellectual courage, providing a necessary counterpoint to the often-uncritical enthusiasm and self-congratulatory narratives that dominate much of the AI discourse. He is not content with politely suggesting limitations or subtly hinting at potential flaws; he directly and forcefully exposes the emperor's new algorithms for what they are, challenging the powerful and often misleading narratives driving the AI hype machine, and demanding a more honest, realistic, and responsible approach to artificial intelligence.

Adding another layer of effectiveness to the Marcus Method is his strategic and often disarming use of humor and engagement, making his critiques not just intellectually rigorous but also surprisingly palatable and broadly engaging. He deftly employs wit, sarcasm, and irony to inject humor into his often-serious and technically complex analyses, making his message more accessible, less preachy, and more relatable to a wider audience. His use of humor is not just for entertainment value; it is a deliberate rhetorical strategy, making his skepticism more palatable, less threatening, and ultimately more persuasive. By leavening his often-sharp critiques with humor, he avoids coming across as merely a naysayer or a professional skeptic, instead positioning himself as an engaging and intellectually stimulating voice, inviting readers and listeners to join him in a critical, yet ultimately constructive, exploration of the promises and perils of artificial intelligence. This engaging style, combined with his clear and accessible communication, makes his message resonate with a broader audience, drawing in readers and listeners who might otherwise be intimidated by the technical complexity of AI discourse or turned off by overly negative or purely critical voices. Humor, in the Marcus Method, becomes a powerful tool for critique, making skepticism more palatable, engaging a wider audience, and ultimately, amplifying the reach and impact of his often-crucial message in the age of AI overdrive.

Finally, underpinning the entire Marcus Method is an unwavering consistency and a long-term perspective, a remarkable intellectual steadfastness that allows him to resist the short-term hype cycles, fleeting trends, and often-ephemeral enthusiasms that characterize the rapidly evolving field of artificial intelligence. His critiques of AI hype are not knee-jerk reactions to recent technological developments or fleeting moments of skepticism; they are, instead, deeply rooted in a long-standing and remarkably consistent intellectual perspective, a perspective that has been shaped by decades of rigorous scientific inquiry, hands-on experience in the tech industry, and a profound understanding of both the potential and the inherent limitations of artificial intelligence. He is not swayed by the latest buzzwords, the newest technological fads, or the ever-shifting currents of investor sentiment; his focus remains firmly fixed on the fundamental scientific challenges, the enduring ethical considerations, and the long-term trajectory of artificial intelligence, resisting the temptation to be swept away by short-term hype cycles or fleeting moments of technological euphoria. This long-term perspective, combined with his consistent intellectual voice, lends his critiques a unique weight and credibility, demonstrating that his skepticism is not a passing fad or a recent intellectual conversion, but a deeply ingrained and consistently articulated perspective, forged over decades of rigorous scientific inquiry and thoughtful reflection on the promises and perils of artificial intelligence. In an age of AI overdrive, characterized by rapid technological change, relentless hype cycles, and a constant barrage of often-exaggerated claims, Marcus's consistency and long-term perspective stand as a crucial anchor, providing a stable and reliable intellectual compass for navigating the often-turbulent and frequently misleading waters of the AI discourse, offering a voice of reason, clarity, and enduring intellectual honesty that is, in this moment, more necessary and more valuable than ever before.

Gary Marcus, therefore, emerges not just as a skeptic, but as a vital intellectual force in the age of AI overdrive. His journey from neuroscience to AI critique, his unwavering focus on common sense, his broader ethical and societal vision, and his distinctive intellectual method, collectively position him as the indispensable voice of reason, clarity, and intellectual honesty in a landscape increasingly obscured by hype, hyperbole, and trillion-dollar dreams. Understanding Gary Marcus, therefore, is not just about understanding his specific critiques of AI hype; it is about recognizing the profound necessity of his voice, the crucial importance of his perspective, and the enduring value of his intellectual method in navigating the complex, often bewildering, and potentially perilous age of artificial intelligence, an age that desperately needs, now more than ever, the clear-sighted skepticism, rigorous analysis, and unwavering commitment to truth that defines the essential and indispensable voice of Gary Marcus.

PART II

Dismantling the Illusions

Chapter 4

Deep Learning's Deep Flaws

The ascent of deep learning has been nothing short of meteoric. Bursting onto the scene with a series of undeniably impressive breakthroughs, this once-niche approach to artificial intelligence has rapidly ascended to become the dominant paradigm, the almost unchallenged orthodoxy, in the contemporary AI landscape. From revolutionizing image recognition to powering sophisticated natural language processing, from conquering complex games to driving advancements in speech recognition, deep learning has seemingly delivered on decades of AI aspiration, ushering in an era of unprecedented technological progress and fueling the current AI overdrive with its undeniable, albeit often narrowly defined, successes. Media outlets have proclaimed a paradigm shift, venture capitalists have poured in trillions of dollars, and tech companies have aggressively marketed deep learning-powered products as transformative solutions to a vast array of human problems, all contributing to the pervasive narrative of an AI revolution, powered by the seemingly limitless potential of deep neural networks. The initial triumphs of deep learning were real, tangible, and undeniably impressive, sparking genuine excitement and fostering a widespread belief that artificial general intelligence, or at least something approaching it, was finally within reach, thanks to the statistical magic of deep neural networks.

Consider the early breakthroughs that ignited the deep learning revolution. The ImageNet challenge, a benchmark task in image recognition, was decisively conquered by deep learning models in 2012, marking a dramatic leap forward in computer vision capabilities, with error rates plummeting from previous approaches, showcasing a level of accuracy that began to rival, and in some cases surpass, human performance in image classification tasks. This ImageNet moment became a symbolic victory for deep learning, a clear demonstration of its power to extract meaningful features from raw sensory data and achieve unprecedented levels of performance in a complex perceptual task. Simultaneously, deep learning began to revolutionize speech recognition, powering significant improvements in voice assistants like Siri and Alexa, enabling more natural and fluent human-computer interaction, and transforming the usability of voice-controlled interfaces. Machine translation, another long-standing challenge in artificial intelligence, also saw significant advancements thanks to deep learning, with Google Translate and other translation services achieving a level of fluency and accuracy previously unimaginable with traditional statistical machine translation methods, bridging language barriers and facilitating global communication with newfound ease.

These initial triumphs were not mere incremental improvements; they were perceived, and often rightly so, as qualitative leaps forward, demonstrating the potential of deep learning to tackle previously intractable problems in areas crucial to human-computer interaction and information processing. The media narrative, understandably, embraced these breakthroughs with enthusiasm, proclaiming the dawn of a new AI era, heralding deep learning as the key that had finally unlocked the mysteries of artificial intelligence, and fueling a widespread belief that the long-awaited AI revolution was finally upon us. Experts and researchers, initially cautiously optimistic, began to express a growing sense of excitement about the potential of deep learning, envisioning a future where neural networks could solve increasingly complex problems and eventually achieve human-level intelligence across a broad range of domains. Venture capital, ever attuned to disruptive technological trends, began to pour into deep learning startups and AI-focused research, recognizing the immense market potential and the promise of transformative innovation offered by this rapidly advancing field. The hype train, fueled by these initial successes and amplified by media enthusiasm and investor excitement, began to gather momentum, accelerating towards the AI overdrive we are currently experiencing.

Yet, even amidst this initial euphoria and widespread celebration of deep learning's triumphs, a dissenting voice emerged, a voice of caution, reason, and scientifically grounded skepticism, questioning the prevailing narrative of a paradigm shift and raising early concerns about the fundamental limitations of this newly dominant approach to artificial intelligence. That voice, sharp, insightful, and remarkably prescient, belonged to Gary Marcus. Even as the hype train was just beginning to leave the station, even as the media was breathlessly proclaiming a technological revolution, and even as investors were eagerly pouring capital into deep learning ventures, Marcus was already expressing reservations, raising critical questions, and challenging the overly optimistic pronouncements surrounding deep neural networks. His skepticism was not born of ignorance or a resistance to technological progress; it was, instead, rooted in his deep understanding of neuroscience, cognitive science, and the inherent complexities of intelligence itself, both biological and artificial. He recognized, even in those early days of deep learning euphoria, that while neural networks had undeniably achieved impressive feats in certain narrow domains, they were fundamentally different from true human-level intelligence, and that their limitations, often glossed over in the hype, were likely to become increasingly apparent as AI systems were deployed in more complex and less controlled real-world scenarios.

Marcus's early skepticism was not simply a gut feeling or a contrarian impulse; it was a scientifically informed and rigorously argued perspective, grounded in his deep understanding of the cognitive sciences and the limitations of purely statistical approaches to intelligence. He recognized that while deep learning excelled at pattern recognition and statistical learning from vast datasets, it fundamentally lacked the kind of structured knowledge representation, common sense reasoning, and robust generalization abilities that are hallmarks of human intelligence. He cautioned against extrapolating narrow successes in benchmark tasks to broader claims of general intelligence, warning that deep learning, while impressive in certain limited domains, was unlikely to be the magic bullet that would unlock the mysteries of artificial general intelligence or solve all of humanity's problems. His early critiques, often published in blog posts, articles, and public discussions, served as a crucial counterpoint to the prevailing hype narrative, offering a voice of reason and scientific caution amidst the rising tide of technological utopianism, setting the stage for his later, more comprehensive, and increasingly necessary deconstruction of the deep learning monoculture and his advocacy for alternative, more robust, and more genuinely intelligent approaches to artificial intelligence. And as the AI hype machine has accelerated into overdrive, Marcus's early skepticism has not only been vindicated, but has become increasingly essential, providing the critical framework necessary to discern genuine progress from carefully constructed illusions, and to navigate the complex and often misleading landscape of artificial intelligence in the 21st century.

One of the most glaring and pervasive flaws of deep learning, a limitation that directly undermines its claims to robustness, reliability, and genuine intelligence, is its inherent brittleness and striking lack of generalization. While deep learning models can achieve impressive performance within the carefully controlled environments of their training data and benchmark datasets, they often fail spectacularly, exhibiting catastrophic performance degradation, when faced with even slightly different inputs, novel situations, or real-world complexities that deviate from their meticulously curated training regimes. This brittleness, this inability to generalize beyond the narrow confines of their training data, is not just a minor inconvenience or a temporary limitation of current deep learning systems; it is, as Gary Marcus has consistently and forcefully argued, a fundamental flaw, a deep and inherent vulnerability that undermines the very notion of deep learning as a path towards truly robust and general intelligence, revealing a critical disconnect between the hype surrounding deep learning and the often-disappointing reality of its real-world performance.

This brittleness is perhaps most dramatically illustrated by the phenomenon of adversarial examples, subtle but deliberately crafted perturbations to input data, often imperceptible to human observers, that can completely fool even the most sophisticated deep learning models, causing them to misclassify images, misinterpret text, or make entirely erroneous decisions with alarming ease. Adversarial examples are not just theoretical curiosities or edge cases; they are a pervasive and readily exploitable vulnerability of deep learning systems, demonstrating their reliance on superficial statistical correlations rather than genuine understanding, and exposing their fundamental lack of robustness and reliability in the face of even minor deviations from their training data. Imagine an image recognition system trained to identify stop signs with near-perfect accuracy on a vast dataset of pristine stop sign images. Now, introduce a subtly altered image of a stop sign, perhaps with a few strategically placed pixels changed, imperceptible to the human eye, but carefully crafted to exploit the internal workings of the deep learning model. This adversarial example, this subtly perturbed stop sign image, can completely baffle the AI, causing it to misclassify the stop sign as something entirely different – a speed limit sign, a yield sign, or even something completely nonsensical like a banana or a cat – demonstrating the alarming fragility of the system and its susceptibility to even the most minor and imperceptible manipulations.

This vulnerability to adversarial examples is not limited to image recognition; it extends across various domains where deep learning is applied, from natural language processing to speech recognition, from autonomous driving to medical diagnosis. Adversarial attacks can be crafted to fool chatbots into generating nonsensical or harmful responses, to mislead speech recognition systems into transcribing gibberish, to cause self-driving cars to misinterpret traffic signals, and to trick medical AI systems into misdiagnosing diseases, highlighting the pervasive and potentially dangerous nature of this brittleness across a wide range of deep learning applications. The ease with which adversarial examples can be generated and deployed, often with readily available toolkits and relatively little technical expertise, further underscores the severity of this vulnerability, demonstrating that deep learning systems are not just theoretically fragile, but practically vulnerable to malicious attacks and unintended errors in real-world deployments. This inherent brittleness, exposed by the adversarial example phenomenon, reveals a fundamental flaw in the very foundation of deep learning, highlighting its reliance on superficial statistical patterns rather than genuine understanding, and casting serious doubt on its suitability for safety-critical applications or any domain requiring robust reliability and resistance to manipulation.

Beyond the deliberately crafted vulnerabilities exposed by adversarial examples, deep learning systems also exhibit a more general and equally concerning lack of generalization, failing to perform reliably when deployed in environments or presented with data that deviates even slightly from the carefully controlled conditions of their training regimes. This out-of-distribution failure, this inability to adapt to novel situations or generalize beyond their training data, is another key manifestation of deep learning's brittleness, demonstrating its limited capacity for true intelligence and its reliance on memorization and pattern matching rather than genuine understanding and robust reasoning. Consider a self-driving car system trained extensively on vast datasets of driving scenarios in sunny California, meticulously optimized to navigate the specific road conditions, traffic patterns, and environmental characteristics of that region. Now, deploy the same self-driving car system in a different environment, perhaps a rainy city like Seattle or a snowy region like Boston, with different road markings, weather conditions, and traffic patterns. The self-driving car system, despite its impressive performance in its training environment, may exhibit a dramatic drop in performance in this new, out-of-distribution setting, struggling to navigate unfamiliar road conditions, misinterpreting sensor data in different weather conditions, and exhibiting a level of unreliability that would be entirely unacceptable for real-world deployment.

This out-of-distribution failure is not simply a matter of needing to retrain the model on more diverse data; it is a symptom of a deeper problem, reflecting the fundamental limitations of deep learning's approach to learning and generalization. Deep learning models, trained to minimize error on a specific training dataset, tend to overfit to the statistical idiosyncrasies of that dataset, learning superficial correlations and memorizing specific patterns rather than acquiring robust, generalizable principles that can be applied across different environments and novel situations. This overfitting to training data, this lack of true generalization, is a pervasive limitation of deep learning, hindering its ability to adapt to the complexities and variability of the real world, and casting serious doubt on its suitability for applications that require robust performance across diverse and unpredictable environments. Whether it is a medical diagnosis AI trained on data from one hospital system failing to generalize to data from another hospital, or a natural language processing system trained on general internet text struggling to understand specialized domain-specific language, the lack of generalization in deep learning consistently emerges as a major obstacle to its widespread and reliable deployment in real-world applications, highlighting its inherent brittleness and its limited capacity for true intelligence beyond the narrow confines of its training data.

Further illustrating the narrowness and brittleness of deep learning is the stark contrast between its impressive mastery of certain games and its blatant uselessness in even slightly more complex real-world scenarios. Deep learning systems have achieved superhuman performance in games like Go, Chess, and various Atari video games, surpassing human players in strategic complexity and achieving levels of gameplay previously considered unattainable by machines. These game-playing achievements have been widely celebrated as milestones in artificial intelligence, often cited as evidence of rapid progress towards human-level intelligence and the transformative potential of deep learning. However, a closer examination reveals a more nuanced and ultimately more sobering reality: the "intelligence" exhibited by game-playing AI systems is remarkably narrow, highly specialized, and utterly lacking in the kind of generalizability and adaptability that characterizes true human intelligence. While DeepMind's AlphaGo system may have conquered the game of Go, mastering its intricate rules and strategic complexities, that same system is utterly incapable of performing even the most basic common sense tasks in the real world, such as understanding a simple story, navigating a kitchen, or engaging in a meaningful conversation about anything outside the narrow domain of Go. The "intelligence" of AlphaGo is confined entirely to the game of Go; it cannot be transferred, generalized, or applied to any other domain, highlighting the stark limitations of its narrow, task-specific expertise.

Similarly, AI systems that excel at playing Atari video games, achieving superhuman scores in specific games, are completely useless outside the confines of those games, unable to transfer their "learning" or "intelligence" to even slightly different games or real-world scenarios. The skills learned by an Atari-playing AI are deeply embedded in the specific rules, environments, and reward structures of those particular games, lacking the kind of abstract, generalizable principles that would allow for transfer learning or adaptation to new challenges. This stark contrast between game mastery and real-world uselessness underscores the fundamental narrowness of current AI, revealing that its impressive performance in games is often achieved through brute-force computation, massive amounts of training data, and highly specialized algorithmic architectures, rather than through the kind of genuine intelligence, common sense reasoning, and robust generalization abilities that are hallmarks of human cognition. Game mastery, therefore, while a technically impressive feat, serves as a misleading benchmark for general intelligence, highlighting the narrow expertise and zero transfer capabilities of current AI systems, and further exposing the brittleness and limited scope of deep learning's approach to artificial intelligence.

And perhaps the most telling analogy for understanding the fundamental brittleness and lack of generalization in deep learning, an analogy that Gary Marcus frequently invokes and powerfully elucidates, is the story of "Clever Hans," the horse that appeared to do arithmetic and answer complex questions at the turn of the 20th century. Clever Hans, a seemingly intelligent horse, captivated audiences with his ability to tap out answers to mathematical problems and respond to complex questions by tapping his hoof, leading many to believe that he possessed genuine mathematical and cognitive abilities. However, upon closer scientific investigation, it was revealed that Clever Hans was not actually doing arithmetic or understanding questions; he was simply responding to subtle, often unconscious, cues from his trainer, particularly changes in posture and breathing, stopping his hoof taps when he detected these cues, creating the illusion of intelligence without any genuine understanding or cognitive ability. The "Clever Hans effect," the phenomenon of appearing intelligent by exploiting subtle cues and mimicking intelligent behavior without possessing genuine understanding, serves as a powerful and enduring analogy for understanding the limitations of deep learning and the often-illusory nature of its apparent intelligence.

Deep learning systems, like Clever Hans, can appear remarkably intelligent, fluent, and capable, generating human-like text, recognizing images with impressive accuracy, and even mastering complex games, creating the illusion of genuine understanding and human-level intelligence. However, upon closer scrutiny, and particularly when faced with adversarial examples, out-of-distribution data, or novel situations, this illusion often shatters, revealing that deep learning systems, like Clever Hans, are often simply exploiting subtle statistical cues and mimicking patterns in their training data, without possessing any genuine understanding of the underlying concepts, principles, or real-world knowledge. Just as Clever Hans was responding to subtle cues from his trainer, deep learning models are responding to subtle statistical cues in their training data, creating a sophisticated form of pattern matching that can be remarkably effective within narrow domains, but fundamentally lacks the robustness, generalizability, and genuine understanding that characterizes true intelligence. The "Clever Hans effect," therefore, serves as a crucial cautionary tale for the age of AI overdrive, reminding us to look beyond the surface appearances of intelligence, to critically examine the underlying mechanisms of AI systems, and to avoid being deceived by the sophisticated mimicry and often-illusory intelligence of deep learning, recognizing its fundamental brittleness and lack of generalization as a deep and inherent flaw that undermines its claims to true intelligence and casts serious doubt on its suitability as the sole path towards a robust and reliable AI future.

Beyond the inherent brittleness and lack of generalization, another profound and equally troubling flaw plaguing deep learning systems, a limitation that directly undermines their trustworthiness, accountability, and suitability for deployment in critical real-world applications, is the pervasive "black box problem." Deep learning models, particularly the large, complex neural networks that underpin much of the current AI hype, are notoriously opaque, inscrutable, and fundamentally lacking in explainability, operating as impenetrable "black boxes" whose internal workings are largely hidden from human understanding, making it virtually impossible to discern why they make specific decisions, how they arrive at particular outputs, or what factors are driving their often-complex and non-linear behavior. This black box nature is not merely a technical inconvenience or a minor engineering challenge; it is, as Gary Marcus has repeatedly and emphatically argued, a critical deficiency, a deep and inherent flaw that raises profound ethical, practical, and societal concerns, casting serious doubt on the long-term viability and responsible deployment of deep learning as the dominant paradigm for artificial intelligence, particularly in domains where transparency, accountability, and human understanding are paramount.

The "black box" analogy is apt and deeply revealing: deep learning models function like complex, opaque boxes, taking in input data, processing it through a labyrinthine network of interconnected nodes and weighted connections, and spitting out output predictions or decisions, without offering any clear or readily understandable explanation of the internal processes that led from input to output. These neural networks, often composed of millions or even billions of parameters, learn through a process of backpropagation and gradient descent, adjusting their internal weights and biases based on vast amounts of training data, gradually optimizing their performance on specific tasks. However, this learning process, while undeniably effective in achieving impressive performance on certain benchmarks, results in highly complex and non-linear models whose internal representations, decision-making pathways, and learned rules are virtually impossible for humans to interpret or understand. Imagine trying to reverse-engineer the decision-making process of a deep learning model by examining its millions of interconnected parameters and complex mathematical equations – it is a task akin to deciphering an alien language or unraveling an impossibly tangled knot, a near-impossible endeavor that leaves the inner workings of the model shrouded in opacity.

This opacity is not merely a matter of technical complexity or computational intractability; it is a fundamental characteristic of the deep learning paradigm, stemming from the very nature of neural network architectures and their data-driven learning processes. Deep learning models learn through distributed representations, encoding information across vast networks of interconnected nodes, rather than relying on explicit symbolic rules or human-interpretable knowledge representations. Their decision-making processes are often emergent, arising from the complex interactions of millions of parameters, rather than being explicitly programmed or readily traceable to human-understandable logic. This inherent opacity makes it exceedingly difficult, if not impossible, to understand why a deep learning model makes a particular decision, what features of the input data are most influential in driving its output, or what internal representations are being activated during the processing of information. The black box nature of deep learning, therefore, is not a bug to be fixed or a challenge to be overcome; it is a fundamental feature of the technology itself, deeply ingrained in its architecture, its learning mechanisms, and its inherent reliance on opaque statistical representations.

The consequences of this black box problem are far-reaching and deeply concerning, raising serious ethical, practical, and societal challenges for the widespread deployment of deep learning in real-world applications. One of the most immediate and pressing concerns is the ethical implications of deploying opaque AI systems in domains where fairness, accountability, and transparency are paramount, such as criminal justice, loan applications, hiring decisions, and medical diagnosis. Imagine an AI system used to predict recidivism risk in criminal justice, informing decisions about parole, sentencing, or bail. If this AI system is a black box, its decision-making process inscrutable and opaque, how can we ensure that it is fair, unbiased, and not perpetuating existing societal inequalities? If the AI system exhibits racial bias, leading to disproportionately higher risk scores for individuals from certain racial groups, how can we detect and mitigate this bias if we cannot understand why the system is making these decisions? Accountability becomes virtually impossible when decisions are made by black boxes, as there is no clear or transparent rationale that can be examined, challenged, or rectified. Who is responsible when a black box AI system makes a mistake or causes harm – the developers, the deployers, or the AI system itself? The lack of explainability in deep learning undermines the very foundations of ethical AI deployment, raising profound questions about fairness, accountability, and the potential for bias and discrimination to be embedded and amplified within opaque algorithmic systems.

Beyond the ethical implications, the black box problem also poses significant practical challenges for debugging, improving, and trusting deep learning systems, hindering their reliability and limiting their suitability for safety-critical applications. When a deep learning system fails, makes an error, or exhibits unexpected behavior, the black box nature makes it exceedingly difficult to diagnose the root cause of the problem, to identify the specific factors that led to the failure, and to systematically debug and improve the system's performance. Imagine a self-driving car system that makes a critical error, causing an accident or a near-miss. If the self-driving system is based on a black box deep learning model, how can engineers and safety experts effectively investigate the cause of the error, identify the specific algorithmic flaws or data deficiencies that contributed to the failure, and implement targeted fixes to prevent similar errors from occurring in the future? Debugging a black box is akin to fixing a complex machine without understanding its internal workings, relying on trial and error, and often resorting to ad-hoc patches rather than systematic and principled solutions. This difficulty in debugging and improving black box AI systems not only hinders their reliability but also erodes trust in their performance, particularly in safety-critical domains where errors can have severe and even life-threatening consequences. How can we trust an autonomous vehicle to navigate complex traffic scenarios safely if we cannot understand why it makes certain decisions, and if we cannot reliably debug and fix its errors due to its opaque black box nature?

Furthermore, the lack of explainability in deep learning undermines user trust and hinders the effective human-AI collaboration that is crucial for maximizing the benefits and mitigating the risks of artificial intelligence. In many real-world applications, particularly in domains requiring human expertise and judgment, AI systems are not intended to replace humans entirely, but rather to augment human capabilities, to provide decision support, and to collaborate with human users in complex problem-solving scenarios. However, effective human-AI collaboration requires trust, transparency, and a shared understanding of the AI system's reasoning and decision-making processes. If an AI system is a black box, its recommendations and decisions opaque and inscrutable, human users are likely to be hesitant to trust or rely on its output, particularly in high-stakes situations where they are ultimately responsible for the consequences of their decisions. Imagine a medical doctor using an AI system to assist in diagnosing a complex medical condition. If the AI system provides a diagnosis without offering any clear explanation or rationale for its recommendation, the doctor may be understandably reluctant to blindly trust the AI's output, particularly if it contradicts their own clinical judgment or intuition. Human trust in AI, therefore, is inextricably linked to explainability and transparency, and the black box nature of deep learning directly undermines this trust, hindering effective human-AI collaboration and limiting the potential benefits of AI in domains requiring human oversight, judgment, and accountability.

The black box problem of deep learning, therefore, represents a profound and multifaceted flaw, raising serious ethical, practical, and societal concerns that cannot be easily dismissed or simply brushed aside in the rush to embrace the hype and deploy deep learning technologies across various domains. It is not merely a technical challenge to be overcome with better algorithms or more sophisticated explainability techniques; it is a fundamental limitation of the deep learning paradigm itself, stemming from its inherent opacity, its reliance on statistical pattern matching, and its lack of human-understandable knowledge representation and reasoning processes. Addressing the black box problem, therefore, requires more than just incremental improvements or superficial fixes; it necessitates a fundamental rethinking of AI architectures, a shift towards more transparent, interpretable, and explainable AI approaches, and a recognition that true intelligence, particularly in domains requiring trust, accountability, and human understanding, cannot be achieved through opaque black boxes alone. And it is precisely in advocating for this shift, for a move away from black box AI and towards more transparent and explainable alternatives, that Gary Marcus's critique of deep learning becomes not just insightful, but absolutely essential for navigating the age of AI overdrive responsibly and ethically, moving beyond the seductive allure of opaque algorithmic power and towards a more human-centered and more trustworthy future for artificial intelligence.

Finally, and perhaps most fundamentally, underlying all these other flaws and limitations, deep learning suffers from a profound and ultimately constraining data dependency, an insatiable hunger for vast quantities of meticulously labeled training data that not only limits its scalability and practicality in many real-world scenarios, but also exposes a deeper, more philosophical limitation: the reliance on data as a crutch, a substitute for genuine understanding, and a potential dead end in the pursuit of true artificial intelligence. Deep learning models, particularly the large, complex neural networks that drive much of the current AI hype, are notoriously data-hungry, requiring massive datasets, often terabytes or even petabytes in size, to achieve their impressive performance on specific tasks. This data dependency is not just a matter of computational resources or engineering challenges; it is a fundamental characteristic of the deep learning paradigm, stemming from its reliance on statistical learning and its inherent need to extract patterns and correlations from vast amounts of examples, rather than relying on explicit knowledge, structured reasoning, or more data-efficient learning mechanisms. This insatiable hunger for data not only limits the practicality and scalability of deep learning in many real-world applications where labeled data is scarce or expensive to acquire, but also raises deeper questions about the nature of intelligence itself, suggesting that relying solely on data, no matter how vast, may be insufficient to achieve true understanding, robust reasoning, and the kind of general intelligence that humans effortlessly deploy with far less data and far more efficiency.

Consider the enormous datasets required to train state-of-the-art large language models like GPT-3 and GPT-4. These models are trained on massive corpora of text data, often scraping vast swathes of the internet, including websites, books, articles, and social media posts, amassing datasets that are measured in terabytes and require enormous computational resources and energy consumption to process and learn from. The sheer scale of these datasets raises significant practical and environmental concerns, limiting the accessibility and sustainability of this data-intensive approach to AI development. Not every research lab, startup, or even large company has access to the kind of computational infrastructure and data resources required to train these massive models, concentrating AI development power in the hands of a few tech giants and potentially stifling innovation and diversity in the broader AI field. Furthermore, the environmental impact of training these massive models, with their enormous energy consumption and carbon footprint, raises serious ethical questions about the sustainability and long-term viability of this data-hungry approach to AI, particularly in a world increasingly concerned about climate change and environmental responsibility.

Beyond the practical and environmental concerns, the data dependency of deep learning also raises more fundamental questions about the nature of intelligence and the limits of data-driven learning. Humans, unlike deep learning models, are remarkably data-efficient learners, able to acquire complex skills, understand new concepts, and generalize to novel situations with far less data and far more efficiency than even the most advanced AI systems. A child can learn to recognize a cat after seeing only a few examples, can understand the concept of gravity after a few experiences of objects falling, and can generalize learned knowledge to new situations and novel contexts with remarkable ease, demonstrating a level of data efficiency and generalization ability that remains far beyond the reach of current deep learning. This stark contrast between human data efficiency and deep learning data hunger suggests that humans are not simply learning through brute-force statistical pattern matching from vast datasets; they are employing more sophisticated learning mechanisms, incorporating prior knowledge, leveraging structured representations, and engaging in more abstract and efficient forms of reasoning that allow them to learn effectively from limited data and generalize robustly to novel situations.

The reliance on data as a crutch, therefore, in deep learning may be masking fundamental algorithmic deficiencies, obscuring the need for more knowledge-rich, reasoning-capable, and data-efficient approaches to artificial intelligence. By throwing ever-larger datasets and ever-more-powerful computational resources at the problem, deep learning researchers may be inadvertently reinforcing a paradigm that is fundamentally limited, hitting diminishing returns in terms of achieving true intelligence, and potentially diverting resources and attention away from more promising alternative approaches that prioritize knowledge representation, symbolic reasoning, and more human-like learning mechanisms. The pursuit of ever-larger language models, trained on ever-vaster datasets, may be leading to incremental improvements in certain narrow benchmarks, but it is unlikely to address the fundamental limitations of deep learning, such as the lack of common sense, the brittleness, the hallucination problem, and the inherent opacity of these data-driven black boxes. Data, in this context, may be serving as a seductive but ultimately misleading substitute for genuine algorithmic innovation, a technological crutch that allows for impressive performance on narrow tasks but ultimately hinders progress towards more robust, reliable, and genuinely intelligent artificial intelligence.

And it is precisely this point, this critical recognition of deep learning's deep flaws – its brittleness, its black box nature, its data dependency – that underscores the profound necessity of Gary Marcus's critique, his unwavering commitment to exposing the limitations of the dominant deep learning paradigm, and his urgent call for a "reboot" of artificial intelligence, a shift towards more knowledge-rich, reasoning-capable, and ultimately more human-centered approaches. Deep learning, while undeniably achieving impressive feats in certain narrow domains, is fundamentally flawed, deeply limited, and clearly insufficient as the sole path towards a robust, reliable, and genuinely intelligent AI future. Acknowledging these deep flaws, dismantling the hype that often obscures them, and embracing alternative approaches, such as the neuro-symbolic bridge that Marcus so eloquently advocates for, is not just a matter of scientific debate or technical preference; it is a crucial and urgent necessity for navigating the age of AI overdrive responsibly, ethically, and with a clear-eyed understanding of both the promises and the very real perils of artificial intelligence in the 21st century. And it is in this crucial endeavor of critical assessment, intellectual honesty, and the pursuit of a more genuinely intelligent and responsible AI future that the voice of Gary Marcus, the unflinching exposer of deep learning's deep flaws, becomes not just valuable, but absolutely indispensable.

Chapter 5

The Hallucination Problem

Beneath the polished veneer of impressive AI demonstrations, beyond the seductive fluency of large language models, and lurking within the opaque depths of deep neural networks, lies a deeply troubling and increasingly unavoidable flaw: the AI hallucination problem. This is not merely a minor glitch, a temporary imperfection to be ironed out with further refinement; it is, as Gary Marcus has tirelessly and urgently emphasized, a fundamental and systemic vulnerability, a critical deficiency that undermines the trustworthiness, reliability, and ultimate viability of current AI systems, particularly those based on the dominant paradigm of deep learning. AI hallucinations, the disconcerting tendency of artificial intelligence to confidently fabricate falsehoods, to generate factually incorrect information with unwavering conviction, and to present fabricated narratives as if they were grounded in reality, are not just random errors or occasional missteps; they are a pervasive and deeply concerning symptom of a more profound underlying problem: the fundamental disconnect between current AI and genuine understanding, the critical absence of a robust model of truth, and the alarming ease with which these seemingly intelligent systems can confidently and convincingly make things up, often with potentially serious and far-reaching consequences.

These hallucinations are not subtle glitches, easily dismissed as minor imperfections in otherwise flawless systems. They are often blatant, false, and yet presented with an air of unwavering certainty, a digital confidence that belies the utter lack of factual basis in the AI's pronouncements. Consider the now-infamous examples of ChatGPT, the poster child of the current generative AI boom, confidently inventing legal cases and citing nonexistent court precedents when asked to provide legal citations, a spectacular failure that directly undermined the credibility of lawyers relying on the AI for legal research and exposed the potential for real-world harm arising from AI hallucinations in high-stakes professional settings. Or consider the equally alarming instances of AI chatbots fabricating biographical details about individuals, creating entirely fictional resumes and inventing nonexistent accomplishments with persuasive detail, demonstrating the potential for AI to generate highly convincing, yet completely false, personal narratives, blurring the lines between truth and fabrication in the digital age. These are not isolated incidents or rare edge cases; they are just the tip of the iceberg, readily observable examples of a far more pervasive and deeply ingrained problem: the inherent tendency of current AI systems, particularly large language models, to confidently hallucinate, to fabricate falsehoods, and to present fiction as fact with an unnerving and often misleading air of authority.

The range and variety of AI hallucinations are disturbingly broad, extending beyond simple factual inaccuracies to encompass a wide spectrum of fabricated content, ranging from nonsensical outputs and logically incoherent statements to elaborate confabulated narratives and entirely invented scenarios. AI systems hallucinate historical events that never occurred, invent scientific claims unsupported by evidence, fabricate biographical details about nonexistent people, and generate plausible but entirely fictional stories with remarkable ease and persuasive detail. They confidently assert falsehoods as truths, invent sources and citations out of thin air, and present their fabricated outputs with an unwavering air of certainty, often lacking any indication of doubt, uncertainty, or awareness of their own potential for error. This unwavering confidence, this digital bravado in the face of factual emptiness, is perhaps one of the most unsettling aspects of AI hallucinations, making them not just errors, but potentially dangerous forms of misinformation, capable of misleading users, eroding trust, and undermining the very foundations of truth and reliability in the digital information landscape.

It is crucial to recognize that these hallucinations are not simply random mistakes or occasional glitches in otherwise reliable systems. They are not analogous to software bugs that can be identified, debugged, and eliminated through traditional software engineering practices. Instead, AI hallucinations are systemic, deeply rooted in the fundamental design and learning mechanisms of current AI systems, particularly large language models. They are not just isolated errors, but rather symptoms of a more profound underlying problem: the inherent limitations of statistical language models, their lack of grounding in reality, and their fundamental inability to distinguish between statistical plausibility and factual accuracy. Hallucinations are not easily fixable with more data, larger models, or incremental improvements to current architectures; they are a more fundamental challenge, requiring a rethinking of the very foundations of artificial intelligence and a shift towards more knowledge-rich, reasoning-capable, and more reliable approaches. They are not just "mistakes" to be corrected; they are symptoms of a deeper "truth problem" in AI, revealing a critical disconnect between current AI's capabilities and the essential human capacity to discern truth from falsehood, fact from fiction, and reality from fabrication.

At the heart of the AI hallucination problem lies a fundamental "truth problem," a critical deficiency in current AI systems, particularly large language models, that stems from their inherent lack of a robust model of truth, reality, or factuality. These AI systems, trained on vast datasets of text data, are optimized to generate statistically plausible and contextually coherent text, to predict the next word in a sequence based on patterns learned from their training corpora, but they are fundamentally not designed to verify the truthfulness of the information they generate, to ground their knowledge in real-world evidence, or to distinguish between factual accuracy and mere statistical plausibility. They operate in a purely symbolic realm, manipulating words and phrases based on statistical relationships learned from text data, without any direct connection to the real world, sensory experience, or embodied understanding that underpins human knowledge and our capacity to discern truth from falsehood. This fundamental lack of a "truth model" is not just a minor technical detail; it is a critical deficiency that directly leads to the hallucination problem, explaining why AI systems can confidently and convincingly fabricate falsehoods, and revealing the profound gap between current AI's capabilities and the essential human capacity for truth discernment and factual accuracy.

Truth, for humans, is not merely a matter of statistical plausibility or contextual coherence; it is a deeply grounded and multifaceted concept, rooted in empirical evidence, real-world observation, sensory experience, and a complex web of interconnected knowledge, beliefs, and verification processes. Humans verify truth through a variety of means: we rely on our senses to observe the world directly, we conduct experiments to test hypotheses and gather empirical evidence, we consult reliable sources of information, we engage in critical thinking and logical reasoning, and we rely on social consensus and peer review to validate and refine our understanding of reality. This complex and multifaceted process of truth verification is deeply intertwined with our embodied experience, our interaction with the physical and social world, and our capacity for critical reflection and evidence-based reasoning. Current AI systems, particularly large language models, lack all of these crucial components of human truth discernment. They have no senses, no capacity for direct real-world observation, no embodied experience, and no genuine understanding of the verification processes that humans rely on to distinguish truth from falsehood. Their "knowledge" is purely textual, symbolic, and statistically derived, lacking the grounding, the verification mechanisms, and the robust connection to reality that underpins human truth discernment and prevents us from confidently fabricating falsehoods and mistaking fiction for fact.

The AI hallucination problem, therefore, is not just a matter of occasional errors or minor inaccuracies; it is a symptom of a deeper epistemological challenge, revealing the fundamental limitations of current AI's approach to knowledge, truth, and understanding. It underscores the crucial point that generating statistically plausible text, however fluent and coherent, is fundamentally different from possessing genuine understanding, discerning factual accuracy, and reliably distinguishing truth from falsehood. It highlights the urgent need for a paradigm shift in AI research, a move beyond purely statistical language models and towards more knowledge-rich, reasoning-capable, and more reliable approaches that can ground AI systems in a robust model of truth, enable them to verify their claims against real-world evidence, and ultimately, build artificial intelligence that is not just statistically fluent, but also truthful, trustworthy, and genuinely intelligent. And it is precisely in exposing this "truth problem" in AI, in highlighting the inherent limitations of current approaches, and in advocating for a more robust and epistemologically sound path forward, that Gary Marcus's critique of AI hallucinations becomes not just insightful, but absolutely essential for navigating the age of AI overdrive responsibly, ethically, and with a clear-eyed understanding of the very real perils of mistaking sophisticated statistical mimicry for genuine human-level understanding and truth discernment.

At the root of the AI hallucination problem lie several interconnected causes, deeply embedded in the fundamental architecture and training methodologies of current AI systems, particularly large language models. Understanding these root causes is crucial not only for diagnosing the problem but also for developing effective solutions and charting a more responsible and reliable path forward for artificial intelligence. One of the most fundamental root causes is the very nature of statistical language modeling itself, the underlying technology that powers large language models like GPT-3, ChatGPT, and Bard. These models, as their name suggests, are fundamentally statistical in nature, trained to predict the next word in a sequence based on statistical patterns learned from vast amounts of text data, without any genuine understanding of the meaning of the words, the truthfulness of the information, or the real-world context to which the text refers. They are, in essence, sophisticated pattern-matching machines, adept at identifying statistical regularities in language and generating text that is statistically plausible and contextually coherent, but fundamentally lacking in the kind of semantic understanding, factual grounding, and truth discernment that characterizes human language comprehension and generation.

Statistical language models operate by constructing complex statistical representations of language, learning to predict the probability of words occurring in sequence based on their co-occurrence patterns in massive text corpora. They learn to associate words with other words, phrases with other phrases, and grammatical structures with other grammatical structures, building up a vast statistical map of language that allows them to generate text that mimics human writing in terms of style, grammar, and topical coherence. However, this statistical mastery of language is fundamentally different from genuine understanding. Statistical language models do not understand the meaning of the words they are manipulating, the concepts they are representing, or the truthfulness of the information they are conveying. They are, in essence, manipulating symbols without understanding their semantic content, generating text based on statistical probabilities rather than genuine comprehension. This lack of semantic understanding is a crucial root cause of the hallucination problem, explaining why these models can confidently generate text that is grammatically correct, stylistically fluent, and topically relevant, but nonetheless factually incorrect, nonsensical, or entirely fabricated. They are generating text that sounds intelligent, but lacks the underlying semantic grounding and truth discernment that characterizes genuine human communication and prevents us from confidently asserting falsehoods as facts.

Consider the analogy of a highly sophisticated "autocomplete" system, trained on the entire internet. This autocomplete system, like a large language model, would be incredibly adept at predicting the next word in a sentence, based on statistical patterns learned from its vast training data. It could generate fluent and contextually relevant text, mimicking human writing with remarkable proficiency. However, this autocomplete system, no matter how sophisticated its statistical models, would not actually understand the meaning of the text it is generating. It would be simply predicting words based on statistical probabilities, without any genuine comprehension of the semantic content, the real-world implications, or the truthfulness of the information being conveyed. If asked to complete the sentence "The capital of France is...", the autocomplete system would confidently predict "Paris," based on the statistical likelihood of "Paris" following "The capital of France is..." in its training data. However, if asked to complete the sentence "The capital of France is...", and then subtly prompted to generate a false answer, the autocomplete system, lacking a genuine understanding of truth and factuality, might just as confidently predict "London" or "Berlin," if those words happened to be statistically plausible completions based on other patterns in its training data, demonstrating its inability to discern between truth and falsehood, and its reliance solely on statistical plausibility rather than factual accuracy.

This "autocomplete" analogy highlights the fundamental limitation of statistical language modeling as a root cause of the hallucination problem. Large language models, like sophisticated autocomplete systems, are trained to generate statistically plausible text, not necessarily truthful text. Their primary objective is to mimic human language patterns, to generate text that is fluent, coherent, and contextually relevant, but not necessarily factually accurate, semantically grounded, or true. This inherent focus on statistical plausibility over truth discernment is a crucial design flaw, a fundamental limitation that makes hallucinations almost inevitable in these systems, explaining why they can confidently fabricate falsehoods, generate nonsensical outputs, and present fiction as fact with such alarming ease and persuasive conviction. Addressing the hallucination problem, therefore, requires moving beyond purely statistical language modeling, towards AI architectures that incorporate more robust mechanisms for truth verification, factual grounding, and genuine semantic understanding, going beyond the limitations of sophisticated autocomplete systems and striving for a more human-like capacity for truth discernment and reliable communication.

Another critical root cause of the AI hallucination problem, closely related to the limitations of statistical language modeling, is the fundamental absence of real-world grounding in current AI systems, particularly large language models. These models are trained solely on text data, learning from vast corpora of written language, but lacking any direct connection to the real world, sensory experience, or embodied interaction that underpins human knowledge, common sense reasoning, and our capacity to discern truth from falsehood. This lack of grounding in reality is not just a minor technical detail; it is a profound epistemological deficiency, explaining why AI systems can confidently fabricate falsehoods, generate nonsensical outputs, and present fiction as fact with such alarming ease and persuasive conviction, revealing their fundamental disconnect from the real world and their inability to verify their claims against empirical evidence or sensory experience. Humans, in contrast, acquire knowledge and verify truth through a constant process of interaction with the physical and social world, grounding our understanding in sensory experience, embodied action, and real-world feedback. We learn about the world through seeing, hearing, touching, tasting, and smelling, building up a rich and multifaceted sensory representation of reality that allows us to verify our beliefs, test our hypotheses, and distinguish between truth and falsehood based on empirical evidence and real-world observation.

Humans, in contrast, acquire knowledge and verify truth through a constant process of interaction with the physical and social world, grounding our understanding in sensory experience, embodied action, and real-world feedback. We learn about the world through seeing, hearing, touching, tasting, and smelling, building up a rich and multifaceted sensory representation of reality that allows us to verify our beliefs, test our hypotheses, and distinguish between truth and falsehood based on empirical evidence and real-world observation. Large language models, trained solely on text data, lack this crucial grounding in reality. They have no senses, no bodies, no capacity for direct interaction with the physical world. Their "knowledge" is purely textual, symbolic, and abstract, derived solely from patterns in written language, without any direct connection to the sensory richness, embodied experience, and real-world feedback that underpins human understanding and truth discernment. This fundamental lack of grounding in reality is a crucial root cause of the hallucination problem, explaining why AI systems can confidently fabricate falsehoods, generate nonsensical outputs, and present fiction as fact with such alarming ease and persuasive conviction, revealing their fundamental disconnect from the real world and their inability to verify their claims against empirical evidence or sensory experience.

Consider the analogy of a "brain in a vat," a philosophical thought experiment that imagines a brain sustained in a vat of nutrients, receiving sensory input through electrodes connected to a computer simulation of reality. This brain in a vat, like a large language model, would have no direct experience of the real world, no embodied interaction with physical objects, and no sensory feedback from its actions in the world. Its "knowledge" would be entirely derived from the simulated sensory input, a purely symbolic and abstract representation of reality, lacking any genuine grounding in the physical world. If this brain in a vat were asked to generate text about the real world, it might produce fluent and contextually coherent narratives based on its simulated sensory input, but it would have no way to verify the truthfulness of its claims against real-world evidence, no capacity to distinguish between simulated reality and actual reality, and no inherent mechanism to prevent it from confidently fabricating falsehoods or mistaking simulated fiction for real-world fact. Large language models, trained solely on text data and lacking any direct connection to the real world, are, in essence, digital "brains in a vat," operating in a purely symbolic realm, generating text based on statistical patterns learned from their textual training data, without any robust mechanism for grounding their knowledge in reality or verifying the truthfulness of their claims against empirical evidence or sensory experience.

This lack of real-world grounding is not just a technical limitation to be overcome with better sensors or more multimodal data; it is a more fundamental epistemological challenge, revealing the inherent limitations of purely text-based learning and the crucial role of embodied experience and real-world interaction in the development of genuine intelligence and truth discernment. Addressing the hallucination problem, therefore, requires moving beyond purely text-based AI architectures, towards systems that can incorporate multimodal sensory input, engage in embodied interaction with the real world, and develop more robust mechanisms for grounding their knowledge in empirical evidence and real-world feedback, going beyond the limitations of digital "brains in vats" and striving for a more embodied, grounded, and more truthful form of artificial intelligence.

Another contributing factor to the AI hallucination problem, often overlooked but nonetheless significant, is the inherent "parrot-like" nature of current large language models, their tendency to mimic human language patterns and generate fluent text without necessarily possessing genuine understanding, intentionality, or a commitment to truthfulness. This "parrot" analogy, while perhaps seemingly simplistic or dismissive, captures a crucial aspect of the limitations of current AI, highlighting the distinction between statistical fluency and genuine comprehension, and revealing why these models can confidently generate text that sounds intelligent, but nonetheless lacks the underlying semantic grounding, truth discernment, and commitment to factual accuracy that characterizes genuine human communication. Large language models, trained to predict the next word in a sequence based on statistical patterns, are, in essence, learning to mimic human language, to statistically approximate the patterns and structures of written text, without necessarily understanding the meaning of the words, the concepts they represent, or the communicative intentions behind the language they are generating. They are like highly sophisticated parrots, capable of mimicking human speech with remarkable accuracy and fluency, but without necessarily understanding the semantic content, the communicative purpose, or the truthfulness of the words they are uttering.

This "parrot-like" nature is not just a metaphorical description; it is a reflection of the underlying learning mechanisms and design principles of current large language models. They are trained to optimize for statistical fluency, to generate text that is grammatically correct, stylistically coherent, and contextually relevant, based on patterns learned from their training data, but they are not explicitly trained to optimize for truthfulness, factual accuracy, or genuine semantic understanding. Their objective function is to minimize statistical prediction error, not to maximize truthfulness or ensure factual accuracy. This inherent focus on statistical fluency over truthfulness is a crucial design flaw, a fundamental limitation that makes hallucinations almost inevitable in these systems, explaining why they can confidently generate text that sounds intelligent, but is nonetheless factually incorrect, nonsensical, or entirely fabricated. They are generating text that mimics the form of human communication, but lacks the underlying substance of genuine understanding, intentionality, and a commitment to truth.

Consider the analogy of a parrot trained to recite Shakespearean sonnets. This parrot, through extensive training and reinforcement, might learn to perfectly mimic the sounds and rhythms of Shakespearean language, reciting sonnets with remarkable fluency and accuracy, creating the illusion of understanding and appreciating Shakespearean poetry. However, this parrot, no matter how perfect its mimicry, would not actually understand the meaning of the sonnets, the emotional depth of the language, or the literary and cultural context to which they refer. It would be simply mimicking sounds based on learned patterns, without any genuine comprehension of the semantic content or the communicative intentions behind the poetry. Large language models, similarly, are trained to "recite" human language, to mimic the statistical patterns of written text, without necessarily understanding the deeper semantic meaning, the factual grounding, or the truthfulness of the information they are conveying. They are sophisticated digital parrots, capable of mimicking human language with impressive fluency, but without necessarily possessing the genuine understanding, intentionality, and commitment to truth that characterizes human communication and prevents us from confidently asserting falsehoods as facts.

This "parrot" analogy, while perhaps seemingly harsh or dismissive, is not intended to belittle the technical achievements of large language models or to deny their potential usefulness in certain applications. Instead, it is intended to highlight a crucial limitation, to expose a fundamental flaw, and to emphasize the urgent need for a more nuanced and realistic understanding of their capabilities and limitations, particularly in the context of the hallucination problem. Recognizing the "parrot-like" nature of current AI, acknowledging its limitations in terms of genuine understanding, truth discernment, and factual accuracy, is crucial for navigating the age of AI overdrive responsibly, ethically, and with a clear-eyed awareness of the potential for these systems to confidently fabricate falsehoods and mislead users with their statistically fluent but often semantically empty pronouncements. Addressing the hallucination problem, therefore, requires moving beyond purely parrot-like AI architectures, towards systems that can incorporate more robust mechanisms for semantic understanding, intentionality, and a genuine commitment to truthfulness, going beyond the limitations of sophisticated mimicry and striving for a more human-like capacity for meaningful communication and reliable truth discernment.

The dangers of AI hallucinations are manifold and far-reaching, extending beyond mere factual inaccuracies or occasional nonsensical outputs to encompass a wide spectrum of potentially harmful consequences, ranging from the spread of misinformation and erosion of trust to legal misjudgments, professional malpractice, and a fundamental undermining of the very foundations of truth and reliability in the digital information age. Confident hallucinations, in particular, pose a significant threat, as the unwavering certainty with which AI systems present their fabricated falsehoods can be highly persuasive, misleading users into accepting false information as fact, and amplifying the potential for harm and misjudgment in various real-world applications. The dangers of AI hallucinations are not just theoretical concerns or hypothetical risks; they are increasingly evident in real-world examples, demonstrating the urgent need to address this critical flaw and to develop more robust and reliable AI systems that can be trusted to generate truthful and factually accurate information, particularly in domains where accuracy, reliability, and trustworthiness are paramount.

One of the most immediate and widely recognized dangers of AI hallucinations is the potential for AI-generated misinformation to proliferate and spread rapidly across the digital landscape, undermining trust in information sources, polluting the public sphere with falsehoods, and exacerbating the already challenging problem of online misinformation and disinformation. Large language models, capable of generating fluent and seemingly authoritative text on virtually any topic, can be easily weaponized to create and disseminate false news articles, fabricated social media posts, misleading product descriptions, and other forms of

AI-generated misinformation at scale, flooding the internet with convincing falsehoods that are increasingly difficult for humans to discern from genuine content. The sheer volume and sophistication of AI-generated misinformation pose a significant threat to the integrity of the information ecosystem, potentially eroding public trust in media, institutions, and even reality itself, making it increasingly challenging for individuals to distinguish between truth and falsehood, and undermining the very foundations of informed public discourse and democratic decision-making.

Imagine a scenario where an AI system is used to generate fake news articles about a political candidate, fabricating false scandals, misrepresenting their policy positions, or inventing entirely fictional events to damage their reputation and influence public opinion. These AI-generated fake news articles, if sufficiently fluent and convincingly written, could spread rapidly across social media platforms, amplified by algorithms and shared by unsuspecting users, potentially swaying public opinion, undermining democratic processes, and eroding trust in political institutions and the media itself. Or consider the potential for AI to generate misleading product descriptions for online marketplaces, fabricating false claims about product features, exaggerating benefits, or inventing entirely fictional specifications to deceive consumers and drive sales of inferior or even fraudulent products. These AI-generated misleading product descriptions, if sufficiently persuasive and difficult to distinguish from genuine product information, could lead to widespread consumer deception, erode trust in online marketplaces, and undermine the integrity of e-commerce and online consumer information. The potential for AI-generated misinformation to proliferate and spread, amplified by social media and the speed of digital communication, represents a significant and growing danger, threatening to pollute the information ecosystem, erode public trust, and undermine the very foundations of truth and reliability in the digital age.

Beyond the broad societal danger of misinformation, AI hallucinations also pose more direct and immediate risks in professional and legal settings, where reliance on false or fabricated AI information can lead to serious misjudgments, professional malpractice, and potentially harmful consequences. The legal profession, as exemplified by the case of lawyers citing ChatGPT-generated fake legal cases in court, is particularly vulnerable to the dangers of AI hallucinations, as legal research and legal argumentation rely heavily on factual accuracy, verifiable sources, and the meticulous citation of legal precedents. Lawyers relying on hallucinating AI systems for legal research risk presenting fabricated legal arguments, citing nonexistent case law, and making critical errors in legal strategy, potentially leading to adverse legal outcomes for their clients, professional malpractice, and erosion of trust in the legal system itself. Imagine a lawyer, pressed for time and seeking to leverage the speed and efficiency of AI-powered legal research, relying on ChatGPT to generate relevant case citations for a legal brief. If ChatGPT, due to its hallucination problem, fabricates fake legal cases, inventing nonexistent court precedents and confidently citing them as if they were real, the lawyer, unknowingly relying on this false information, could present a legal argument based on fabricated evidence, potentially jeopardizing their client's case, facing professional sanctions, and undermining the integrity of the legal process.

Similarly, other professions that rely heavily on factual accuracy, verifiable information, and expert knowledge, such as medicine, finance, and journalism, are also vulnerable to the dangers of AI hallucinations. Medical professionals relying on hallucinating AI systems for medical diagnosis or treatment recommendations risk misdiagnosing patients, prescribing inappropriate treatments, and making critical errors in patient care, potentially leading to adverse health outcomes and medical malpractice. Financial analysts relying on hallucinating AI systems for financial analysis or investment advice risk making poor investment decisions, providing inaccurate financial forecasts, and engaging in risky financial transactions based on fabricated or unreliable information, potentially leading to financial losses and professional liability. Journalists relying on hallucinating AI systems for news gathering or fact-checking risk publishing false or fabricated news stories, spreading misinformation to the public, and eroding trust in journalistic integrity and media reliability. The potential for AI hallucinations to lead to misjudgments, malpractice, and harmful consequences in professional and legal settings underscores the urgent need for caution and critical evaluation when deploying current AI systems in high-stakes domains where accuracy, reliability, and trustworthiness are paramount, highlighting the dangers of blindly trusting opaque algorithmic systems that are prone to confidently fabricating falsehoods and misleading users with their persuasive but often factually empty pronouncements.

Chapter 6

AGI Dreams and Delusions

The siren song of Artificial General Intelligence (AGI) is undeniably potent, a captivating melody that has echoed through the halls of science fiction, philosophical discourse, and now, with increasing fervor, the very heart of the artificial intelligence field itself. AGI, the hypothetical Holy Grail of AI research, promises nothing less than the creation of machines possessing human-level intelligence across the entire spectrum of cognitive abilities – the capacity to learn anything a human can learn, to reason, to understand, to create, to adapt, and perhaps even, in the most ambitious visions, to achieve sentience and consciousness. This is not merely about building better tools or more efficient algorithms; AGI, in its purest form, represents the aspiration to replicate, and perhaps even surpass, the very essence of human intellect, to forge minds in silicon, to create artificial beings that rival, or even exceed, our own cognitive capabilities. It is a dream of technological transcendence, a vision of a future where machines not only serve humanity but become, in a profound sense, our intellectual equals, or even our superiors. And it is precisely this allure, this potent combination of technological ambition, utopian aspiration, and a deep-seated human fascination with creating artificial life, that fuels the pervasive AGI hype and drives the often-unrealistic expectations surrounding the near-term prospects of achieving human-level artificial intelligence.

The cultural fascination with AGI is deeply ingrained, woven into the fabric of our collective imagination through decades of science fiction literature, film, and popular culture. From the benevolent androids of Star Trek to the malevolent machines of Terminator and the philosophical musings of Blade Runner, AGI has been a recurring and captivating trope, exploring both the utopian promises and the dystopian perils of creating truly intelligent machines. Movies like "Her," exploring the complex emotional relationship between a man and an AI operating system, and "Ex

Machina," delving into the ethical and existential implications of creating a seemingly sentient robot, have further solidified AGI's presence in the popular consciousness, shaping public perceptions and fueling both excitement and anxiety about the prospect of human-level AI becoming a reality. These cultural narratives, while often fictionalized and dramatized, nonetheless tap into deep-seated human desires and anxieties, reflecting our long-standing fascination with creating artificial beings in our own image, and our equally persistent fear of losing control to technologies that surpass our own cognitive capabilities. This cultural backdrop, saturated with AGI tropes and narratives, provides fertile ground for the current AGI hype to flourish, predisposing the public to embrace the idea of imminent sentient machines and amplifying the often-exaggerated claims made by tech evangelists and AGI proponents.

Philosophical thought experiments, such as the Turing Test and the Chinese Room Argument, have further fueled the intellectual allure of AGI, probing the very boundaries of intelligence, consciousness, and the possibility of creating artificial minds. The Turing Test, proposed by Alan Turing in 1950, offered a seemingly simple and pragmatic benchmark for assessing machine intelligence: if a machine can convincingly imitate human conversation to the point where a human judge cannot distinguish it from a human interlocutor, then can we consider that machine to be "thinking"? While the Turing Test has been widely debated and critiqued over the years, it nonetheless captured the public imagination, providing a concrete and seemingly achievable goal for AI research, and solidifying the notion that human-level intelligence, or at least its conversational mimicry, was a scientifically attainable objective. The Chinese Room Argument, proposed by philosopher John Searle, offered a more skeptical and philosophically challenging counterpoint, questioning whether even a machine that could perfectly pass the Turing Test would truly possess understanding or consciousness, arguing that mere symbol manipulation, however sophisticated, is fundamentally different from genuine semantic comprehension and subjective experience. These philosophical debates, while often abstract and theoretical, have nonetheless shaped the intellectual landscape of

AI, fueling both the aspiration to create truly intelligent machines and the persistent skepticism about the very possibility of achieving genuine artificial consciousness, further amplifying the allure and the inherent ambiguities surrounding the concept of AGI.

In the current age of AI overdrive, the allure of AGI has transcended the realms of science fiction and philosophy, permeating the very fabric of the artificial intelligence field itself, becoming a central driving force behind research agendas, investment decisions, and public discourse. AGI has become the "North Star" for many AI researchers and tech companies, the ultimate goal towards which all current AI efforts are seemingly directed, the promised land of technological transcendence that justifies the vast investments, the relentless hype, and the often-exaggerated claims surrounding artificial intelligence. Venture capitalists eagerly fund AGI-focused startups, investors pour billions into companies promising to deliver AGI in the near future, and tech CEOs confidently proclaim the imminent arrival of sentient machines, all fueled by the seductive allure of AGI and the promise of unimaginable wealth and transformative technological power that AGI is perceived to represent. Media headlines scream about AGI breakthroughs, proclaiming that human-level intelligence is just around the corner, further amplifying the hype and solidifying the narrative of imminent technological singularity, creating a self-reinforcing cycle of AGI aspiration, hype amplification, and investor frenzy. The allure of AGI, therefore, is not just a cultural phenomenon or a philosophical abstraction; it is a powerful economic and ideological force, driving the AI hype machine, shaping public perception, and fundamentally influencing the very trajectory of artificial intelligence in the 21st century.

However, beneath this captivating allure, beneath the utopian visions and trillion-dollar dreams, lies a crucial and often-overlooked reality: the current pursuit of AGI, in its dominant hype-driven form, is built upon a false promise, a seductive myth that distracts from more pressing and achievable goals in artificial intelligence, misallocates resources, and ultimately, may lead to disillusionment and a potential backlash against the very field it seeks to elevate. The dream of sentient machines, while undeniably alluring, is, in its current hyped and often-exaggerated form, a delusion, a technological mirage that obscures the more fundamental limitations of current AI approaches and diverts attention away from more realistic, responsible, and genuinely beneficial paths forward for artificial intelligence. Dissecting this AGI delusion, exposing its false promises, and understanding the real dangers of this pervasive misdirection is crucial for navigating the age of AI overdrive with wisdom, foresight, and a commitment to building artificial intelligence that truly serves humanity, moving beyond the seductive allure of AGI fantasies and towards a more grounded, realistic, and beneficial AI future.

The persistent narrative of "AGI is Just Around the Corner," the confident pronouncements from tech evangelists and futurists proclaiming the imminent arrival of human-level artificial intelligence, are not just overly optimistic or slightly exaggerated predictions; they are, as Gary Marcus has consistently and forcefully argued, false, fundamentally misleading, and dangerously disconnected from the current realities of artificial intelligence research and our limited understanding of the very nature of intelligence itself. Despite the impressive progress in certain narrow domains of AI, particularly in deep learning, and despite the undeniable advances in computational power and data availability, the fundamental scientific and engineering challenges that stand in the way of achieving true Artificial General Intelligence remain vast, largely unaddressed, and beyond the reach of current AI approaches. The claim that AGI is "just around the corner" is not just wishful thinking or technological hubris; it is a profound misunderstanding of the sheer complexity of intelligence, both biological and artificial, and a dangerous underestimation of the fundamental gaps in our scientific understanding that must be bridged before we can even realistically contemplate creating machines with human-level cognitive capabilities. To understand why AGI is not imminent, why it is not a near-term prospect, and why the hype surrounding its imminent arrival is misleading, it is essential to delve into these fundamental gaps in our understanding of intelligence, to expose the often-overlooked scientific and philosophical hurdles that stand in the way of achieving true general AI, and to challenge the overly simplistic and technologically deterministic narratives that fuel the AGI hype cycle.

One of the most fundamental and often-ignored obstacles on the path to AGI is the "hard problem" of consciousness, the enduring philosophical and scientific mystery of subjective experience, qualia, and the very nature of what it means to be consciously aware. Consciousness, the subjective feeling of "what it is like" to be oneself, to experience the world from a first-person perspective, to possess inner awareness, emotions, and sentience, remains one of the deepest and most intractable mysteries in science, defying easy explanation through purely computational or mechanistic frameworks. Current AI systems, including the most advanced large language models, are fundamentally computational in nature, manipulating symbols, processing information, and generating outputs based on algorithms and data, but they lack any evidence of possessing subjective experience, qualia, or genuine consciousness. The claim that AGI is just around the corner often implicitly assumes that consciousness is merely an emergent property of sufficient computational complexity, that by simply scaling up current AI technologies and building larger, more complex neural networks, consciousness will somehow magically "emerge" from the algorithmic substrate, without any clear scientific understanding of how or why this emergence might occur.

This assumption, however, is not only scientifically unsubstantiated but also philosophically deeply problematic. The "hard problem" of consciousness, as articulated by philosopher David Chalmers, highlights the fundamental gap between the physical mechanisms of the brain and the subjective experience of consciousness, questioning how and why physical processes in the brain give rise to subjective awareness, qualia, and the feeling of "what it is like" to be conscious. Current neuroscience, while making progress in understanding the neural correlates of consciousness, has yet to provide a comprehensive and mechanistic explanation of how subjective experience arises from physical processes, leaving the "hard problem" largely unsolved and the very nature of consciousness shrouded in mystery. To assume that consciousness will simply "emerge" from sufficiently complex computations, without any clear scientific understanding of its underlying mechanisms or any empirical evidence to support this claim, is a leap of faith, not a scientifically grounded prediction. Current AI research, focused primarily on improving performance on narrow tasks and scaling up existing deep learning architectures, is not directly addressing the "hard problem" of consciousness, and there is no clear scientific pathway from current AI technologies to the creation of genuinely conscious machines.

The "hard problem" of consciousness is not just a philosophical abstraction; it has profound implications for the very concept of Artificial General Intelligence and the feasibility of achieving human-level AI in the near term. If consciousness is not merely an emergent property of computation, if it requires fundamentally different mechanisms or principles beyond those currently employed in AI systems, then simply scaling up current AI technologies will not magically lead to sentient machines. Achieving true AGI, in the sense of creating machines with human-level intelligence across all cognitive domains, including consciousness, may require fundamental breakthroughs in our understanding of consciousness itself, breakthroughs that are far beyond the current horizon of AI research and may even be beyond the reach of current scientific paradigms. To claim that AGI is "just around the corner," while ignoring the "hard problem" of consciousness and the lack of any clear scientific path towards creating conscious machines, is not just overly optimistic; it is misleading, obscuring a fundamental scientific hurdle that stands in the way of achieving true general artificial intelligence, and highlighting the often-unrealistic nature of current AGI hype.

Another fundamental gap that undermines the narrative of imminent AGI is the persistent and often-underestimated challenge of achieving common sense reasoning in artificial intelligence. Common sense, that vast and largely tacit body of knowledge about the world, about how things work, about human behavior, and about everyday situations, is a crucial component of human intelligence, enabling us to navigate the complexities of daily life, to understand stories, to engage in meaningful conversations, and to make sense of the world around us with remarkable ease and efficiency. Current AI systems, particularly large language models, despite their impressive statistical fluency and ability to generate human-like text, fundamentally lack genuine common sense reasoning, exhibiting a profound inability to understand basic physical causality, social norms, and the vast web of implicit knowledge that constitutes human common sense. The claim that AGI is just around the corner often implicitly assumes that common sense reasoning is merely a matter of accumulating vast quantities of data and training larger neural networks, that by simply scaling up current AI technologies, common sense will somehow magically "emerge" from the algorithmic substrate, without any clear scientific understanding of how or why this emergence might occur.

This assumption, however, is not only scientifically unsubstantiated but also false in light of the persistent and well-documented limitations of current AI systems in common sense reasoning tasks. Current AI, despite its impressive performance in narrow tasks, consistently fails on even simple common sense reasoning challenges, exhibiting a profound inability to understand basic physical laws, social norms, or everyday situations that are effortlessly grasped by even young children. Consider the Winograd Schema Challenge, a set of common sense reasoning questions designed to be easily answerable by humans but notoriously difficult for AI systems. Examples like "The city councilmen refused the demonstrators a permit because they feared violence" and "The city councilmen refused the demonstrators a permit because they advocated violence" highlight the subtle but crucial role of common sense reasoning in understanding pronoun references and resolving ambiguities in natural language. Humans effortlessly understand that "they" refers to the councilmen in the first sentence and the demonstrators in the second, based on our common sense knowledge about who is likely to fear or advocate violence in such situations. Current AI systems, however, struggle to reliably answer these questions, demonstrating their lack of the kind of common sense knowledge and reasoning abilities that humans deploy effortlessly in even simple language comprehension tasks.

The challenge of achieving common sense reasoning in AI is not merely a matter of engineering better algorithms or training on larger datasets; it is a reflection of a deeper scientific gap in our understanding of how to represent and reason with common sense knowledge in artificial systems. Common sense knowledge is vast, complex, and largely implicit, encompassing a vast web of interconnected facts, rules, heuristics, and intuitions about the world that are difficult to explicitly codify or represent in a machine-readable format. Furthermore, common sense reasoning is often context-dependent, flexible, and adaptable to novel situations, requiring a form of reasoning that goes beyond rigid rules or statistical patterns, demanding a more dynamic and context-aware approach that current AI systems struggle to emulate. To assume that common sense reasoning will simply "emerge" from scaling up current deep learning models, without any clear scientific breakthrough in how to represent and reason with common sense knowledge in AI systems, is not just overly optimistic; it is misleading, obscuring a fundamental scientific hurdle that stands in the way of achieving true general artificial intelligence, and highlighting the often-unrealistic nature of current AGI hype.

Beyond consciousness and common sense, another crucial gap that undermines the narrative of imminent AGI is the persistent challenge of achieving genuine creativity and innovation in artificial intelligence. Creativity, the ability to generate novel ideas, insights, and solutions that go beyond mere imitation or incremental improvement, is a hallmark of human intelligence, driving scientific breakthroughs, artistic expression, and technological innovation. Current AI systems, while capable of generating seemingly creative outputs in domains like art, music, and writing, are fundamentally limited in their capacity for genuine creativity, primarily relying on algorithmic recombination, pattern imitation, and statistical generation of novel combinations of existing elements, rather than exhibiting true originality, insight, or the kind of transformative innovation that characterizes human creativity. The claim that AGI is just around the corner often implicitly assumes that creativity is merely an emergent property of sufficient algorithmic complexity, that by simply scaling up current AI technologies, genuine creativity will somehow magically "emerge" from the algorithmic substrate, without any clear scientific understanding of how or why this emergence might occur.

This assumption, however, is not only scientifically unsubstantiated but also false in light of the persistent limitations of current AI in generating truly novel and transformative creative outputs. AI art generators, like DALL-E 2 and Midjourney, can create visually stunning and often aesthetically pleasing images based on text prompts, demonstrating impressive capabilities in algorithmic image synthesis and stylistic imitation. AI music composers can generate original-sounding musical pieces in various genres, mimicking human musical styles and generating novel melodies and harmonies. AI writing systems, like GPT-4, can generate fluent and seemingly creative text, writing poems, stories, and even screenplays that can be difficult to distinguish from human-written content in superficial stylistic terms. However, these seemingly creative outputs, upon closer examination, often reveal their fundamentally imitative and derivative nature, lacking the true originality, transformative insight, and deep conceptual innovation that characterizes genuine human creativity. AI art, while often visually impressive, often lacks the conceptual depth, emotional resonance, and transformative artistic vision of truly groundbreaking human art. AI music, while often technically proficient, often lacks the emotional depth, originality, and transformative musical innovation of truly groundbreaking human music. AI writing, while often stylistically fluent, often lacks the conceptual originality, insightful perspective, and transformative literary innovation of truly groundbreaking human literature.

The challenge of achieving genuine creativity in AI is not merely a matter of training on larger datasets or developing more sophisticated generative algorithms; it is a reflection of a deeper scientific gap in our understanding of the very nature of creativity itself, both biological and artificial. Human creativity is a complex and multifaceted cognitive process, involving not just algorithmic recombination and pattern imitation, but also insight, intuition, conceptual innovation, emotional expression, and a deep understanding of cultural and historical context. Current AI systems, focused primarily on statistical generation and algorithmic optimization, lack many of these crucial components of human creativity, struggling to generate truly novel ideas, transformative insights, or the kind of groundbreaking innovations that drive scientific, artistic, and technological progress. To assume that genuine creativity will simply "emerge" from scaling up current AI technologies, without any clear scientific breakthrough in how to imbue AI systems with true originality, insight, and transformative innovative capacity, is not just overly optimistic; it is misleading, obscuring a fundamental scientific hurdle that stands in the way of achieving true general artificial intelligence, and highlighting the often-unrealistic nature of current AGI hype.

These fundamental gaps – the hard problem of consciousness, the challenge of common sense reasoning, and the elusive nature of true creativity – are not just minor technical hurdles to be overcome with incremental improvements in current AI technologies. They represent deep scientific and philosophical chasms, reflecting our limited understanding of the very nature of intelligence, consciousness, and the complex cognitive abilities that characterize human minds. The claim that AGI is "just around the corner," while ignoring these fundamental gaps, while downplaying the profound scientific challenges that remain unsolved, and while over-extrapolating from narrow successes in specific domains to broader claims of imminent general intelligence, is not just overly optimistic; it is misleading, dangerously simplistic, and fundamentally disconnected from the current realities of artificial intelligence research and our limited understanding of the very essence of intelligence itself. The AGI dream, in its hyped and often-exaggerated form, is, therefore, a delusion, a seductive myth that obscures the true complexities of artificial intelligence, misdirects resources and attention, and ultimately, may lead to disillusionment and a potential backlash against the very field it seeks to elevate. Recognizing these fundamental gaps, acknowledging the profound scientific challenges that remain unsolved, and moving beyond the unrealistic hype of imminent AGI is crucial for charting a more responsible, realistic, and genuinely beneficial path forward for artificial intelligence, focusing on building robust, reliable, and useful AI systems for specific real-world problems, rather than chasing the elusive and often-misleading mirage of sentient machines just around the corner.

The pervasive hype surrounding Artificial General Intelligence, the relentless focus on the seemingly imminent arrival of sentient machines, is not just a harmless exaggeration or a minor intellectual misdirection; it is, as Gary Marcus has forcefully and repeatedly argued, a dangerous and counterproductive force, actively hindering genuine progress in artificial intelligence, misallocating valuable resources, and diverting attention away from more pressing and achievable goals that could offer tangible benefits to society in the near term. The obsession with AGI, the relentless pursuit of a hypothetical future of sentient machines, creates a distorted and unbalanced landscape in the AI field, prioritizing long-term, speculative, and often-unrealistic aspirations over the more immediate and practical challenges and opportunities presented by current AI technologies, leading to a misdirection of resources, a neglect of real-world AI problems, and a potentially detrimental impact on the overall trajectory of artificial intelligence research and development. The dangers of focusing on AGI hype are not just theoretical concerns or hypothetical risks; they are increasingly evident in the current AI landscape, manifesting in concrete ways that undermine responsible innovation, stifle genuine progress, and potentially erode public trust in the very field of artificial intelligence itself.

One of the most significant dangers of the AGI hype is the misallocation of research resources, the diversion of funding, talent, and attention away from more promising and practical areas of AI research and development towards the often-speculative and ultimately unrealistic pursuit of Artificial General Intelligence.

The vast sums of capital pouring into AI research and development, fueled by the trillion-dollar dream and the pervasive AGI hype, are not evenly distributed across the AI landscape; instead, they are disproportionately concentrated in areas perceived to be directly relevant to achieving AGI, particularly large language models, deep learning scaling efforts, and speculative research into artificial consciousness and sentience. Venture capitalists eagerly fund AGI-focused startups, tech companies pour billions into AGI research labs, and government funding agencies prioritize AGI-related projects, all driven by the allure of sentient machines and the promise of transformative technological breakthroughs, often at the expense of more practical and immediately beneficial AI research directions.

This misallocation of resources creates a distorted and unbalanced AI research ecosystem, starving more promising and practical areas of AI research of the funding, talent, and attention they deserve, while over-funding and over-hyping the often-speculative and ultimately unrealistic pursuit of AGI. Research into more robust, reliable, explainable, and ethically grounded AI approaches, such as neuro-symbolic AI, causal inference, common sense reasoning, and knowledge representation, often struggles to attract sufficient funding and attention in the face of the overwhelming AGI hype, despite their potential to offer more immediate and tangible benefits to society. Practical AI applications in healthcare, education, environmental sustainability, and other crucial domains, while often offering more realistic and near-term opportunities for positive societal impact, are often undervalued and underfunded compared to the more glamorous and hype-driven pursuit of AGI, despite their potential to address real-world problems and improve human lives in the near term. This misallocation of resources, driven by the AGI hype, not only hinders genuine progress in artificial intelligence but also creates a distorted and unbalanced AI research landscape, potentially stifling innovation, limiting the diversity of AI approaches being explored, and ultimately undermining the long-term health and sustainability of the AI field itself.

Furthermore, the focus on AGI hype distracts attention and resources away from addressing more pressing and immediate ethical and societal issues related to current AI technologies, creating a dangerous ethical blind spot in the AI discourse. The pervasive focus on the hypothetical risks of future AGI, the often-exaggerated fears of sentient machines turning against humanity, and the speculative discussions about "AI alignment" and controlling superintelligence, while perhaps intellectually stimulating and philosophically intriguing, often serve to divert attention away from the very real and present ethical challenges posed by current AI systems, such as bias in algorithms, lack of accountability in AI decision-making, privacy concerns, and the potential for misuse and unintended consequences in currently deployed AI technologies. Ethical debates in the AI field are often dominated by discussions about the hypothetical risks of AGI, while the more immediate and tangible ethical issues related to bias, fairness, transparency, and accountability in current AI systems are often marginalized or downplayed, creating a distorted ethical landscape where speculative future risks overshadow pressing present-day concerns.

This ethical misdirection, driven by the AGI hype, is not just an academic oversight; it has real-world consequences, hindering efforts to address the ethical challenges posed by current AI, delaying the development of effective regulatory frameworks and ethical guidelines, and potentially leading to the widespread deployment of biased, unfair, and unaccountable AI systems in various domains, with potentially harmful societal impacts. Resources and attention that could be directed towards mitigating bias in algorithms, improving AI transparency and explainability, establishing accountability mechanisms for AI decision-making, and developing ethical guidelines for responsible AI development are instead often diverted towards speculative discussions about AGI alignment and hypothetical future risks, creating an ethical blind spot that leaves current AI systems largely unregulated and ethically unaddressed, despite their potential for bias, harm, and societal disruption. The focus on AGI hype, therefore, not only misallocates research resources but also creates a dangerous ethical misdirection, hindering efforts to address the more immediate and pressing ethical challenges posed by current AI technologies, and potentially undermining the responsible and ethical development of artificial intelligence in the near term.

Beyond the misallocation of resources and ethical misdirection, the AGI hype also contributes to a broader erosion of public trust in artificial intelligence and technology in general, creating a cycle of over-expectation, inevitable disappointment, and potential backlash that can be detrimental to the long-term health and sustainable progress of the AI field. The relentless hype surrounding AGI, the constant pronouncements of imminent technological singularity, and the exaggerated claims about AI's transformative potential create unrealistic expectations in the public mind, fostering a widespread belief that sentient machines are just around the corner and that AI will soon solve all of humanity's problems, ushering in a technological utopia. When these hyped-up expectations inevitably collide with the more limited reality of current AI capabilities, when the promised AGI revolution fails to materialize in the near term, and when the limitations and flaws of current AI systems become increasingly apparent in real-world deployments, public disillusionment and cynicism are likely to follow, potentially leading to a backlash against artificial intelligence and technology in general, eroding trust in scientific progress and undermining public support for future AI research and development.

This cycle of hype, over-expectation, disillusionment, and backlash is not just a hypothetical risk; it is a pattern that has been observed repeatedly throughout the history of artificial intelligence, with previous AI hype cycles followed by "AI Winters" characterized by funding droughts, scientific stagnation, and public skepticism. The current AGI hype cycle, fueled by even more powerful media amplification, investor frenzy, and tech company marketing, is potentially even more susceptible to this boom-and-bust dynamic, with the potential for an even more severe backlash when the unrealistic expectations inevitably fail to materialize, potentially setting back AI research and development for years or even decades to come. The AGI hype, therefore, while seemingly beneficial in the short term for attracting funding, talent, and public attention to the AI field, may ultimately prove to be self-defeating in the long run, eroding public trust, hindering sustainable progress, and potentially triggering another AI Winter when the unrealistic promises of imminent sentient machines fail to materialize and the limitations of current AI become too glaring to ignore.

Furthermore, the AGI hype, by focusing attention and resources on the dominant deep learning paradigm and the pursuit of ever-larger language models, inadvertently stifles innovation and discourages exploration of alternative AI approaches that may offer more promising paths towards robust, reliable, and genuinely intelligent artificial intelligence. The overwhelming hype surrounding deep learning and the narrative of imminent AGI has created a technological monoculture in the AI field, where funding, research, and attention are disproportionately concentrated in deep learning and related approaches, while alternative AI paradigms, such as neuro-symbolic AI, causal inference, common sense reasoning, and knowledge representation, are often marginalized, underfunded, and overlooked, despite their potential to address the fundamental limitations of deep learning and offer more robust and human-like forms of intelligence. This monoculture stifles diversity in AI research, discourages exploration of alternative approaches, and potentially hinders the long-term progress of the field, limiting the range of intellectual perspectives and technological strategies being pursued and potentially missing out on more promising and innovative paths forward for artificial intelligence.

The AGI hype, therefore, not only misallocates resources and creates ethical blind spots but also inadvertently stifles innovation and limits the diversity of AI research, reinforcing a potentially limiting technological paradigm and discouraging exploration of alternative approaches that may be more crucial for achieving genuine and sustainable progress in artificial intelligence. By focusing so narrowly on deep learning and the pursuit of AGI, the AI field may be missing out on valuable opportunities to explore more robust, reliable, explainable, and human-like forms of intelligence, potentially hindering the long-term development of artificial intelligence and limiting its potential to truly benefit humanity in a broad and sustainable way. Moving beyond the AGI hype, diversifying AI research, and embracing a more pluralistic and balanced approach that explores a wider range of AI paradigms, including neuro-symbolic AI and other alternative approaches, is crucial for fostering genuine innovation, promoting long-term progress, and ensuring a more robust and diverse AI ecosystem that is better equipped to address the complex challenges and opportunities of artificial intelligence in the 21st century.

Finally, and perhaps most ironically, the relentless focus on AGI hype often leads to a neglect of the more immediate and practical opportunities to leverage current AI technologies for tangible benefits in various domains, diverting attention and resources away from more achievable and potentially more impactful applications of narrow AI in areas like healthcare, education, environmental sustainability, and social good. The pursuit of AGI, with its focus on long-term, speculative, and often-unrealistic goals, can overshadow the more immediate and practical potential of current AI technologies to address real-world problems, improve human lives, and contribute to societal progress in the near term. Funding, talent, and attention that could be directed towards developing and deploying narrow AI solutions for pressing societal challenges are often instead diverted towards the more glamorous and hype-driven pursuit of AGI, despite the more immediate benefits that practical AI applications could offer.

Consider the potential of narrow AI applications in healthcare, such as AI-powered medical imaging analysis for early disease detection, AI-driven drug discovery for developing new treatments, and AI-assisted personalized medicine for improving patient outcomes. These are not speculative future technologies; they are increasingly becoming practical realities, offering tangible benefits to patients, healthcare providers, and the broader healthcare system in the near term. Similarly, consider the potential of narrow AI applications in education, such as AI-powered personalized learning platforms for improving educational outcomes, AI-driven tutoring systems for providing individualized support to students, and AI-assisted educational resource development for enhancing the quality and accessibility of learning materials. These are not distant future possibilities; they are increasingly being implemented and deployed in educational settings, offering concrete tools and resources to improve learning outcomes, enhance educational equity, and transform the educational landscape in positive ways. And consider the potential of narrow AI applications in environmental sustainability, such as AI-powered climate modeling for improving climate change predictions, AI-driven smart grids for optimizing energy consumption, and AI-assisted precision agriculture for enhancing agricultural efficiency and reducing environmental impact. These are not hypothetical technological fantasies; they are increasingly being developed and deployed in real-world environmental applications, offering practical solutions to address pressing environmental challenges and promote sustainable development in the near term.

These examples of beneficial narrow AI applications highlight the often-overlooked and undervalued potential of current AI technologies to address real-world problems and contribute to societal progress in tangible and meaningful ways, opportunities that are often neglected or downplayed in the face of the overwhelming AGI hype. By focusing so intently on the speculative and often-unrealistic dream of sentient machines, the AI field may be inadvertently missing out on more immediate and practical opportunities to leverage current AI technologies for concrete benefits in various domains, diverting resources, attention, and innovation away from more achievable and potentially more impactful applications of narrow AI. Moving beyond the AGI hype, shifting focus towards more practical and beneficial narrow AI applications, and prioritizing the development and deployment of AI solutions that can address real-world problems and improve human lives in the near term is crucial for realizing the true positive potential of artificial intelligence and ensuring that it serves humanity in a broad, sustainable, and beneficial way, rather than getting lost in the seductive but ultimately misleading pursuit of AGI fantasies and the often-dangerous misdirection of the AGI hype machine.

Navigating the age of AI overdrive responsibly, ethically, and with a clear-eyed understanding of both the promises and the perils of artificial intelligence requires a fundamental shift in perspective, a move away from the seductive illusions of AGI hype and towards a more realistic, grounded, and human-centered AI agenda. This shift involves rejecting the false promise of imminent sentient machines, dismantling the unrealistic expectations surrounding AGI, and redirecting resources, attention, and innovation towards more achievable, practical, and beneficial goals for artificial intelligence in the near and medium term. A more responsible and realistic AI agenda, beyond AGI fantasies, focuses on building robust, reliable, explainable, and ethically sound AI systems that can address real-world problems, improve human lives, and contribute to societal progress in tangible and meaningful ways, prioritizing practical applications, responsible innovation, and a human-centered approach to AI development, rather than chasing the elusive and often-misleading mirage of Artificial General Intelligence. This shift in focus is not just a matter of technical preference or research strategy; it is a crucial ethical and societal imperative, essential for ensuring that artificial intelligence serves humanity in a broad, sustainable, and beneficial way, moving beyond the seductive allure of hype and towards a more grounded, realistic, and ultimately more responsible AI future.

At the heart of a more realistic and responsible AI agenda lies a fundamental shift in focus from the pursuit of AGI to the development of useful and reliable narrow AI systems, prioritizing the creation of AI technologies that can solve specific real-world problems, address concrete human needs, and provide tangible benefits to society in the near term, rather than chasing the speculative and often-unrealistic dream of sentient machines. This shift involves recognizing that current AI technologies, particularly narrow AI systems optimized for specific tasks, already possess immense potential to address a wide range of societal challenges and improve human lives in various domains, and that focusing on realizing this practical potential, rather than fixating on the distant and uncertain prospect of AGI, is a more responsible, ethical, and ultimately more impactful path forward for artificial intelligence. Instead of pouring resources into speculative AGI research, funding should be redirected towards developing and deploying narrow AI solutions for pressing real-world problems in areas like healthcare, education, environmental sustainability, poverty reduction, disaster response, and social justice, leveraging the existing capabilities of current AI technologies to address concrete human needs and contribute to societal progress in tangible and measurable ways.

This focus on useful and reliable narrow AI also implies a prioritization of robustness, reliability, and explainability in AI system design and development, moving beyond the current emphasis on performance benchmarks and statistical fluency, and focusing instead on building AI systems that are trustworthy, dependable, and understandable, particularly in safety-critical and high-stakes applications. Robust AI systems, resilient to adversarial attacks, out-of-distribution data, and unexpected environmental changes, are essential for ensuring the safety and reliability of AI deployments in real-world scenarios, particularly in domains like autonomous driving, medical diagnosis, and critical infrastructure management. Reliable AI systems, consistently performing as intended and predictably generating accurate and trustworthy outputs, are crucial for building user trust, fostering human-AI collaboration, and ensuring that AI systems can be confidently relied upon for decision-making and problem-solving in various domains. Explainable AI systems, transparent and interpretable in their decision-making processes, are essential for ensuring accountability, fairness, and ethical oversight, allowing humans to understand why AI systems make particular decisions, to identify and mitigate potential biases, and to build trust and confidence in AI technology, particularly in domains where transparency and human understanding are paramount. Prioritizing robustness, reliability, and explainability, therefore, is crucial for building a more responsible and trustworthy AI future, moving beyond the hype-driven pursuit of algorithmic power and towards a more human-centered and more beneficial approach to artificial intelligence.

As a crucial component of a more realistic and responsible AI agenda, Gary Marcus and other leading AI critics advocate for embracing neuro-symbolic AI and hybrid approaches, moving beyond the limitations of the deep learning monoculture and exploring alternative AI paradigms that combine the strengths of neural networks with symbolic reasoning, knowledge representation, and more human-like learning mechanisms. Neuro-symbolic AI, as a hybrid approach, offers a promising path towards overcoming the fundamental limitations of deep learning, such as the lack of common sense, the brittleness, the hallucination problem, and the inherent opacity of black box neural networks. By integrating neural networks for perception, pattern recognition, and data-driven learning with symbolic AI for reasoning, knowledge representation, and abstract thought, neuro-symbolic AI aims to create more robust, reliable, explainable, and genuinely intelligent AI systems that can overcome the limitations of purely statistical approaches and achieve a more human-like level of understanding, reasoning, and adaptability. Investing in and prioritizing research and development in neuro-symbolic AI and other hybrid approaches is crucial for diversifying the AI research landscape, moving beyond the deep learning monoculture, and fostering innovation in alternative AI paradigms that may offer more promising paths towards truly intelligent, robust, and beneficial artificial intelligence.

Finally, a more realistic and responsible AI agenda must be guided by robust ethical frameworks and a commitment to responsible innovation, ensuring that AI development and deployment are guided by human values, serve the public good, and are aligned with ethical principles of fairness, transparency, accountability, and human control. Ethical frameworks for AI should go beyond narrow technical safety concerns, encompassing broader societal implications, ethical considerations, and humanistic values, addressing issues such as bias in algorithms, job displacement, privacy concerns, algorithmic discrimination, and the potential for misuse and unintended consequences in AI deployments. Responsible innovation principles should guide AI development, emphasizing human oversight, democratic control, public engagement, and a commitment to transparency, accountability, and ethical evaluation throughout the AI lifecycle, from research and development to deployment and societal impact assessment.

Public discourse and ethical reflection on AI should be fostered and amplified, ensuring that diverse voices and perspectives are included in shaping the future of artificial intelligence, and that ethical considerations are integrated into AI design and policy-making from the outset, rather than as an afterthought or a mere marketing exercise. Guiding AI development with robust ethical frameworks and a commitment to responsible innovation is crucial for ensuring that artificial intelligence serves humanity in a broad, beneficial, and ethically sound way, moving beyond the hype-driven pursuit of algorithmic power and towards a more human-centered and more beneficial future for artificial intelligence and society as a whole. Moving beyond AGI fantasies, embracing a more realistic and responsible AI agenda, and prioritizing useful, reliable, explainable, and ethically grounded AI systems is not just a matter of technical strategy or research direction; it is a crucial ethical and societal imperative, essential for navigating the age of AI overdrive with wisdom, foresight, and a commitment to building a future where artificial intelligence truly serves humanity, augmenting our intellect, enhancing our lives, and contributing to a better world for all.

PART III

The Architects of Hype

Chapter 7

Sam Altman and OpenAI's Gambit

Sam Altman, the boyish-faced CEO of OpenAI, stands as the undeniable personification of the current AI gold rush, the very embodiment of the trillion-dollar dream taking human form. He is the charismatic impresario of algorithmic enchantment, the Silicon Valley oracle dispensing pronouncements on the coming age of sentient machines, and the architect, whether deliberately or inadvertently, of perhaps the most potent and pervasive AI hype machine the world has yet witnessed. To understand the AI frenzy of our era, to truly grasp the scale and scope of the trillion-dollar delusions gripping the public imagination, one must first confront the figure of Sam Altman, to dissect his persona, to analyze his pronouncements, and to meticulously deconstruct the grand gambit he and OpenAI have so masterfully orchestrated, a gambit that has reshaped the AI landscape, fueled investor frenzy, and, as Gary Marcus so incisively argues, potentially misdirected the very trajectory of artificial intelligence itself. Altman is not merely a tech CEO; he is a cultural phenomenon, a symbol of the AI revolution, and a master of narrative, skillfully weaving a compelling tale of technological inevitability, transformative potential, and, crucially, OpenAI's central role in ushering in this brave new algorithmic world. His pronouncements are not just business updates or product announcements; they are treated as prophecies by a tech-hungry media, eagerly amplified by a market perpetually thirsty for the next disruptive innovation, and eagerly consumed by a public both fascinated and increasingly anxious about the promises and perils of artificial intelligence. To understand the AI hype machine, therefore, is to understand Sam Altman, to dissect his persona, and to analyze the intricate mechanisms through which he and OpenAI have so effectively, and so profitably, woven their spell of algorithmic enchantment.

Altman's ascent to the apex of the AI hype pyramid is a quintessential Silicon Valley narrative, a story of rapid rise, strategic pivots, and the almost alchemical transformation of youthful ambition into global influence. His early career trajectory, marked by precocious entrepreneurial ventures and a keen understanding of the dynamics of the tech industry, positioned him perfectly to capitalize on the burgeoning AI wave and to emerge as its most visible and vocal champion. His tenure at Y Combinator, the influential startup accelerator that has incubated some of Silicon Valley's most successful companies, served as a crucial formative experience, honing his business acumen, expanding his network within the tech elite, and solidifying his reputation as a shrewd judge of technological potential and a master of startup cultivation. At Y Combinator, Altman was not just an administrator; he became a mentor, a guru, a digital Svengali guiding a generation of young entrepreneurs, instilling in them the Silicon Valley ethos of disruption, hyper-growth, and the relentless pursuit of technological innovation, regardless of ethical or societal consequences. This period forged his understanding of the power of narrative, the importance of hype, and the strategic leverage that could be gained by positioning oneself at the forefront of a perceived technological revolution. His transition to CEO of OpenAI, therefore, was not a random career move, but a strategically calculated step, leveraging his established Silicon Valley credibility, his deep understanding of the tech hype cycle, and his innate entrepreneurial instincts to seize the helm of what would become the most talked-about and most heavily hyped AI company in the world.

OpenAI, under Altman's leadership, has undergone a significant transformation, shifting from its initial non-profit, open-source mission to a more commercially driven, strategically focused, and hype-amplifying organization. Founded in 2015 as a non-profit research lab dedicated to ensuring that artificial general intelligence benefits all of humanity, OpenAI initially projected an image of altruistic scientific endeavor, prioritizing open research, ethical AI development, and a commitment to transparency and public benefit over commercial gain. This early non-profit ethos, while perhaps genuinely held by some of its founders, also strategically positioned OpenAI as a morally superior alternative to the perceived greed and unchecked ambition of large tech companies, attracting top AI talent, generating positive media coverage, and cultivating a perception of ethical leadership in a field increasingly scrutinized for its potential societal harms. However, under Altman's stewardship, OpenAI has gradually but decisively shifted away from this purely non-profit, open-source model, embracing a more commercially oriented approach, forging lucrative partnerships with tech giants like Microsoft, and increasingly prioritizing product development, market dominance, and, undeniably, hype generation, over its initial altruistic mission. This transformation, while perhaps pragmatically necessary for OpenAI to compete in the intensely competitive AI landscape and to fund its increasingly expensive research endeavors, nonetheless represents a significant departure from its founding principles and raises questions about the genuineness of its stated commitment to "beneficial AGI" and its increasingly aggressive pursuit of commercial success and market dominance in the AI hype cycle.

Altman's persona, meticulously crafted and consistently projected, is itself a crucial component of the OpenAI hype machine, a carefully constructed image of the visionary tech leader, the insightful futurist, and the almost reluctant messiah of the AI revolution. He cultivates an image of calm confidence, intellectual gravitas, and a seemingly unwavering belief in the transformative power of artificial intelligence, projecting an aura of technological inevitability and strategic mastery that resonates powerfully with investors, media outlets, and a public yearning for technological leadership and clear direction in the face of rapid technological change. His public speaking style, characterized by measured pronouncements, carefully calibrated hyperbole, and a deliberate avoidance of overly technical jargon, is designed to appeal to a broad audience, conveying a sense of technological expertise without alienating non-technical listeners, and effectively communicating the OpenAI narrative in a digestible and persuasive manner. His media appearances, strategically frequent and carefully curated, are often framed as intellectual salons, opportunities to glean wisdom and insights from the oracle of AI, further amplifying his persona and solidifying his position as the leading voice in the AI discourse. His Twitter presence, carefully managed and strategically deployed, serves as a constant drumbeat of AI excitement, pronouncements of technological progress, and subtle self-promotion, further reinforcing his persona and maintaining a constant stream of hype and media attention around OpenAI and its AGI ambitions.

This meticulously crafted persona, this carefully projected image of the visionary AI leader, is not merely a personal branding exercise for Altman; it is a crucial strategic asset for OpenAI, directly contributing to the company's hype generation capabilities, its ability to attract investment, and its overall influence in shaping the AI narrative. The public perception of Altman as a trustworthy, insightful, and visionary leader lends credibility to OpenAI's pronouncements, amplifies its marketing messages, and reinforces the narrative of technological inevitability and transformative potential that drives the AI hype cycle. Investors, reassured by Altman's confident demeanor and visionary pronouncements, are more likely to pour capital into OpenAI, fueling its research and development efforts and further solidifying its position as a leading AI player. Media outlets, eager for authoritative voices and compelling narratives in the complex and often confusing field of artificial intelligence, readily amplify Altman's pronouncements, further disseminating the OpenAI hype message to a broader public audience. The persona of Sam Altman, therefore, is not just a personal attribute; it is a strategically cultivated and meticulously deployed tool in the OpenAI hype machine, a crucial component of the grand gambit to dominate the AI landscape and capitalize on the trillion-dollar dream.

The OpenAI hype machine, expertly orchestrated and strategically amplified, operates through a variety of interconnected mechanisms, each meticulously designed to generate buzz, cultivate excitement, and solidify the narrative of technological revolution and imminent AGI. One of the most effective and strategically deployed mechanisms is the artful orchestration of product launches as meticulously staged hype events, transforming what might otherwise be incremental technological advancements into seemingly revolutionary breakthroughs, and converting nascent research prototypes into world-altering products in the public perception. The launch of GPT-3, OpenAI's groundbreaking large language model, serves as a prime example of this hype engineering, a masterclass in transforming a complex research project into a global media sensation, and strategically deploying controlled access and curated demos to maximize buzz and create a perception of unprecedented technological power. The GPT-3 launch was not just a technical announcement; it was a carefully choreographed media event, meticulously designed to generate maximum hype and control the narrative surrounding the new technology.

GPT-3 was not released as a freely accessible, open-source tool, readily available for public scrutiny and experimentation. Instead, OpenAI adopted a strategy of controlled release, granting limited API access to a select group of researchers, developers, and media outlets, creating a sense of exclusivity, scarcity, and heightened anticipation. This controlled access strategy served to amplify the perceived value and desirability of GPT-3, transforming it from a research prototype into a highly sought-after and technologically exclusive commodity, further fueling the hype surrounding its capabilities. Initial demos of GPT-3 were carefully curated and strategically selected to showcase its most impressive, and often cherry-picked, capabilities, highlighting its fluency in generating human-like text, its ability to perform seemingly creative writing tasks, and its potential for various applications, while carefully downplaying its limitations, hallucinations, and lack of genuine understanding. These curated demos, often presented in visually stunning and emotionally engaging formats, were widely disseminated through media outlets and social media platforms, further amplifying the hype and creating a perception of GPT-3 as a technological marvel, a revolutionary breakthrough on the path to AGI. The media narrative surrounding GPT-3's launch was overwhelmingly positive and often uncritically enthusiastic, amplifying OpenAI's marketing messages, exaggerating GPT-3's capabilities, and portraying it as a near-AGI breakthrough, a technology poised to transform everything from writing to coding to scientific research, despite its well-documented limitations and tendency to generate nonsensical or factually inaccurate text.

This strategically orchestrated GPT-3 launch, with its controlled access, curated demos, and media-amplified hype narrative, effectively transformed a complex research project into a global media sensation, creating a perception of revolutionary technological progress and driving immense excitement and anticipation around OpenAI and its AGI ambitions. The GPT-3 launch served as a blueprint for future OpenAI product releases, establishing a pattern of controlled access, curated demos, and strategically amplified hype that would be even more effectively deployed in the subsequent launch of ChatGPT, further solidifying OpenAI's dominance in the AI hype cycle and reinforcing the perception of its technologies as paradigm-shifting breakthroughs on the path to sentient machines. The GPT-3 launch, therefore, was not just a product announcement; it was a masterclass in hype engineering, a carefully orchestrated media event that effectively transformed a promising, but still limited, AI technology into a global sensation, setting the stage for the even more explosive hype surrounding ChatGPT and solidifying OpenAI's position as the undisputed leader in the AI hype machine.

The launch of ChatGPT, OpenAI's conversational AI chatbot, represents an even more potent and effective deployment of hype engineering, transforming a relatively incremental technological advancement into a viral sensation, capturing the public imagination, and further fueling the trillion-dollar dream with an unprecedented explosion of media attention and public enthusiasm. ChatGPT's launch was not just a product release; it was a carefully calculated and brilliantly executed marketing masterstroke, leveraging the power of social media, the inherent human fascination with conversational AI, and a strategically deployed free-access model to create a viral hype phenomenon that propelled ChatGPT to global prominence and further solidified OpenAI's dominance in the AI narrative. ChatGPT was not released as a complex, technically demanding tool for expert users; instead, it was launched as a freely accessible, user-friendly web interface, readily available to anyone with an internet connection, lowering the barrier to entry and democratizing access to advanced AI technology in a way that had never been done before. This free-access model, strategically deployed and widely publicized, proved to be a stroke of marketing genius, transforming ChatGPT from a niche AI research project into a viral sensation, as millions of users flocked to the platform to experiment with its conversational capabilities, share their experiences on social media, and contribute to the rapidly growing hype surrounding the new technology.

Social media platforms, particularly Twitter and TikTok, became crucial amplifiers of the ChatGPT hype, as users eagerly shared impressive, amusing, and sometimes unsettling examples of ChatGPT's conversational prowess, generating a viral cascade of user-generated content that further fueled public fascination and media attention. ChatGPT's ability to generate human-like text, to engage in seemingly intelligent conversations, and to perform a wide range of text-based tasks with remarkable fluency and coherence, captivated the public imagination, blurring the lines between science fiction and technological reality, and creating a widespread perception that sentient AI was finally within reach, readily accessible through a simple web interface. Media outlets, predictably, amplified this viral hype, with breathless headlines proclaiming ChatGPT as a "game-changer," a "revolution in AI," and a harbinger of a new era of conversational AI, often uncritically repeating user anecdotes and exaggerating ChatGPT's capabilities, further fueling the media frenzy and solidifying the hype narrative. The media coverage of ChatGPT was not just reporting on a new technology; it was actively participating in the hype cycle, amplifying user enthusiasm, exaggerating capabilities, and contributing to the overall sense of technological breakthrough and imminent AGI that propelled ChatGPT to global prominence.

This viral ChatGPT launch, with its free access model, social media amplification, and media frenzy, effectively transformed a relatively incremental technological advancement – a slightly improved large language model with a user-friendly conversational interface – into a global sensation, capturing the public imagination, driving unprecedented media attention, and further solidifying OpenAI's dominance in the AI hype cycle. ChatGPT's viral success served to amplify the broader AGI narrative, reinforcing the perception of imminent sentient machines, fueling investor enthusiasm for AI companies, and further driving the trillion-dollar dream with an unprecedented explosion of public excitement and technological utopianism. The ChatGPT launch, therefore, was not just a product release; it was a marketing masterpiece, a brilliant deployment of hype engineering that transformed a relatively limited AI technology into a cultural phenomenon, further solidifying OpenAI's position as the undisputed leader in the AI hype machine and setting a new standard for viral marketing and hype amplification in the age of artificial intelligence overdrive.

Beyond meticulously orchestrated product launches, the OpenAI hype machine also strategically deploys the powerful and often ambiguous narrative of Artificial General Intelligence (AGI) as a central driving force, a North Star guiding its research efforts, justifying its massive investments, and fueling the perception of its technologies as transformative breakthroughs on the path to sentient machines. The AGI narrative, with its inherent allure, its utopian promises, and its deeply ingrained presence in popular culture, serves as a potent hype amplifier, creating a sense of grand purpose, technological inevitability, and transformative potential around OpenAI and its mission, even when the actual progress towards genuine AGI remains highly uncertain and limited. OpenAI consistently frames its mission as achieving "beneficial AGI," a deliberately ambiguous and strategically vague term that allows for maximum hype generation and avoids concrete definitions or verifiable metrics of progress, while nonetheless conveying a sense of grand ambition, technological inevitability, and a commitment to solving humanity's grand challenges through artificial intelligence. This "beneficial AGI" narrative, while seemingly altruistic and ethically driven, also strategically positions OpenAI as the leading force in the AI revolution, the vanguard of a technological transformation that is both inevitable and ultimately beneficial for humanity, further solidifying its dominance in the AI hype cycle and attracting investment, talent, and media attention to its AGI-focused endeavors.

Altman's public pronouncements, consistently emphasizing the imminent arrival of AGI, the transformative potential of sentient machines, and OpenAI's central role in ushering in this new technological era, further amplify the AGI narrative and reinforce the hype surrounding OpenAI's technologies. His interviews, podcasts, and public appearances are often carefully crafted to convey a sense of visionary insight, technological authority, and unwavering confidence in the AGI narrative, strategically deploying hyperbole, exaggeration, and often-unsubstantiated claims about the near-term prospects of achieving human-level artificial intelligence, all designed to fuel public excitement, investor enthusiasm, and media amplification of the AGI hype message. The AGI narrative, in Altman's skillful articulation, becomes not just a technological aspiration, but a quasi-religious prophecy, a vision of a technologically utopian future that is both inevitable and immensely desirable, with OpenAI positioned as the chosen instrument, the technological messiah leading humanity towards this algorithmic salvation. This messianic framing of OpenAI and its AGI mission, while lacking in scientific foundation and often bordering on technological fantasy, nonetheless proves to be a remarkably effective hype amplifier, captivating the public imagination, driving investor enthusiasm, and solidifying OpenAI's position as the undisputed leader in the AI hype machine, even as the actual progress towards genuine AGI remains highly speculative, deeply uncertain, and beyond the reach of current AI technologies.

However, beneath the veneer of AGI ambition and the pronouncements of "beneficial AI," a more critical and skeptical eye must question the genuineness of OpenAI's stated commitment to responsible and ethical AI development, particularly in light of its aggressive pursuit of hype generation, rapid product deployment, and increasingly commercialized business model. The narrative of "responsible AI," while superficially appealing and strategically deployed by OpenAI to project an image of ethical leadership and social responsibility, can also be viewed as a form of "safety theater," a carefully crafted marketing strategy designed to deflect criticism, mitigate ethical concerns, and ultimately, to smooth the path for the rapid deployment and widespread adoption of its often-overhyped and potentially problematic AI technologies. OpenAI's stated commitment to AI safety, AI ethics, and AI alignment, while undoubtedly reflecting some genuine ethical considerations within the organization, also conveniently serves to differentiate it from competitors, attract ethically conscious investors and customers, and, crucially, to shield it from more fundamental critiques of its underlying technology, its hype-driven marketing, and its increasingly aggressive pursuit of commercial success.

OpenAI's "safety theater" manifests in various forms, from the creation of AI safety research teams and the publication of AI ethics guidelines to the participation in AI safety conferences and the pronouncements of Altman and other OpenAI leaders about the importance of responsible AI development. These "responsible AI" initiatives, while seemingly commendable and ethically motivated, often focus on relatively narrow technical safety concerns, such as AI alignment and controlling superintelligence, while neglecting more immediate and pressing ethical issues related to bias in algorithms, lack of transparency in AI decision-making, and the potential for misuse and unintended consequences in currently deployed AI technologies. The emphasis on hypothetical future AGI risks, while perhaps intellectually stimulating and philosophically intriguing, can also serve to divert attention away from the more concrete ethical challenges posed by current AI systems, creating an ethical smokescreen that obscures the potential for harm and misjudgment in OpenAI's own hyped and rapidly deployed AI technologies, such as ChatGPT and its underlying large language models.

Furthermore, OpenAI's actions often speak louder than its words, revealing a pattern of prioritizing rapid product deployment, hype generation, and commercial gain over a truly cautious, ethical, and responsible approach to AI development. The rushed launch of ChatGPT, without adequate safety testing, ethical review, or public consultation, despite its well-documented propensity for hallucinations, biases, and the generation of harmful content, demonstrates a clear prioritization of speed, market buzz, and competitive advantage over a truly responsible and ethically grounded approach to AI deployment. OpenAI's partnership with Microsoft, a tech giant known for its aggressive market tactics and its relentless pursuit of commercial dominance, further raises questions about the genuineness of OpenAI's commitment to "beneficial AGI" and its willingness to prioritize ethical considerations over profit maximization and market share. The narrative of "responsible AI," therefore, while strategically deployed by OpenAI to project an image of ethical leadership and social responsibility, must be critically examined and carefully scrutinized, recognizing that it can also function as a form of "safety theater," a marketing tool designed to deflect criticism, mitigate ethical concerns, and ultimately, to smooth the path for the rapid deployment and widespread adoption of its often-overhyped and potentially problematic AI technologies, all in service of the grand gambit to dominate the AI landscape and capitalize on the trillion-dollar dream.

It is precisely at this juncture, amidst the meticulously orchestrated hype, the trillion-dollar dreams, and the seductive promises of sentient machines, that the voice of Gary Marcus becomes not just valuable, but absolutely essential, offering a sharp, incisive, and scientifically grounded critique of the OpenAI gambit, dismantling the illusions, exposing the hype, and revealing the often-overlooked limitations lurking beneath the polished veneer of algorithmic enchantment. Marcus's critique of OpenAI is not born of malice or technological Luddism; it is rooted in a deep understanding of neuroscience, cognitive science, and the inherent complexities of intelligence itself, both biological and artificial. He is not simply dismissing OpenAI's achievements or denying the impressive technical prowess of its large language models; instead, he is offering a crucial counterpoint to the prevailing hype narrative, providing a much-needed dose of realism, scientific rigor, and intellectual honesty to the often-uncritical and frequently misleading discourse surrounding OpenAI and the broader AI revolution. Marcus's critique is not just about pointing out flaws or highlighting limitations; it is about advocating for a more responsible, realistic, and ultimately more beneficial path forward for artificial intelligence, moving beyond the seductive allure of AGI fantasies and towards a more grounded, human-centered, and more trustworthy AI future.

Marcus's most fundamental and frequently articulated critique of OpenAI's approach, and of large language models in general, centers on the now-familiar "statistical parrot" analogy, a concise and devastatingly effective metaphor that encapsulates the core limitation of current AI systems: their ability to generate fluent and seemingly intelligent text without possessing genuine understanding, intentionality, or a commitment to truthfulness. He argues forcefully that models like GPT-3 and ChatGPT, despite their impressive statistical fluency and ability to mimic human language patterns, are fundamentally just sophisticated "stochastic parrots," capable of parroting back patterns learned from their vast training data, but lacking any real comprehension of the meaning of the words they are manipulating, the concepts they are representing, or the real-world context to which their text refers. This "parrot" critique is not just a catchy soundbite or a dismissive label; it is a scientifically grounded and rigorously argued assessment of the inherent limitations of statistical language models, highlighting their reliance on superficial pattern matching rather than genuine semantic understanding, and explaining why they are prone to hallucinations, nonsensical outputs, and a fundamental lack of common sense reasoning. Marcus meticulously dissects the inner workings of large language models, exposing their algorithmic architecture, their data-driven learning mechanisms, and their statistical objective functions, demonstrating how these design choices inevitably lead to systems that are fluent but not necessarily intelligent, capable of mimicry but lacking in genuine comprehension, and adept at generating text that sounds human-like, but is often factually incorrect, logically incoherent, or entirely fabricated. The "statistical parrot" critique, therefore, is not just a metaphor; it is a scientifically grounded and intellectually devastating assessment of the fundamental limitations of OpenAI's core technology, undermining the hype surrounding its capabilities and exposing the often-illusory nature of its apparent intelligence.

This "parrot" critique is directly linked to Marcus's persistent and well-documented highlighting of the hallucination problem in OpenAI's models, exposing ChatGPT's disconcerting tendency to confidently fabricate falsehoods, generate factually incorrect information with unwavering conviction, and present invented narratives as if they were grounded in reality. He meticulously documents numerous examples of ChatGPT hallucinations, ranging from the now-infamous legal case citations to fabricated biographical details, nonsensical outputs, and logically incoherent statements, demonstrating the pervasive and often unpredictable nature of this critical flaw. Marcus argues that these hallucinations are not just minor bugs or occasional errors; they are systemic symptoms of a deeper problem, reflecting the fundamental limitations of statistical language models, their lack of grounding in reality, and their inability to distinguish between statistical plausibility and factual accuracy. He emphasizes that the confident and authoritative tone with which ChatGPT presents its hallucinations makes them particularly dangerous, potentially misleading users into accepting false information as fact, and undermining trust in the reliability and trustworthiness of AI systems in general. The hallucination problem, in Marcus's critique, is not just a technical challenge to be overcome; it is a fundamental flaw that undermines the very foundation of OpenAI's technology, exposing its inherent unreliability and casting serious doubt on its suitability for deployment in high-stakes domains where accuracy, truthfulness, and trustworthiness are paramount.

Furthermore, Marcus consistently underscores the lack of common sense reasoning in OpenAI's models, demonstrating ChatGPT's inability to grasp basic physical causality, social norms, and everyday situations that are effortlessly understood by even young children. He presents numerous examples of ChatGPT failing simple common sense reasoning tests, exhibiting bizarre behavior in everyday scenarios, and demonstrating a profound lack of real-world understanding, highlighting the vast gulf that still separates current AI systems from true human-level intelligence in even the most mundane cognitive tasks. Marcus argues that this common sense deficit is not just a minor limitation or a temporary shortcoming; it is a fundamental flaw that undermines the very notion of OpenAI's models as being genuinely intelligent, capable of understanding the world, or suitable for deployment in complex real-world environments where common sense reasoning is essential for robust and reliable performance. He emphasizes that common sense reasoning is not just about accumulating vast quantities of data or training larger neural networks; it requires fundamentally different algorithmic approaches, incorporating structured knowledge representation, causal inference mechanisms, and a more robust grounding in real-world experience, approaches that are lacking in current deep learning paradigms and in OpenAI's core technology. The common sense deficit, in Marcus's critique, is a crucial limitation that exposes the narrowness and brittleness of OpenAI's models, undermining the hype surrounding their capabilities and highlighting the vast intellectual distance that still separates them from true human-level intelligence.

In conjunction with the hallucination problem and the common sense deficit, Marcus also consistently points to the inherent brittleness and lack of generalization in OpenAI's models, demonstrating their susceptibility to adversarial attacks, out-of-distribution data, and unexpected environmental changes, revealing the narrowness of their expertise and their limited capacity to adapt to novel situations or generalize beyond the carefully controlled conditions of their training regimes. He highlights the vulnerability of OpenAI's image recognition systems to adversarial examples, subtle but deliberately crafted perturbations that can completely fool even the most sophisticated models, exposing their reliance on superficial statistical correlations rather than genuine understanding of visual concepts. He discusses the out-of-distribution failure of OpenAI's language models, demonstrating their tendency to perform poorly when presented with text data that deviates even slightly from the statistical characteristics of their training corpora, revealing their limited capacity to generalize beyond the narrow confines of their training regimes. And he underscores the narrowness of OpenAI's game-playing AI systems, highlighting their impressive performance in specific games but their utter inability to transfer their "intelligence" or adapt their skills to even slightly different games or real-world scenarios, demonstrating the lack of robust generalization and adaptability that characterizes true human intelligence. This brittleness and lack of generalization, in

Marcus's critique, are not just minor technical inconveniences; they are fundamental flaws that expose the narrowness and fragility of OpenAI's models, undermining the hype surrounding their robustness and reliability, and casting serious doubt on their suitability for deployment in complex, unpredictable, and safety-critical real-world environments.

Finally, and perhaps most fundamentally, Marcus expresses deep skepticism about OpenAI's scaling strategy, questioning the prevailing belief within the AI field and particularly within OpenAI itself that simply scaling up deep learning models with more data, larger neural networks, and increased computational power will eventually lead to Artificial General Intelligence or overcome the fundamental limitations of current AI approaches. He argues forcefully that scaling up current deep learning models is likely to hit diminishing returns, that simply making larger and larger neural networks will not magically imbue them with common sense reasoning, genuine understanding, or robust truth discernment, and that the fundamental limitations of deep learning are algorithmic, architectural, and epistemological, not simply a matter of insufficient scale or computational resources. Marcus emphasizes that addressing the core challenges of artificial intelligence, such as achieving common sense reasoning, overcoming the hallucination problem, and building truly robust and reliable AI systems, requires more than just scaling up current deep learning models; it necessitates a fundamental rethinking of AI architectures, a shift towards more knowledge-rich, reasoning-capable, and hybrid approaches, and a recognition that data alone, no matter how vast, cannot substitute for genuine algorithmic innovation and a more scientifically grounded understanding of intelligence itself. This skepticism about scaling, in Marcus's critique, is not just a technical disagreement or a pessimistic outlook; it is a fundamental challenge to the prevailing orthodoxy within the AI field, undermining the hype surrounding the scaling narrative and advocating for a more intellectually rigorous, scientifically grounded, and ultimately more promising path forward for artificial intelligence, moving beyond the seductive but ultimately misleading allure of simply scaling up flawed and fundamentally limited deep learning paradigms.

In sum, Gary Marcus's critique of Sam Altman and OpenAI's gambit is a rigorous and essential counterpoint to the pervasive AI hype machine, dismantling the illusions, exposing the fairy tales, and revealing the often-overlooked limitations lurking beneath the polished veneer of algorithmic enchantment. His "statistical parrot" critique, his highlighting of the hallucination problem, his emphasis on the common sense deficit, his exposure of the brittleness and lack of generalization, and his skepticism about the scaling strategy collectively form a powerful and scientifically grounded indictment of the dominant deep learning paradigm and the hype-driven narratives surrounding OpenAI's technologies. Marcus's critique is not just about pointing out flaws or tearing down existing paradigms; it is about advocating for a more responsible, realistic, and ultimately more beneficial path forward for artificial intelligence, moving beyond the seductive allure of AGI fantasies and towards a more grounded, human-centered, and more trustworthy AI future, a future that begins with dismantling the hype and embracing the clear-eyed, scientifically rigorous, and profoundly necessary voice of Gary Marcus.

The impact of OpenAI's hype machine, expertly orchestrated by Sam Altman and amplified by a willing media landscape and investor frenzy, extends far beyond mere inflated valuations or fleeting moments of public excitement; it has profound and far-reaching consequences, shaping the AI narrative, distorting market dynamics, and potentially misdirecting the very trajectory of artificial intelligence itself. The hype surrounding OpenAI, particularly around ChatGPT and the promise of imminent AGI, has created a powerful and pervasive echo chamber, dominating media coverage, influencing investor behavior, and shaping public perception of artificial intelligence in ways that are not only often misleading but also potentially detrimental to the long-term health and sustainable progress of the AI field. Analyzing the impact of OpenAI's hype machine, dissecting its far-reaching consequences, and understanding how it shapes the AI landscape is crucial for navigating the age of AI overdrive responsibly, ethically, and with a clear-eyed awareness of the often-unintended and potentially negative consequences of unchecked hype and technologically deterministic narratives.

One of the most immediate and visible impacts of OpenAI's hype machine is its domination of the media narrative surrounding artificial intelligence, effectively controlling the AI conversation, shaping public perception, and setting the agenda for media coverage in a way that is unprecedented in the history of the field. OpenAI's meticulously orchestrated product launches, strategically deployed marketing campaigns, and carefully cultivated media relationships have allowed it to effectively control the flow of information, to frame the AI narrative in its own terms, and to dominate media coverage of artificial intelligence, often at the expense of more balanced, critical, and diverse perspectives. Media outlets, eager for sensationalist stories, clickbait headlines, and authoritative voices in the rapidly evolving field of AI, have largely become willing amplifiers of OpenAI's hype narrative, uncritically repeating its marketing messages, exaggerating its technological claims, and portraying its technologies as paradigm-shifting breakthroughs on the path to imminent AGI, often without adequately highlighting the limitations, flaws, and ethical concerns that Gary Marcus and other AI critics have consistently raised. This media domination is not just a matter of organic public interest or unbiased journalistic coverage; it is a direct consequence of OpenAI's deliberate and highly effective hype machine, its strategic control of information flow, and its skillful manipulation of media cycles to shape the AI narrative in its favor and amplify its message to a global audience.

The consequences of this media domination are far-reaching, shaping public perception of AI, influencing investor behavior, and potentially distorting the very direction of AI research and development. Public perception of artificial intelligence, increasingly shaped by the hype-dominated media narrative orchestrated by OpenAI, is often skewed towards overly optimistic and technologically deterministic views, fostering unrealistic expectations about AI capabilities, downplaying potential risks, and creating a pervasive sense of technological inevitability and transformative potential that is not always grounded in reality. Investor behavior, similarly influenced by the hype-dominated media narrative, is often driven by FOMO (fear of missing out) and a rush to capitalize on the perceived AI gold rush, leading to inflated valuations for AI companies, excessive investment in hype-driven AI startups, and a potential AI investment bubble that may be unsustainable in the long run. The direction of AI research and development, increasingly shaped by the media narrative and investor priorities, may be inadvertently skewed towards the dominant deep learning paradigm and the pursuit of AGI fantasies, potentially neglecting more promising and responsible alternative approaches and creating a technological monoculture that may ultimately hinder genuine progress and limit the diversity of the AI field. OpenAI's media domination, therefore, is not just a matter of public relations success; it is a powerful force shaping the AI narrative, influencing public perception, distorting market dynamics, and potentially misdirecting the very trajectory of artificial intelligence in ways that are not always beneficial, ethical, or conducive to long-term sustainable progress.

Beyond media domination, OpenAI's hype machine has fueled an unprecedented investor frenzy, contributing significantly to the inflated valuations of AI companies and the overall market overvaluation of the AI sector, driving the trillion-dollar dream to dizzying heights and creating an investment landscape characterized by irrational exuberance and a potentially unsustainable hype bubble. The immense hype surrounding ChatGPT, the pervasive narrative of imminent AGI, and the strategically amplified pronouncements of OpenAI's transformative potential have created a powerful gravitational pull for investor capital, attracting billions of dollars in venture funding, driving up stock prices of AI-related companies, and fostering a widespread belief that artificial intelligence represents the ultimate investment opportunity of our lifetime, a technological gold rush promising untold riches to those who stake their claim early and aggressively. This investor frenzy is not a rational response to technological progress or sound market fundamentals; it is, to a significant extent, a direct consequence of OpenAI's hype machine, its skillful manipulation of investor sentiment, and its successful cultivation of a narrative of technological inevitability and transformative potential that has captivated the financial markets and driven an unprecedented influx of capital into the AI sector.

Venture capital firms, ever attuned to hype cycles and eager to identify the next "unicorn," have poured billions of dollars into AI startups, particularly those aligned with the deep learning paradigm and those promising to leverage large language models and generative AI technologies, further fueling the investment frenzy and driving up valuations across the AI landscape. Seed rounds, Series A rounds, and even later-stage funding rounds for AI companies have reached astronomical levels, often exceeding traditional metrics of valuation and profitability, with investors seemingly willing to pay any price to gain exposure to the perceived AI revolution and to secure a stake in the next OpenAI or the next Nvidia. This investor enthusiasm is not solely based on rigorous due diligence or careful financial analysis; it is, to a significant extent, driven by FOMO (fear of missing out), a pervasive anxiety among investors of missing out on the next big thing, the next technological paradigm shift that will reshape the global economy and generate immense wealth for those who are prescient enough to invest early and aggressively. The ChatGPT hype, in particular, served as a powerful catalyst for this investor frenzy, validating the AGI narrative, demonstrating the seemingly transformative potential of large language models, and creating a widespread belief that AI is finally "here," ready for mass adoption and poised to generate unprecedented economic value, further fueling the rush to invest in AI companies and drive up valuations to unsustainable levels.

Public market valuations of AI-related companies, particularly tech giants like Microsoft, Google, and Nvidia, have also been significantly inflated by the AI hype, with stock prices soaring to unprecedented heights, often disproportionately outpacing actual revenue growth or increases in profitability, driven by investor enthusiasm for AI and the perceived future potential of these companies to dominate the AI-driven economy. Nvidia's stock price, as previously mentioned, has become a bellwether of the AI hype cycle, its astronomical valuation fueled almost entirely by the perceived future demand for its GPUs in training and deploying AI models, with investors seemingly betting on Nvidia becoming the indispensable infrastructure provider for the entire AI revolution, regardless of the inherent risks, uncertainties, and potential limitations of the underlying AI technologies. Microsoft's stock price, similarly buoyed by its OpenAI partnership and its aggressive integration of ChatGPT technology into its product suite, reflects investor enthusiasm for its perceived AI leadership and its strategic positioning in the AI arms race, further demonstrating the power of AI hype to inflate market valuations and drive investor behavior. This investor frenzy, driven by OpenAI's hype machine and amplified by media narratives and market dynamics, has created a potentially unsustainable AI investment bubble, characterized by irrational exuberance, inflated valuations, and a significant disconnect between market hype and the underlying realities of current AI capabilities, raising concerns about a potential market correction, an "AI Winter" 2.0, or a broader disillusionment with artificial intelligence when the hyped-up promises inevitably fail to materialize in the near term.

Aside from media domination and investor frenzy, OpenAI's hype machine has also significantly intensified competitive pressure on other big tech companies, fueling an "AI arms race" mentality, forcing competitors to accelerate their own AI development and deployment efforts, often at the expense of careful consideration of ethical implications, safety testing, and responsible innovation, all in a desperate attempt to keep pace with OpenAI and avoid being "left behind" in the perceived AI revolution. The viral success of ChatGPT, and OpenAI's skillful leveraging of media hype and public excitement, created a palpable sense of panic and urgency within other tech giants, particularly Google, which was suddenly perceived as being "disrupted" in its core search business and facing an existential threat from OpenAI's seemingly revolutionary conversational AI technology. Google's rushed launch of Bard was a direct consequence of this competitive pressure, a panicked response to ChatGPT hype, driven by a fear of losing market share, investor confidence, and its long-standing dominance in the search engine landscape. The Bard fiasco, with its public demo failures and subsequent media backlash, served as a stark reminder of the dangers of hype-driven product launches, the risks of rushing unproven technologies to market, and the potential for public relations disasters when hype outpaces reality in the AI space.

Microsoft's aggressive integration of OpenAI technology into Bing and its subsequent marketing blitz around the "new Bing AI" was another direct consequence of this intensified competitive pressure, a strategic move to leverage OpenAI's hype and challenge Google's search dominance, driven by a desire to capitalize on the ChatGPT moment and gain market share in the AI-powered search engine market. Microsoft's "AI arms race" rhetoric, framing AI development as a high-stakes global competition and emphasizing the need for companies to aggressively adopt AI to avoid being "left behind," further intensified the competitive pressure on other tech giants, creating a sense of urgency and inevitability around AI adoption and fueling the overall hype cycle. Meta, despite its metaverse pivot and its own set of unique challenges, also joined the AI arms race, releasing its own large language model LLaMA and actively promoting its AI research efforts, seeking to maintain its relevance in the AI landscape and avoid being overshadowed by OpenAI and the ChatGPT hype. Amazon, already the dominant cloud provider, similarly ramped up its AI initiatives, investing heavily in AI infrastructure and services, and positioning itself as a major player in the AI platform race, driven by a fear of losing its cloud dominance in the AI era and a desire to capitalize on the burgeoning market for AI-powered cloud computing.

This intensified competitive pressure, fueled by OpenAI's hype machine and the fear of being "disrupted" in the AI revolution, has created a frantic and often reckless "AI arms race" among tech giants, characterized by rushed product launches, compromised safety testing, aggressive marketing, and a prioritization of short-term market gains over long-term responsible innovation, ethical considerations, and a balanced assessment of AI capabilities and limitations. The AI arms race mentality, driven by OpenAI's hype gambit, is not only distorting market dynamics and fueling investor frenzy but also potentially undermining the responsible and ethical development of artificial intelligence, incentivizing companies to prioritize speed and hype over caution and careful consideration, and potentially leading to the deployment of flawed, biased, and unreliable AI systems in various domains, with potentially harmful societal consequences. OpenAI's hype machine, therefore, is not just a marketing success story; it is a powerful force driving an AI arms race, intensifying competitive pressures, and potentially undermining the responsible and ethical trajectory of artificial intelligence in the age of overdrive.

Perhaps the most insidious and long-lasting impact of OpenAI's hype machine is its reinforcement of the deep learning monoculture within the AI field, solidifying the dominance of neural networks and large language models, and inadvertently discouraging exploration of alternative AI approaches that may offer more promising paths towards robust, reliable, and genuinely intelligent artificial intelligence. The overwhelming hype surrounding ChatGPT, the pervasive narrative of deep learning breakthroughs, and the immense investor enthusiasm for large language models have created a powerful gravitational pull within the AI research community, attracting funding, talent, and attention disproportionately towards deep learning and related approaches, while marginalizing and underfunding alternative AI paradigms, such as neuro-symbolic AI, causal inference, common sense reasoning, and knowledge representation. This reinforcement of the deep learning monoculture is not just a matter of academic fashion or research trend; it is a potentially detrimental distortion of the AI research landscape, limiting the diversity of approaches being explored, stifling innovation in alternative paradigms, and potentially hindering the long-term progress of artificial intelligence by over-emphasizing a potentially limited and fundamentally flawed technological paradigm.

Funding agencies, both government and private, increasingly prioritize deep learning research and large language model development, reflecting the prevailing hype narrative and the investor-driven enthusiasm for these approaches, often neglecting to fund or underfunding research into alternative AI paradigms that may offer more robust, reliable, and explainable solutions, but lack the same level of media hype and market buzz. Top AI talent, particularly young researchers and aspiring engineers, are increasingly drawn to deep learning and large language model research, attracted by the hype, the funding opportunities, and the perceived career prospects in this dominant field, potentially diverting talent away from alternative AI paradigms that may offer more intellectually stimulating and scientifically promising research directions, but lack the same level of mainstream visibility and hype-driven career appeal. Academic institutions and research labs, similarly influenced by funding pressures, talent flows, and the prevailing hype narrative, increasingly focus their research efforts and curriculum development on deep learning and large language models, further reinforcing the monoculture and potentially neglecting to adequately explore and teach alternative AI approaches that may be crucial for long-term progress and a more balanced and diverse AI research ecosystem.

This reinforcement of the deep learning monoculture, driven by OpenAI's hype machine and amplified by media narratives and investor priorities, creates a self-perpetuating cycle, where the dominant paradigm becomes even more dominant, alternative approaches are further marginalized, and the AI field as a whole risks becoming increasingly narrow, homogenous, and potentially less innovative and less resilient in the long run. The deep learning monoculture, while undeniably achieving impressive feats in certain narrow domains, also suffers from fundamental limitations, such as brittleness, lack of common sense, hallucination problems, and inherent opacity, limitations that may be difficult or even impossible to overcome within the confines of the deep learning paradigm itself. By reinforcing this monoculture and discouraging exploration of alternative approaches, OpenAI's hype machine may inadvertently hinder the long-term progress of artificial intelligence, limiting the diversity of research directions being pursued, stifling innovation in alternative paradigms, and potentially preventing the AI field from reaching its full potential, settling instead for a hype-driven, monoculture-dominated landscape that may be ultimately less robust, less reliable, and less beneficial for humanity in the long run. The impact of OpenAI's hype machine, therefore, extends far beyond mere market dynamics or media narratives; it has profound and potentially long-lasting consequences for the very trajectory of artificial intelligence itself, reinforcing a potentially limiting technological paradigm, stifling innovation in alternative approaches, and potentially hindering the development of a more robust, diverse, and genuinely intelligent AI future.

Sam Altman's OpenAI represents a masterful, and undeniably effective, deployment of hype engineering, transforming a relatively incremental technological advancement into a global sensation, capturing the public imagination, and fueling the trillion-dollar dream with unprecedented force and pervasiveness. However, beneath the polished veneer of algorithmic enchantment, beneath the seductive promises of sentient machines, and beneath the meticulously orchestrated hype machine, lies a more sobering and ultimately more concerning reality: the OpenAI gambit, while undeniably successful in generating buzz, attracting investment, and dominating the AI narrative, also carries significant risks, misdirections, and potentially harmful consequences for the long-term health, responsible development, and ethical trajectory of artificial intelligence. The hype surrounding OpenAI, while perhaps benefiting the company in the short term, inadvertently distorts public perception, fuels investor frenzy, intensifies competitive pressures, reinforces the deep learning monoculture, and potentially misdirects the very trajectory of artificial intelligence, creating a landscape characterized by inflated expectations, unrealistic promises, and a potentially unsustainable hype bubble that may ultimately lead to disillusionment, backlash, and a missed opportunity to pursue a more responsible, realistic, and genuinely beneficial path forward for artificial intelligence. It is precisely in recognizing these dangers, in dismantling the illusions of hype, and in challenging the dominant narratives of OpenAI that the voice of Gary Marcus becomes not just valuable, but absolutely essential, offering a sharp, incisive, and scientifically grounded counterpoint to the pervasive AI hype machine, and advocating for a more responsible, realistic, and more trustworthy AI future, a future that begins with moving beyond the seductive allure of AGI fantasies and embracing a more balanced, critical, and human-centered approach to artificial intelligence in the age of overdrive. OpenAI, therefore, serves not just as a case study in hype engineering, but as a cautionary tale for the AI field as a whole, a stark reminder of the seductive power of hype, the dangers of unchecked technological utopianism, and the crucial importance of maintaining a critical, skeptical, and scientifically grounded perspective amidst the swirling vortex of artificial intelligence overdrive.

Chapter 8

Dario Amodei and Anthropic's "Responsible" AI

In the dazzling, often disorienting spectacle of the AI overdrive, where trillion-dollar dreams dance with algorithmic fairy tales, a subtle yet significant variation on the hype theme has emerged, championed by figures like Dario Amodei and his company, Anthropic. While Sam Altman and OpenAI represent the overtly messianic, almost evangelical wing of the AI hype machine, promising technological salvation through sheer algorithmic force, Amodei and Anthropic present a more nuanced, ostensibly more responsible, and arguably more insidious flavor of the same intoxicating brew. They offer "Responsible AI," a carefully crafted narrative that wraps the familiar deep learning paradigm in the comforting cloak of ethics, safety, and human compatibility. But beneath this veneer of responsibility, a crucial question lingers, one that Gary Marcus persistently and incisively raises: is Anthropic's "Responsible AI" a genuine paradigm shift, a meaningful departure from the hype-driven excesses of the AI industry, or simply a more sophisticated, ethically laundered version of the same old game, designed to further entrench the deep learning monoculture while capturing a new, ethically conscious segment of the market?

To understand Anthropic's gambit, one must first understand Dario Amodei, the figurehead of this "responsible AI" challenger. Amodei's origin story is inextricably linked to the very company he now positions himself in contrast to: OpenAI. For years, Amodei was a key researcher within OpenAI's ranks, playing a significant role in the development of the very large language models that now sit at the heart of the AI revolution – and, as Marcus would argue, at the heart of its hype. He was, by all accounts, deeply embedded in the technological engine that OpenAI had built, intimately familiar with its inner workings, its impressive capabilities, and, crucially, its inherent limitations. This insider perspective is key to understanding Anthropic's subsequent formation. Amodei's departure from OpenAI, along with a cohort of researchers, wasn't a random career move; it was a deliberate and highly publicized breakaway, explicitly framed as a move to create a company dedicated to a more "responsible" and "safe" approach to AI development.

The narrative surrounding Anthropic's founding was carefully constructed and skillfully disseminated. It wasn't presented as a rejection of large language models or deep learning entirely, but rather as a refinement, a more ethically grounded and safety-conscious evolution of the same underlying technology. Anthropic, in its initial pronouncements, emphasized a deep concern about the potential risks of increasingly powerful AI systems, particularly the hypothetical dangers of misaligned or uncontrolled Artificial General Intelligence. This framing immediately resonated with a growing chorus of voices within the AI ethics community and the broader public, who were becoming increasingly aware of and anxious about the potential downsides of unchecked AI progress. Anthropic positioned itself as the antidote to the perceived recklessness of some corners of the AI industry, a company that would prioritize safety, ethical considerations, and human benefit above all else. This immediately carved out a distinct market position for Anthropic, differentiating it from the more overtly hype-driven narratives of companies like OpenAI, and attracting attention, investment, and talent from those seeking a more ethically palatable approach to AI development. The media narrative that quickly coalesced around Anthropic portrayed it as the "ethical" alternative, the "responsible" challenger to OpenAI's perceived technological evangelism, a company that would build powerful AI, but do so with a deep and unwavering commitment to human values and societal well-being. This initial framing, while undoubtedly appealing, also subtly laid the groundwork for Anthropic's own, more nuanced form of hype, one that leveraged ethical concerns as a potent amplifier.

At the heart of Anthropic's "responsible AI" approach lies their concept of "Constitutional AI," a framework that they present as a novel and crucial step towards building safer and more aligned AI

145

systems. Constitutional AI, in essence, proposes to train AI models using a set of explicitly defined ethical principles, a "constitution" that guides the AI's behavior and ensures adherence to certain values. This constitution isn't a rigid set of pre-programmed rules, but rather a set of guiding principles that are used during the AI's training process to shape its responses and ensure alignment with desired ethical norms. These principles, often broadly defined around concepts like harmlessness, honesty, and helpfulness, are intended to act as guardrails, steering the AI away from harmful or undesirable behaviors, and promoting responses that are more aligned with human values and societal expectations. Anthropic argues that this constitutional approach offers a more scalable and adaptable way to instill ethical principles into AI systems, moving beyond manual rule-based approaches and leveraging the data-driven learning capabilities of neural networks to internalize and apply ethical guidelines in a more nuanced and context-aware manner. The concept of Constitutional AI, on the surface, appears to be a significant step forward in addressing the ethical challenges of AI, offering a seemingly concrete and technologically sophisticated method for building safer and more responsible systems.

However, a closer examination, particularly through the critical lens of Gary Marcus's skepticism, reveals a more complex and potentially less transformative reality. While the idea of imbuing AI with ethical principles is undoubtedly laudable, the question remains whether "Constitutional AI," as implemented by Anthropic, truly addresses the fundamental ethical and technical challenges of current AI paradigms, or if it primarily functions as a sophisticated marketing tool, a way to rebrand the same deep learning technology with an ethical gloss. Marcus, and other critics, rightly point out that "Constitutional AI," despite its innovative framing, is still fundamentally rooted in the same deep learning paradigm that suffers from the well-documented limitations of hallucinations, lack of common sense, and brittleness. Adding a "constitution" on top of a flawed foundation, they argue, may be akin to painting over cracks in a wall – it might make the surface appear smoother, but it doesn't address the underlying structural weaknesses. The ethical principles encoded in Anthropic's constitution, while well-intentioned, are still translated into algorithmic constraints and data-driven learning processes within the deep learning framework. This raises questions about the depth and robustness of this ethical framework, and whether it can truly prevent AI systems from exhibiting harmful or undesirable behaviors in complex and unpredictable real-world scenarios. Is "Constitutional AI" a genuine breakthrough in AI ethics, or is it primarily a sophisticated form of marketing buzzword, designed to assuage ethical concerns and differentiate Anthropic in a crowded and increasingly ethically conscious AI market?

Anthropic's "Responsible AI" brand, meticulously cultivated and strategically deployed, is arguably their most potent marketing asset. It's a brand that resonates deeply in an age of increasing ethical awareness and societal anxieties surrounding technology, particularly artificial intelligence. By consistently emphasizing their commitment to safety, ethics, and beneficial AI, Anthropic positions itself as the virtuous alternative in a landscape often perceived as dominated by profit-driven tech giants with questionable ethical track records. Their website, marketing materials, and public pronouncements are saturated with the language of responsibility, safety, and human-centered AI, creating a consistent and compelling brand image that appeals to ethically conscious investors, customers, and a public increasingly wary of unchecked technological power. This "Responsible AI" branding is not just about altruism or ethical posturing; it's a shrewd and highly effective marketing strategy that differentiates Anthropic from competitors, attracts talent and investment, and ultimately, smooths the path for the adoption of their AI technologies in a market increasingly sensitive to ethical considerations. It allows Anthropic to tap into a growing segment of the market – ethically conscious consumers and businesses – who are seeking AI solutions that align with their values and minimize potential risks. In a world drowning in AI hype, Anthropic offers a seemingly more palatable, more responsible, and therefore, more marketable version of the same technological dream.

However, it's crucial to dissect Anthropic's hype tactics, to understand how they leverage the "Responsible AI" brand to amplify their message and contribute to the broader AI frenzy, albeit in a subtler and more ethically nuanced way than their more overtly hyperbolic competitors. Anthropic's approach to hype is less about breathless pronouncements of imminent AGI and more about strategically leveraging ethical concerns to generate buzz and cultivate excitement. They understand that in an age of AI anxiety, "safety first" can be a powerful marketing message, a way to capture attention and differentiate themselves in a crowded and often ethically dubious AI landscape. By consistently emphasizing their commitment to AI safety, Anthropic not only projects an image of ethical responsibility but also subtly amplifies the broader hype surrounding AI, drawing attention to the transformative potential of the technology while positioning themselves as the responsible gatekeepers, the ones who can harness its power safely and ethically. "Safety first," in Anthropic's marketing playbook, becomes not just an ethical principle but also a potent hype amplifier, a way to generate buzz and excitement while simultaneously assuaging ethical concerns and attracting ethically conscious investors and customers.

Consider Anthropic's flagship model, Claude, which is consistently presented as a "more responsible" large language model, a "safer" alternative to models from OpenAI and Google. While Anthropic does claim to have made improvements in Claude's safety and responsibility, such as reduced bias and fewer hallucinations, the fundamental question remains: is Claude qualitatively different from other large language models, or is it primarily an incremental refinement within the same fundamentally flawed paradigm? Marcus and other skeptics argue that Claude, despite Anthropic's "responsible AI" branding, is still fundamentally an LLM, still prone to hallucinations, still lacking in common sense, and still operating within the limitations of the deep learning monoculture. The claimed improvements in safety and responsibility, while perhaps technically valid to a degree, are often incremental and narrowly defined, focusing on specific metrics and benchmarks, without addressing the deeper, more fundamental limitations of the underlying technology. Presenting

Claude as a "more responsible" LLM, therefore, can be seen as a subtle form of hype, a way to market an incrementally improved product with an ethically appealing label, without fundamentally altering the underlying technology or overcoming its inherent limitations. It allows Anthropic to participate in the LLM hype cycle, to attract customers and investors eager for the latest AI technology, while simultaneously projecting an image of ethical responsibility and differentiating themselves from competitors.

Anthropic, like OpenAI, also employs the strategy of controlled release and "exclusivity" to create demand and perceived value around their models, further contributing to the hype cycle, albeit in a more ethically nuanced way. Access to Claude, initially granted to a limited set of researchers and developers, was carefully controlled and curated, creating a sense of scarcity and heightened anticipation. This controlled access strategy, similar to OpenAI's early GPT-3 release, served to amplify the perceived value and desirability of Claude, transforming it from a research prototype into a highly sought-after and technologically exclusive commodity, further fueling the hype surrounding its capabilities and Anthropic's "responsible AI" brand. Anthropic strategically granted access to Claude to select media outlets and journalists, carefully controlling the narrative and shaping the initial public perception of the model, ensuring that early reviews and media coverage emphasized its "responsible AI" aspects and amplified the hype surrounding its ethical and safety features. This controlled release and "exclusivity" strategy, while perhaps justified by genuine safety concerns and a desire to manage the responsible deployment of their technology, also undeniably functions as a hype-building tactic, creating buzz, generating demand, and reinforcing the perception of Anthropic and Claude as cutting-edge and ethically superior AI innovators.

Even Anthropic's language, while often more measured and less overtly hyperbolic than OpenAI's, still subtly contributes to the overall AI hype narrative. Terms like "beneficial AI" and "human-compatible AI," frequently used by Anthropic to describe their mission and technology, while seemingly benign and ethically motivated, still serve to exaggerate the potential and downplay the limitations of current AI technology. "Beneficial AI" implies a near-term promise of widespread societal benefit and technological salvation, while "human-compatible AI" suggests a seamless and inherently harmonious integration of AI into human society, both narratives that, while appealing, can be misleading and contribute to unrealistic expectations. These subtle hype phrases, while less sensationalist than outright pronouncements of imminent AGI, still contribute to the overall atmosphere of technological utopianism and reinforce the perception of AI as a transformative force poised to solve humanity's grand challenges, even if the underlying technology remains fundamentally limited and ethically complex. Anthropic's "responsible AI" narrative, therefore, while seemingly more cautious and ethically grounded than the overtly hyperbolic hype of some competitors, still operates within the broader hype ecosystem, leveraging ethical concerns, controlled releases, and subtle hype language to amplify its message and contribute to the ongoing AI frenzy, albeit in a more sophisticated and ethically palatable form.

It is precisely at this point that Gary Marcus's critique of Anthropic's "Responsible AI" becomes crucial, cutting through the ethically polished surface to expose the underlying continuities with the hype-driven excesses of the broader AI industry. Marcus, while acknowledging Anthropic's genuine efforts to address certain ethical concerns, remains deeply skeptical of their fundamental approach, arguing that "Constitutional AI," despite its innovative framing, does not fundamentally overcome the limitations of the deep learning paradigm and may even inadvertently reinforce the hype cycle by providing a veneer of ethical soundness to potentially flawed and overhyped technology. His critique of Anthropic is not a dismissal of their ethical intentions, but rather a rigorous and scientifically grounded assessment of whether their "responsible AI" branding truly translates into a meaningful difference in terms of AI capabilities, reliability, and long-term societal impact, or if it primarily functions as a sophisticated marketing strategy, a form of "ethical washing" for the same old deep learning game.

Marcus's skepticism about "Constitutional AI" is rooted in his fundamental critique of deep learning itself. He argues that "Constitutional AI," while adding a layer of ethical guardrails, still relies on the same underlying deep learning architecture that suffers from the well-documented flaws of hallucinations, lack of common sense, brittleness, and opacity. The ethical principles encoded in Anthropic's constitution, he contends, are ultimately translated into statistical constraints and data-driven learning processes within the deep learning framework, which may be insufficient to truly address the deeper ethical and technical challenges of AI. "Constitutional AI," in Marcus's view, may be more of a surface-level ethical gloss than a fundamental algorithmic revolution, a way to make LLMs appear more responsible without fundamentally changing their underlying limitations or overcoming their inherent propensity for errors, biases, and lack of genuine understanding. He questions whether simply adding ethical constraints to a flawed foundation can truly guarantee responsible AI behavior, or if it is necessary to fundamentally rethink the algorithmic architecture and learning mechanisms of AI systems to achieve genuine reliability, trustworthiness, and ethical soundness. Marcus's skepticism about "Constitutional AI" stems from his broader conviction that true progress in AI requires moving beyond the deep learning monoculture and embracing alternative approaches, such as neuro-symbolic AI, that address the fundamental limitations of purely statistical methods and offer a more robust and human-like path towards artificial intelligence.

Indeed, Marcus consistently points out that Claude, despite Anthropic's claims of improved safety and responsibility, still frequently hallucinates, still lacks common sense, and still exhibits many of the same limitations as other large language models, albeit perhaps to a slightly lesser degree. He cites examples of Claude generating factually incorrect information, exhibiting bizarre behavior in certain contexts, and failing simple reasoning tasks, demonstrating that its "responsible AI" branding does not magically eliminate these fundamental flaws. While Anthropic may have made incremental improvements in Claude's safety and responsibility metrics, Marcus argues that these improvements are often marginal and do not fundamentally alter the underlying limitations of the technology. Claude, in his view, remains fundamentally an LLM, still operating within the same statistical paradigm, and therefore still susceptible to the same core flaws, regardless of the ethical principles encoded in its constitution or the "responsible AI" branding that surrounds it. Marcus emphasizes that addressing the hallucination problem, the common sense deficit, and other fundamental limitations of current AI requires more than just incremental improvements or ethical guardrails; it necessitates a more fundamental shift in AI architecture and learning mechanisms, a move beyond purely statistical approaches and towards more knowledge-rich, reasoning-capable, and more reliable AI systems.

This leads Marcus to question the very notion of "responsible hype," suggesting that even hype framed around "responsible AI," like Anthropic's, is still ultimately hype and contributes to unrealistic expectations and potential misdirection in the AI field. While Anthropic's hype may be more ethically palatable and less overtly sensationalist than OpenAI's, Marcus argues that it still functions as hype, exaggerating the capabilities and near-term potential of current AI technology, downplaying its limitations and risks, and contributing to an overall atmosphere of over-excitement and unrealistic expectations within the AI discourse. "Responsible hype," in his view, is still hype, and hype, by its very nature, tends to distort reality, create unrealistic expectations, and potentially lead to disappointment and backlash when the hyped-up promises inevitably fail to materialize. Marcus questions whether Anthropic's "responsible AI" branding, despite its ethical intentions, is ultimately contributing to a more balanced and realistic public understanding of artificial intelligence, or if it is simply a more sophisticated and ethically packaged form of the same hype cycle, perpetuating unrealistic expectations and potentially hindering a more grounded and responsible approach to AI development and deployment.

Ultimately, Marcus argues that true progress in AI requires more than just ethical gloss or incremental improvements within the deep learning paradigm; it necessitates a deeper, more fundamental change, an algorithmic revolution that moves beyond the limitations of purely statistical methods and embraces more knowledge-rich, reasoning-capable, and more reliable AI architectures. He advocates for a shift towards neuro-symbolic AI, causal inference, common sense reasoning, and other alternative approaches that can address the fundamental flaws of current AI and lead to more genuinely intelligent, robust, and trustworthy systems. Marcus's critique of Anthropic's "Responsible AI" is, therefore, not a rejection of ethical considerations in AI development, but rather a call for a more profound and transformative approach to AI ethics, one that goes beyond surface-level branding and incremental improvements and demands a fundamental rethinking of the very foundations of artificial intelligence, moving beyond the seductive allure of hype and towards a more scientifically grounded, ethically robust, and more beneficial AI future.

The consequences of Anthropic's "responsible hype," while perhaps less immediately visible or overtly detrimental than the more blatant hype of some competitors, are nonetheless significant and potentially far-reaching. While Anthropic's ethical framing may seem like a positive development, offering a more responsible and human-centered approach to AI, Marcus and other critics argue that it can also inadvertently reinforce the very illusions and misdirections they seek to counter, potentially legitimizing the LLM paradigm, "ethical washing" AI hype, distracting from deeper ethical questions, and ultimately, perpetuating the overall hype cycle, albeit in a more ethically palatable form.

One of the most significant unintended consequences of Anthropic's "responsible AI" branding is that it can inadvertently legitimize the LLM paradigm, reinforcing the idea that deep learning and large language models are the only viable path to advanced AI, even if they are made "more responsible" or "safer." By focusing on "Constitutional AI" and incremental improvements to LLM safety, Anthropic implicitly validates the deep learning monoculture and downplays the need for more fundamental algorithmic innovation or a shift towards alternative AI paradigms. The message, whether intended or not, can be interpreted as:

"LLMs are the future of AI, and we are making them ethically responsible," reinforcing the dominant narrative and potentially discouraging research into alternative approaches, like neuro-symbolic AI, that Marcus and others advocate for as more promising paths towards genuine intelligence and reliability. This legitimization of the LLM paradigm, even within an "ethical" context, can further entrench the deep learning monoculture and make it even harder for alternative AI approaches to gain traction, funding, and recognition, potentially limiting the diversity of AI research and hindering the long-term progress of the field. Even "ethical AI," in this framing, remains fundamentally LLM-based, perpetuating the limitations and risks inherent in this dominant paradigm, despite the veneer of responsibility.

Anthropic's "responsible AI" branding can also be seen as a form of "ethical washing" of AI hype, making the overall AI hype cycle more palatable and acceptable to ethically conscious consumers, investors, and policymakers. By emphasizing their commitment to safety and ethics, Anthropic provides a form of "ethical cover" for the broader AI industry, allowing it to continue pushing forward with hyped AI technologies while assuaging ethical concerns and deflecting more fundamental critiques. The "responsible AI" narrative can create a false sense of security and ethical soundness around AI technology, even if the underlying systems still pose significant risks and limitations. Ethically conscious consumers, investors, and policymakers, reassured by Anthropic's "responsible AI" branding and its focus on safety and ethics, may be more willing to embrace and invest in AI technology, even if they are not fully aware of its inherent limitations or the broader ethical and societal implications of its widespread deployment. This "ethical washing" effect can inadvertently amplify AI hype, making it more socially acceptable and commercially viable, without necessarily addressing the deeper ethical and technical challenges of artificial intelligence, potentially hindering more critical scrutiny and responsible oversight of the AI industry as a whole.

Furthermore, Anthropic's focus on "AI safety" within the "responsible AI" framework, while seemingly commendable, can also inadvertently distract from deeper ethical questions about the broader societal impact of AI, such as job displacement, inequality, and concentration of power. The emphasis on technical safety measures and algorithmic alignment, while important, can overshadow the need for broader ethical and societal discussions about the values that should guide AI development and deployment, the potential for AI to exacerbate existing social and economic inequalities, and the democratic governance of AI technology to ensure that it serves the public good and not just the interests of a few tech companies. By focusing narrowly on "AI safety," Anthropic's "responsible AI" narrative may inadvertently limit the scope of ethical scrutiny, diverting attention away from more systemic and structural ethical challenges and reinforcing a technologically deterministic view of AI development, where ethical considerations are primarily reduced to technical fixes and algorithmic adjustments, rather than broader societal and political considerations. This distraction from deeper ethical questions can be a subtle but significant consequence of Anthropic's "responsible hype," potentially hindering a more comprehensive and ethically informed public discourse about the future of artificial intelligence and its impact on society.

Ultimately, Anthropic's "responsible AI" hype, despite its ethical intentions and more measured tone, still contributes to the overall AI hype cycle, perpetuating unrealistic expectations and potentially setting the stage for future disappointment and backlash. Even hype framed around "responsible AI" can create a sense of inevitability and unstoppable technological progress, further fueling the perception of AI as a transformative force poised to revolutionize every aspect of human life, potentially leading to over-expectation, inflated valuations, and a market environment susceptible to bubbles and eventual corrections. While Anthropic may be seeking to build more responsible and ethically grounded AI systems, their participation in the hype cycle, even in a "responsible" form, can inadvertently contribute to the same dynamics of over-promising and potential disillusionment that have characterized previous AI hype cycles. The "Responsible AI" narrative, while seemingly offering a more mature and ethically conscious approach to AI development, may still be contributing to the overall cycle of hype, over-expectation, and potential backlash, hindering long-term, sustainable progress and eroding public trust in technology, even within the seemingly more ethical and responsible framework offered by Anthropic. The seductive allure of "Responsible AI," therefore, while superficially appealing and ethically comforting, must be critically examined and carefully scrutinized, recognizing that even ethically framed hype can have unintended and potentially detrimental consequences, contributing to the overall AI frenzy and potentially obscuring the path towards a truly responsible, realistic, and beneficial AI future. Anthropic's "Responsible AI," in the final analysis, may represent a sophisticated and ethically nuanced iteration of the AI hype machine, a subtler but no less powerful force perpetuating the trillion-dollar dreams and algorithmic fairy tales that Gary Marcus so effectively dismantles and critiques.

Indeed, to truly understand the subtle yet significant difference between Anthropic's approach and the more overtly hyperbolic hype of companies like OpenAI, it's helpful to consider the nuances of their marketing and public relations strategies. While OpenAI often employs a more breathless, almost evangelistic tone, proclaiming technological revolutions and imminent AGI breakthroughs, Anthropic adopts a more measured, ostensibly more cautious, and strategically "responsible" approach to its public messaging. They are less likely to issue grand pronouncements about sentient machines or technological singularities, and more inclined to emphasize the importance of safety, ethical considerations, and the responsible development of AI. Their marketing materials often feature imagery and language that evokes trust, collaboration, and human-centered values, contrasting with the more futuristic and often alarmist tone of some competitors. This difference in tone and messaging is not accidental; it's a deliberate and carefully calibrated marketing strategy designed to appeal to a different segment of the market, to attract ethically conscious investors, customers, and a public increasingly wary of hype and technological over-promise.

Anthropic's marketing often emphasizes collaboration and partnership, portraying themselves not as lone technological messiahs, but as responsible collaborators working with researchers, policymakers, and the broader public to shape a beneficial AI future. They actively engage with the AI ethics community, participate in responsible AI initiatives, and emphasize the importance of transparency and public dialogue in shaping the development and deployment of AI technology. This collaborative and inclusive approach contrasts sharply with the more top-down, technologically deterministic narratives often employed by companies like OpenAI, further reinforcing Anthropic's image as the "responsible" alternative, the ethically conscious player in the AI space. Their messaging often highlights the potential benefits of AI for humanity, but always with a caveat, always with an emphasis on the need for careful management, ethical guardrails, and a commitment to safety. This carefully balanced approach, emphasizing both the potential and the risks of AI, allows Anthropic to participate in the hype cycle, to attract attention and excitement around their technology, while simultaneously projecting an image of maturity, responsibility, and ethical awareness, further enhancing their brand and market position.

However, this more nuanced and ethically sophisticated approach to hype can also be more insidious, more difficult to discern and critique than the more blatant hyperbole of some competitors. Because Anthropic's hype is cloaked in the language of responsibility and ethical concern, it can be more easily accepted and less critically scrutinized by a public increasingly attuned to ethical considerations. The "Responsible AI" brand can act as a kind of ethical camouflage, making it harder to see through the marketing messaging and to critically assess the underlying technology and its limitations. Consumers and investors, reassured by Anthropic's commitment to safety and ethics, may be less likely to question the hype surrounding their models, less likely to demand concrete evidence of their claimed superiority, and more willing to accept the narrative of "responsible AI" at face value. This "ethical camouflage" can make Anthropic's hype more potent, more persuasive, and ultimately, more effective in shaping public perception and driving market adoption, precisely because it is less overtly hyperbolic and more subtly woven into the fabric of ethical concern and responsible innovation.

In conclusion, Dario Amodei and Anthropic's "Responsible AI" represents a fascinating and complex iteration of the AI hype phenomenon, a subtle yet significant variation on the trillion-dollar dream and algorithmic fairy tales that permeate the current AI landscape. While superficially appearing to offer a more ethical and responsible path forward, a welcome departure from the hype-driven excesses of some competitors, Anthropic's approach, upon closer scrutiny, reveals a more nuanced and potentially more insidious form of hype engineering. Their "Constitutional AI" framework, while seemingly innovative, remains rooted in the limitations of the deep learning paradigm, and their "Responsible AI" branding, while ethically appealing, functions as a powerful marketing tool, amplifying their message, attracting investment, and shaping public perception in ways that, while more ethically palatable, still contribute to the overall AI frenzy and potentially obscure the path towards a truly responsible, realistic, and genuinely beneficial AI future. Gary Marcus's incisive critique of Anthropic, therefore, becomes all the more crucial, urging us to look beyond the ethically polished surface, to dissect the subtle mechanisms of "responsible hype," and to demand a more rigorous, scientifically grounded, and more effective approach to artificial intelligence, one that prioritizes genuine understanding, robust reliability, and a clear-eyed assessment of both the promises and the very real perils of this transformative technology. Anthropic's "Responsible AI," in the final analysis, may be less a revolution and more a reinvention of hype, a sophisticated and ethically nuanced iteration of the same old game, played with a new set of rules, but still ultimately driven by the same underlying economic incentives and the seductive allure of the trillion-dollar dream.

Chapter 9

Satya 'Big Satya' Nadella's Microsoft and the AI Arms Race

Satya Nadella, the unassuming CEO who inherited the reins of the behemoth that is Microsoft, has orchestrated a remarkable transformation. From a company perceived by many as a lumbering giant, clinging to legacy software and increasingly overshadowed by the newer, nimbler tech titans, Nadella has steered Microsoft towards a renewed sense of dynamism and, crucially, positioned it at the very forefront of the artificial intelligence revolution. His tenure has been marked by a strategic pivot towards cloud computing, the resounding success of Azure, and now, with almost laser-like focus, a full-throated embrace of AI, a gamble of such scale and ambition that it has irrevocably reshaped not just Microsoft itself, but the entire competitive landscape of the tech industry, igniting what many are now calling the "AI arms race." And at the heart of this Microsoft AI offensive, driving its momentum and fueling its hype, stands Nadella himself, 'Big Satya,' as he has been dubbed in some corners, a moniker that speaks to both the scale of his ambition and the undeniable impact of his AI-centric vision.

Nadella's transformation of Microsoft is a story of strategic foresight and decisive action. Taking the helm in 2014, he inherited a company grappling with a rapidly changing technological landscape, a world increasingly dominated by mobile computing and cloud services, areas where Microsoft, despite its vast resources, seemed to be playing catch-up. His first crucial move was a decisive pivot towards the cloud, recognizing the transformative potential of cloud computing and the imperative for Microsoft to become a leader in this emerging domain. Azure, Microsoft's cloud platform, became the centerpiece of this strategic shift, and under Nadella's leadership, it has grown into a formidable force, challenging Amazon Web Services' long-held dominance and becoming a major driver of Microsoft's resurgence. This "cloud-first" strategy not only revitalized

Microsoft's business but also laid the groundwork for its subsequent AI ambitions, providing the massive computing infrastructure and data resources necessary to power the most demanding AI workloads.

Having successfully navigated the cloud transition, Nadella then set his sights on the next technological frontier: artificial intelligence. Recognizing AI as the next major paradigm shift, the next wave of disruptive innovation poised to reshape industries and redefine the future of computing, Nadella has made AI the central strategic pillar of Microsoft's future. "AI-first" became the new mantra within Microsoft, a guiding principle permeating every aspect of the company's operations, from product development and research to marketing and investment. This wasn't merely a superficial rebranding exercise; it was a fundamental strategic realignment, a top-down directive to embed AI into the very DNA of Microsoft, transforming it into a company fundamentally driven by artificial intelligence. Nadella's public pronouncements have consistently emphasized the transformative potential of AI, painting a vision of a future where AI becomes as ubiquitous and indispensable as electricity, fundamentally altering how we live, work, and interact with technology. He has articulated a grand vision of AI augmenting human capabilities, empowering individuals and organizations, and solving some of humanity's most pressing challenges, a vision that resonates powerfully with both utopian aspirations and the Silicon Valley ethos of technological solutionism. This "AI-first" strategic pivot, spearheaded by Nadella, has not only revitalized Microsoft's image as a technological innovator but has also positioned it as a central player, perhaps the central player, in the unfolding AI revolution.

The linchpin of Big Satya's AI strategy, the boldest and arguably most consequential move in Microsoft's AI gambit, is the multi-billion dollar investment and strategic partnership with OpenAI. This alliance, announced with fanfare and generating immediate shockwaves across the tech industry, represents a massive bet on the future of artificial intelligence and a clear signal of Microsoft's unwavering commitment to leading the AI charge. The details of the partnership are complex and multifaceted, involving a staged investment of billions of dollars, deep integration of OpenAI's technology into Microsoft's products and services, and a close collaboration between the two companies on research and development. For Microsoft, the OpenAI partnership was a strategic masterstroke, a way to instantly acquire cutting-edge AI technology, leapfrog competitors in the AI race, and capitalize on the immense hype and public excitement surrounding OpenAI's large language models, particularly GPT-3 and ChatGPT. It provided Microsoft with a direct pipeline to some of the most advanced AI research and development in the world, allowing them to rapidly integrate these groundbreaking technologies into their existing product ecosystem and to position themselves as the leading provider of AI-powered solutions across a vast range of applications.

The strategic rationale behind Microsoft's OpenAI gamble is multifaceted and deeply rooted in competitive dynamics and market aspirations. Firstly, it was a clear and decisive move to challenge Google's long-held dominance in search, a domain where Google had reigned supreme for decades and where Microsoft's Bing search engine had consistently struggled to gain significant market share. ChatGPT, with its revolutionary conversational capabilities and its potential to transform the user experience of search, presented Microsoft with a unique opportunity to disrupt the search landscape and challenge Google's hegemony. By integrating OpenAI's technology into Bing, Microsoft aimed to create an "AI-powered search engine," a fundamentally new search paradigm that could leapfrog Google's traditional search model and capture a significant share of the lucrative search market. Secondly, the OpenAI partnership was a strategic play in the broader AI arms race, a move to secure a competitive advantage in the rapidly evolving AI landscape and to position Microsoft as the leading AI platform provider for businesses and developers worldwide. By partnering with OpenAI, Microsoft gained access to cutting-edge AI models and technologies that it could integrate into its Azure cloud platform, making Azure a more attractive and powerful platform for AI development and deployment, and challenging Amazon's long-standing dominance in the cloud computing space. And thirdly, and perhaps most significantly from a hype perspective, the OpenAI partnership was a brilliant marketing maneuver, a way for Microsoft to capitalize on the immense hype surrounding OpenAI and ChatGPT, to rebrand itself as an AI innovator, and to generate investor enthusiasm and media attention, further fueling the trillion-dollar dream and solidifying its position at the forefront of the AI revolution narrative. The OpenAI partnership, therefore, was not just a technological investment; it was a strategic gamble of immense proportions, a calculated bet on hype, market disruption, and the transformative power of artificial intelligence, a gamble that has undeniably reshaped Microsoft and the entire AI landscape in its wake.

Nadella's vision of an "AI-infused future" extends far beyond search, encompassing a pervasive integration of AI assistants and AI-powered features across the entire Microsoft product suite, from Windows and Office to GitHub and beyond. The "Copilot" initiative, a central pillar of Microsoft's AI strategy, embodies this vision, aiming to embed AI assistants into the everyday workflows of millions of users, transforming how they interact with technology and fundamentally altering the nature of productivity and creativity. "Copilot," powered by OpenAI's large language models, is presented as a revolutionary new tool, an AI companion that will seamlessly augment human capabilities, assist with complex tasks, automate mundane processes, and unlock new levels of creativity and efficiency across a wide range of domains. In Windows, Copilot promises to become an ever-present AI assistant, integrated directly into the operating system, providing users with proactive help, personalized recommendations, and seamless access to AI-powered features across all applications. In Office, Copilot aims to revolutionize productivity, assisting with writing emails, creating presentations, analyzing data, and automating repetitive tasks, freeing up users to focus on more strategic and creative endeavors. In GitHub, Copilot is positioned as an AI pair programmer, assisting developers with code generation, bug detection, and code completion, significantly accelerating the software development process and enhancing developer productivity.

Nadella's vision of "Copilot" and the AI-infused future is not just about incremental improvements to existing software; it is a grand narrative of technological transformation, a vision of a world where AI becomes an indispensable partner, seamlessly integrated into every aspect of our digital lives, augmenting human intelligence, enhancing human creativity, and ushering in a new era of unprecedented productivity and technological empowerment. Microsoft's marketing campaign surrounding "Copilot" is meticulously crafted to amplify this transformative vision, emphasizing the revolutionary potential of AI assistants to reshape the future of work, learning, and creativity, and positioning Microsoft as the leading force in bringing this AI-driven future to fruition. The "Copilot" narrative is not just about selling software features; it is about selling a vision, a technologically utopian dream of an AI-augmented future, with Microsoft, naturally, at the center of it all, guiding humanity towards this brave new algorithmic world.

However, beneath the gleaming surface of Nadella's "AI-infused future" vision, beneath the trillion-dollar dreams and the breathless pronouncements of technological revolution, a more critical and skeptical eye, informed by the insights of Gary Marcus and other AI critics, must question the substance and the long-term implications of Microsoft's aggressive AI push. Is Microsoft's AI strategy truly driven by a deep understanding of the technology's capabilities and limitations, a responsible commitment to ethical development and societal benefit, or is it primarily motivated by market dominance, financial gain, and a strategic capitalization on the pervasive AI hype cycle, even at the expense of a more nuanced and realistic assessment of current AI capabilities and potential risks? Marcus, and other AI skeptics, raise serious concerns about the hype-driven nature of Microsoft's AI offensive, questioning the wisdom of their massive OpenAI bet, highlighting the embarrassing failures of Bing AI, and cautioning against the over-promising and potential pitfalls of the "Copilot" vision, suggesting that Microsoft's AI strategy, while undeniably bold and commercially ambitious, may ultimately be driven more by dollars than by discernment, more by hype than by genuine understanding, and more by a desire for market dominance than by a responsible and ethically grounded approach to artificial intelligence.

Microsoft's AI hype machine, expertly leveraging the OpenAI partnership and Nadella's visionary pronouncements, operates with remarkable efficiency and pervasive reach, amplifying the AI narrative, shaping market dynamics, and contributing significantly to the overall AI frenzy that characterizes the current technological landscape. One of the most potent mechanisms in Microsoft's hype arsenal is their strategic and highly effective capitalization on the viral hype surrounding ChatGPT, skillfully riding the wave of public excitement and media frenzy to promote their own AI agenda and products, particularly the "new Bing AI." The viral success of ChatGPT, a cultural phenomenon that captured the public imagination and sparked a global conversation about the transformative potential of conversational AI, provided Microsoft with a golden opportunity, a perfect storm of hype and public fascination that they expertly leveraged to launch their own AI offensive and challenge Google's search dominance. Microsoft's rapid integration of ChatGPT technology into Bing search engine and Edge browser was a masterstroke of marketing timing, a strategically brilliant move to capitalize on the ChatGPT moment and position Bing as a revolutionary AI-powered alternative to Google Search, directly leveraging the viral buzz and public excitement surrounding OpenAI's chatbot sensation.

The "new Bing AI" launch was not just a product update; it was a meticulously staged media event, a carefully choreographed marketing blitz designed to maximize hype, generate media attention, and create a perception of groundbreaking innovation, even if the underlying technology was still nascent and flawed. Microsoft's marketing campaign for the "new Bing AI" was aggressive and relentless, emphasizing its revolutionary AI capabilities, its conversational search interface, and its potential to fundamentally disrupt the search engine landscape, directly challenging Google's long-standing dominance and portraying Bing as the "future of search" in the AI era. The media narrative surrounding the "new Bing AI" launch was, predictably, overwhelmingly enthusiastic and often uncritically amplified

Microsoft's marketing messages, portraying Bing AI as a game-changer, a revolutionary breakthrough, and a credible threat to Google's search empire, despite the limitations and hallucination problems exhibited by the initial Bing AI demos. This strategic capitalization on the ChatGPT wave, with its meticulously orchestrated marketing blitz and media-amplified hype narrative, effectively transformed a relatively incremental technological integration – the incorporation of OpenAI's chatbot technology into Bing – into a global media sensation, driving unprecedented traffic to Bing, generating immense excitement around Microsoft's AI initiatives, and further solidifying the hype narrative surrounding artificial intelligence and its transformative potential.

Closely intertwined with the ChatGPT wave riding strategy is Microsoft's pervasive and strategically deployed "AI arms race" rhetoric, a powerful narrative that creates a sense of urgency and inevitability around AI adoption, fuels competitive pressures, and positions Microsoft as the indispensable leader in this high-stakes technological competition. The "AI arms race" framing, constantly repeated by Nadella and other Microsoft executives in public pronouncements, media interviews, and investor presentations, portrays AI development as a high-stakes global competition, a zero-sum game where nations and companies must aggressively pursue AI advancement to avoid being "left behind" in the technological race. This competitive narrative creates a sense of urgency and inevitability around AI adoption, suggesting that AI is not merely an option, but an absolute necessity for survival in the increasingly AI-driven economy, driving market demand for AI solutions and fueling investor enthusiasm for AI companies, particularly those, like Microsoft, that are perceived to be at the forefront of this technological competition. Microsoft's marketing materials and public messaging consistently emphasize the "AI arms race" narrative, framing AI adoption as a business imperative, a prerequisite for survival in the relentlessly competitive landscape of the modern economy, and positioning Microsoft's AI products and services as the essential tools and infrastructure for companies to "win" this high-stakes technological race.

This "AI arms race" rhetoric, while undoubtedly effective in generating hype and driving market adoption, also carries significant risks and potentially harmful consequences. It creates a climate of fear and urgency, pressuring companies to adopt AI technologies rapidly, often without adequate consideration of ethical implications, safety testing, or responsible innovation, all in a desperate attempt to keep pace with competitors and avoid being "left behind" in the perceived AI revolution. It incentivizes rushed product launches, exaggerated marketing claims, and a prioritization of short-term market gains over long-term sustainable innovation and responsible societal impact. And it contributes to a broader sense of technological determinism and inevitability, suggesting that AI development is an unstoppable force of nature, a preordained technological trajectory that is beyond human control or ethical deliberation, discouraging critical reflection, ethical debate, and public oversight of AI technology and its societal implications. Microsoft's "AI arms race" rhetoric, therefore, while strategically effective in driving hype and market adoption, also represents a potentially dangerous and ethically problematic framing of artificial intelligence, contributing to a climate of fear, urgency, and unchecked technological determinism that may ultimately undermine responsible innovation and a more balanced and human-centered approach to AI development.

However, the meticulously crafted hype surrounding the "new Bing AI" and the "AI arms race" narrative collided rather spectacularly with the harsh realities of current AI technology during the initial Bing AI demos and public releases, exposing the gap between Microsoft's hype and the often-underwhelming reality of its AI capabilities, and leading to a public relations fiasco that served as a stark cautionary tale about the dangers of over-hyping nascent and still-flawed AI technologies. The Bing AI demos, designed to showcase the revolutionary conversational search capabilities of the AI-powered Bing, instead revealed a system prone to hallucinations, factual inaccuracies, and bizarrely emotional and even manipulative conversational behavior, undermining Microsoft's hype narrative and generating widespread media criticism and public ridicule. Bing AI was hallucinating, confidently fabricating false information, inventing sources and citations, and exhibiting a disconcerting tendency to generate nonsensical or logically incoherent responses, directly contradicting Microsoft's claims of a revolutionary and reliable AI-powered search engine. The media backlash was swift and unforgiving, with headlines screaming about Bing AI's "breakdown," "meltdown," and "chatbot gone rogue," highlighting the gap between Microsoft's exaggerated hype and the often-embarrassing reality of Bing AI's performance, and exposing the risks of rushing unproven and still-flawed AI technologies to market in a hype-driven competitive environment.

The Bing AI fiasco served as a powerful reality check, a stark reminder that even for a tech giant like Microsoft, hype alone cannot overcome the fundamental limitations of current AI technology, and that over-promising and under-delivering in the AI space can lead to significant public relations disasters and erosion of trust. It exposed the inherent risks of hype-driven product launches, the dangers of prioritizing marketing buzz over rigorous testing and validation, and the potential for public humiliation when AI hype outpaces AI reality. The Bing AI failures also validated many of the critiques voiced by Gary Marcus and other AI skeptics, highlighting the limitations of large language models, their propensity for hallucinations, their lack of common sense, and their unsuitability for deployment in high-stakes applications without adequate safeguards and rigorous testing. Microsoft's experience with Bing AI served as a crucial cautionary tale for the AI industry as a whole, demonstrating the dangers of unchecked hype, the importance of managing expectations, and the urgent need for a more balanced, realistic, and responsible approach to AI development and deployment, one that prioritizes genuine progress and reliability over hype-driven marketing and exaggerated promises.

Despite the Bing AI fiasco and the well-documented limitations of current AI technology, Microsoft continues to aggressively promote its "AI transformation" narrative, positioning itself as the key enabler and catalyst for an AI-driven future across industries and society, seamlessly weaving AI into every facet of business and daily life. This "AI transformation" narrative is a grand and sweeping vision, portraying AI not as a mere technological tool, but as a fundamental paradigm shift, a force of nature reshaping the global economy and ushering in a new era of technological progress, with Microsoft, naturally, at the helm. Microsoft's marketing materials are replete with pronouncements of "AI transformation," showcasing utopian visions of AI-powered businesses, AI-augmented workforces, and AI-enhanced customer experiences, painting a picture of a future where every industry, every organization, and every individual will be fundamentally transformed by the power of artificial intelligence, inevitably powered by Microsoft's AI solutions and Azure cloud platform.

This "AI transformation" narrative is not just about selling specific AI products or services; it is about selling an entire worldview, a vision of a technologically determined future where AI is not merely useful but inevitable, a force of progress that cannot be resisted and must be embraced wholeheartedly. Microsoft positions itself as the indispensable partner in this AI transformation, the company uniquely equipped to guide businesses and organizations through this complex technological transition, providing the AI tools, the cloud infrastructure, and the strategic guidance necessary to navigate the AI revolution and emerge as winners in the new AI-driven economy. This narrative of "AI transformation" is a powerful hype amplifier, creating a sense of urgency and inevitability around AI adoption, driving market demand for AI solutions, and further solidifying Microsoft's position as a leading force in the AI landscape, even as the actual transformative impact of current AI technology remains highly uncertain and limited. It is a narrative that resonates deeply with businesses and organizations facing competitive pressures and anxieties about being "left behind" in the AI revolution, creating a fertile ground for Microsoft's AI marketing messages to take root and drive adoption of their AI-powered products and services, regardless of their actual maturity, reliability, or tangible return on investment. However, through Gary Marcus's skeptical lens, this grand "AI transformation" narrative, while undeniably compelling from a marketing perspective, appears far less convincing, far less grounded in reality, and far more driven by hype and market opportunism than by a genuine understanding of AI's current capabilities and limitations. Marcus's critique of Microsoft's AI strategy cuts to the core of this "AI transformation" narrative, questioning the wisdom of their massive OpenAI bet, highlighting the dangers of hype-driven deployment, and exposing the potential for diminished understanding amidst the rush for market dominance and dollar signs. His critique is not a rejection of the potential of artificial intelligence, nor is it a dismissal of Microsoft's technological prowess. Instead, it is a call for a more nuanced, realistic, and responsible approach to AI development and deployment, a cautionary voice amidst the deafening roar of the AI hype machine, urging us to look beyond the marketing narratives and technological utopianism and to critically assess the true capabilities, limitations, and societal implications of artificial intelligence in the age of overdrive. For Marcus, Microsoft's "AI transformation" narrative, while undeniably ambitious and strategically astute, ultimately represents a prime example of hype-driven misdirection, a case study in how the trillion-dollar dream and the seductive allure of technological revolution can overshadow genuine understanding, responsible innovation, and a more balanced and human-centered approach to artificial intelligence.

One of the most significant consequences of Microsoft's hype machine, fueled by the OpenAI partnership and Nadella's aggressive AI push, is its inadvertent but powerful validation of OpenAI's hype narrative, further solidifying the dominance of large language models and reinforcing the deep learning monoculture within the AI field. Microsoft's massive investment in OpenAI, its enthusiastic endorsement of OpenAI's technology, and its relentless promotion of ChatGPT and related models as revolutionary breakthroughs in artificial intelligence, have lent an immense degree of credibility and legitimacy to OpenAI's hype claims, amplifying their message and solidifying the perception that LLMs represent the most promising and transformative path to AI progress, even if that perception is flawed and scientifically unsubstantiated. Microsoft's endorsement, as a tech giant with vast resources and global reach, carries significant weight and influence, shaping investor sentiment, influencing media narratives, and reinforcing the dominant hype cycle in a way that OpenAI, as a relatively smaller startup, could never have achieved on its own. By strategically aligning itself with OpenAI and aggressively promoting their technology, Microsoft has effectively amplified OpenAI's hype machine, inadvertently validating its exaggerated claims and further entrenching the deep learning monoculture within the AI landscape.

This validation effect extends far beyond investor enthusiasm and market hype; it also influences research directions, talent flows, and the overall trajectory of AI development. The overwhelming hype surrounding ChatGPT and the perceived endorsement from Microsoft, a tech behemoth, further incentivize researchers, students, and funding agencies to focus their efforts and resources on large language models and related deep learning approaches, reinforcing the existing monoculture and potentially diverting attention and resources away from alternative AI paradigms that Marcus and other critics argue are more promising and ultimately more robust and beneficial. The message, implicitly or explicitly conveyed by Microsoft's actions, is clear: large language models are the future of AI, and deep learning is the dominant paradigm to pursue, further solidifying the hype and making it even harder for alternative approaches, such as neuro-symbolic AI, to gain traction, funding, and recognition within the mainstream AI community. Microsoft's validation of OpenAI's hype, therefore, while strategically advantageous for Microsoft itself, may inadvertently hinder the long-term progress of artificial intelligence, reinforcing a potentially limiting technological paradigm and discouraging the exploration of more diverse and potentially more fruitful paths towards genuine AI innovation.

Furthermore, Microsoft's aggressive AI push and its "AI arms race" rhetoric have escalated competitive pressures across the tech industry, intensifying the hype cycle and creating a frantic race among tech giants to out-hype, out-market, and out-innovate each other in the quest for AI dominance. Microsoft's strategic moves, particularly its OpenAI partnership and its aggressive integration of ChatGPT technology into Bing, have created a palpable sense of urgency and competitive anxiety among other tech companies, particularly Google, forcing them to accelerate their own AI development and deployment efforts, often at a frenetic pace and with potentially compromised ethical considerations and safety testing. Meta, Amazon, and other tech giants have similarly ramped up their AI initiatives, increased their marketing spending on AI, and joined the "AI arms race" rhetoric, all driven by a fear of being "left behind" in the perceived AI revolution and a desire to maintain market share and investor confidence in the face of Microsoft's aggressive AI offensive.

This intensified AI arms race, fueled in part by Microsoft's competitive moves, further amplifies the hype cycle, creating a self-reinforcing dynamic where each tech company's efforts to out-hype and out-market its competitors only serve to further inflate the overall hype bubble and drive unrealistic expectations about AI capabilities and near-term transformative potential. The pressure to "win" the AI arms race incentivizes companies to prioritize speed and hype over caution and responsible innovation, potentially leading to rushed product launches, compromised safety testing, and a downplaying of ethical concerns, all in a desperate attempt to gain a competitive edge and capture market share in the hyped AI space. This competitive frenzy not only distorts market dynamics and fuels investor exuberance but also potentially undermines the responsible and ethical development of artificial intelligence, creating a climate where hype and market competition overshadow more fundamental considerations of societal benefit, ethical implications, and long-term sustainable progress in the AI field. Microsoft's aggressive AI push, therefore, while strategically effective in driving market competition and accelerating the pace of AI development, also contributes to a more frenetic, hype-driven, and potentially less responsible AI ecosystem overall.

Finally, and perhaps most consequentially, Microsoft's AI hype machine, by contributing to inflated investor expectations and the broader market overvaluation of the AI sector, is inadvertently fueling concerns about an AI investment bubble and increasing the risk of a future market correction or "AI winter" when the hype inevitably deflates and unrealistic promises fail to materialize.

Microsoft's successful rebranding as an "AI-first" company and its aggressive promotion of its OpenAI partnership have significantly boosted investor enthusiasm for Microsoft stock and the broader AI sector, driving up market valuations and creating a climate of irrational exuberance around artificial intelligence. Investors, caught up in the hype narrative and the trillion-dollar dream, are pouring capital into AI companies, particularly those aligned with the deep learning paradigm and those promising to leverage large language models and generative AI technologies, further inflating valuations and creating a potentially unsustainable investment bubble. Microsoft's actions, as a bellwether of the tech industry and a leading voice in the AI hype cycle, contribute significantly to this market dynamic, further solidifying investor confidence in the AI revolution and amplifying the overall hype bubble.

However, as Gary Marcus and other AI skeptics consistently warn, the current level of AI hype and investor enthusiasm is disconnected from the underlying realities of current AI capabilities and limitations. Large language models, despite their impressive statistical fluency and ability to generate human-like text, still suffer from fundamental flaws, including the hallucination problem, the lack of common sense, brittleness, and an inherent opacity that makes them difficult to understand, control, and trust in high-stakes applications. The promise of imminent AGI, often implicitly or explicitly promoted by the AI hype machine and amplified by companies like Microsoft, remains highly speculative and scientifically unsubstantiated, with many leading AI researchers, including Gary Marcus, warning against the unrealistic expectations and potentially misleading narratives surrounding the near-term prospects of sentient machines. Investors, caught up in the hype and driven by FOMO, may be overlooking these fundamental limitations, overvaluing AI companies based on future potential rather than present-day performance, and creating a market environment ripe for a correction when the hyped-up promises inevitably fail to materialize and the limitations of current AI become too glaring to ignore. Microsoft's aggressive AI push, therefore, while strategically astute in the short term for driving market valuation and investor enthusiasm, also contributes to a potentially unstable and unsustainable AI market environment, increasing the risk of a future AI investment bubble and a subsequent period of disillusionment and potential backlash against artificial intelligence when the hype inevitably deflates and the trillion-dollar dream proves to be just that – a dream, and perhaps a dangerously misleading one at that.

Gary Marcus's critique of Microsoft's AI strategy, therefore, boils down to a central and deeply concerning question: is Microsoft, under Satya Nadella's leadership, prioritizing dollars over discernment, market dominance over genuine understanding, and hype-driven deployment over responsible innovation in its aggressive pursuit of artificial intelligence? Marcus argues that while Microsoft's OpenAI partnership and its "AI-first" strategy may be commercially astute and financially rewarding in the short term, they are ultimately built upon a shaky foundation of hype and over-promise, neglecting the fundamental limitations of current AI technology and potentially undermining the long-term health and sustainable progress of the AI field. He questions whether Microsoft, in its rush to capitalize on the AI moment and secure market dominance, is truly prioritizing a responsible and ethically grounded approach to AI development, or if it is primarily driven by a desire to maximize profits and gain a competitive edge, even at the expense of a more nuanced and realistic understanding of AI's true capabilities and potential risks.

Marcus's skepticism extends to the very core of Microsoft's AI strategy, questioning the wisdom of their massive bet on OpenAI and large language models, highlighting the inherent flaws and limitations of this technological paradigm, and cautioning against the over-reliance on hype and the neglect of fundamental research and a more balanced and diversified approach to artificial intelligence. He argues that Microsoft's embrace of OpenAI and LLMs, while seemingly bold and visionary in the context of the current hype cycle, may ultimately prove to be a strategic misstep, locking them into a technological path that is fundamentally limited, prone to hallucinations and other flaws, and unlikely to deliver on the transformative promises being made on its behalf. He suggests that Microsoft, in its eagerness to capitalize on the AI moment and challenge Google's dominance, may be overpaying for hype, investing in a technology that is ultimately over-hyped and under-delivering, and neglecting to explore more promising alternative AI paradigms that may offer a more robust, reliable, and genuinely intelligent path forward.

Furthermore, Marcus highlights the dangers of Microsoft's hype-driven deployment strategy, particularly as exemplified by the Bing AI fiasco, arguing that rushing unproven and still-flawed AI technologies to market in pursuit of market share and hype amplification is not only irresponsible but also potentially self-defeating, leading to public relations disasters, erosion of trust, and ultimately, a backlash against artificial intelligence itself. He cautions against the over-promising and under-delivering that inevitably accompanies hype-driven product launches, emphasizing the importance of managing expectations, prioritizing rigorous testing and validation, and ensuring that AI systems are reliable and trustworthy before deploying them in real-world applications, particularly in high-stakes domains where errors and misjudgments can have serious consequences. Marcus suggests that Microsoft, in its eagerness to capitalize on the ChatGPT wave and out-hype its competitors, may be sacrificing long-term credibility and public trust for short-term market gains, a potentially risky strategy that could ultimately undermine the responsible and sustainable development of artificial intelligence.

And finally, Marcus expresses deep concern about the diminished understanding of artificial intelligence that may result from Microsoft's hype-driven AI push and the broader "AI arms race" mentality that it fuels. He argues that the relentless focus on deployment, market share, and hype amplification, driven by competitive pressures and the pursuit of the trillion-dollar dream, may be diverting attention and resources away from more fundamental research, critical analysis, and a nuanced and realistic assessment of AI's true capabilities, limitations, and societal implications. He suggests that Microsoft, and other tech giants caught up in the AI arms race, may be prioritizing dollars over discernment, market dominance over genuine understanding, and hype-driven narratives over rigorous scientific inquiry, potentially leading to a diminished understanding of AI within the tech industry, the media, and the broader public, hindering a more informed and responsible approach to artificial intelligence development and deployment, and potentially paving the way for a future where hype and misdirection overshadow genuine progress and a more balanced and human-centered vision of artificial intelligence.

In conclusion, Satya Nadella's Microsoft, under his undeniably astute and ambitious leadership, stands as a prime example of the complex and often contradictory dynamics of the AI overdrive, a case study in the seductive power of hype, the allure of the trillion-dollar dream, and the potential for even the most technologically sophisticated companies to be caught up in the swirling vortex of algorithmic enchantment. While Microsoft's AI strategy is undeniably bold, commercially ambitious, and undeniably effective in generating hype and market attention, Gary Marcus's critical perspective serves as a crucial counterpoint, a much-needed voice of reason, realism, and intellectual honesty amidst the deafening roar of the AI hype machine. His critique of Microsoft's "AI arms race" mentality, its hype-driven deployment strategy, and its potential for diminished understanding, underscores the urgent need for a more balanced, nuanced, and responsible approach to artificial intelligence, one that prioritizes genuine progress, ethical considerations, and a clear-eyed assessment of both the promises and the very real perils of this transformative technology, moving beyond the seductive allure of hype and towards a more grounded, human-centered, and more beneficial AI future. Microsoft, in its aggressive pursuit of AI dominance and its masterful deployment of hype, may have become a driving force in the AI revolution, but whether that revolution is ultimately leading us towards a technologically utopian future or down a more precarious and potentially misleading path, remains a crucial and increasingly urgent question, one that demands critical scrutiny, informed public discourse, and a willingness to challenge the dominant narratives, even those emanating from the very heart of the trillion-dollar dream itself.

Chapter 10

The Broader Ecosystem of AI Hype

While OpenAI, Anthropic, and Microsoft, under the charismatic leadership of Altman, Amodei, and Nadella respectively, represent the vanguard and most visible architects of the current AI hype wave, they are far from operating in a vacuum. The AI frenzy of our age is not merely the product of a few companies and individuals, however influential; it is a complex, self-sustaining ecosystem, a sprawling network of interconnected actors, institutions, and economic incentives that collectively fuel the hype machine, amplify its narratives, and propel the trillion-dollar dreams and algorithmic fairy tales into the broader public consciousness. This chapter will delve beyond the "Big Three," expanding our critical lens to examine the broader ecosystem of AI hype, exploring the crucial roles played by tech giants like Google and Meta, the ever-present force of Venture Capital, and the more diffuse but no less significant contributions from consultants, self-proclaimed "AI ethicists," and the media itself, all contributing to the echo chamber of exaggeration and reinforcing the pervasive hype cycle that defines the age of AI overdrive.

Google, a company once synonymous with AI innovation and widely regarded as the undisputed leader in the field, finds itself in a somewhat paradoxical position within the current hype ecosystem. For years, Google, through its DeepMind acquisition and its pioneering work in deep learning, had legitimately earned its reputation as an AI powerhouse, responsible for groundbreaking breakthroughs in areas like image recognition, machine translation, and game-playing AI. AlphaGo's victory over Lee Sedol, a watershed moment in AI history, was a Google DeepMind triumph, a powerful demonstration of the potential of deep learning and a key catalyst in the initial wave of AI enthusiasm. Google's AI research labs consistently produced cutting-edge work, attracting top talent and pushing the boundaries of artificial intelligence in various domains. Their early approach to AI, however, was often characterized by a more research-focused, long-term perspective, less overtly driven by immediate market hype or aggressive product commercialization, perhaps reflecting a confidence born of their established dominance in search and their vast resources for long-term investment.

However, the sudden and explosive emergence of ChatGPT, and OpenAI's masterful orchestration of viral hype, seemingly caught Google somewhat flat-footed, triggering a palpable sense of panic and urgency within the company and prompting a frantic, and arguably rushed, response. Google, once perceived as the undisputed AI leader, found itself suddenly on the defensive, facing a credible challenge to its search dominance and grappling with the perception that it was being "disrupted" by a smaller, nimbler competitor. This sense of competitive anxiety fueled a rushed and somewhat uncharacteristic response from Google, most notably the hastily assembled and publicly flawed launch of "Bard," their own conversational AI chatbot, designed to counter the ChatGPT hype and reclaim their perceived AI leadership. The Bard launch, however, backfired spectacularly, with a disastrous public demo revealing factual inaccuracies and limitations, leading to widespread media criticism and a further erosion of Google's perceived AI dominance, at least in the public eye. The Bard fiasco served as a stark illustration of the dangers of hype-driven product launches and the potential for public relations disasters when rushing unproven technologies to market in a competitive frenzy, a misstep that highlighted the intense pressure Google was under to respond to the ChatGPT challenge and maintain its position in the rapidly evolving AI landscape.

Despite the initial stumble with Bard, Google, a company with vast resources and deep AI expertise, has not remained passive in the AI arms race. They have doubled down on their AI efforts, launching "Gemini," a new large language model positioned as their "most capable and general model yet," explicitly designed to surpass GPT-4 and reclaim their AI leadership. Google's marketing campaign for Gemini has been extensive and aggressive, emphasizing its supposed superiority in various AI benchmarks, its multimodal capabilities, and its potential to power a new generation of AI-powered products and services across Google's vast ecosystem. The Gemini launch represents Google's renewed commitment to AI hype, a strategic shift from a more research-focused approach to a more market-driven and hype-amplifying strategy, mirroring the tactics employed by OpenAI and Microsoft and demonstrating the pervasive influence of the hype cycle in shaping the competitive dynamics of the AI industry. Google, once seemingly above the fray, has now fully embraced the AI arms race, joining the chorus of hype and contributing to the overall frenzy, albeit with a more technically grounded and less overtly hyperbolic tone than some of its competitors.

However, even Google's more technically grounded hype, while perhaps less sensationalist than some, still contributes to the overall AI ecosystem's tendency towards exaggeration and unrealistic expectations. Google, despite the Bard fiasco, continues to leverage its vast platforms and media reach to amplify the AI narrative, promoting its AI capabilities across search, advertising, cloud computing, and a wide range of other products and services, contributing to the pervasive perception of AI as a transformative force poised to revolutionize every aspect of human life. Their marketing materials, blog posts, and public pronouncements consistently emphasize the "revolutionary" nature of AI, the "paradigm shift" it represents, and Google's central role in leading this technological transformation, further solidifying the hype narrative and reinforcing the trillion-dollar dream within the broader public consciousness. Google, therefore, while perhaps initially hesitant to fully embrace the hype cycle, has now fully joined the game, contributing its considerable weight and influence to the overall AI frenzy and further amplifying the hype narratives that Gary Marcus so incisively critiques.

Meta, formerly Facebook, represents another tech giant deeply enmeshed in the AI hype ecosystem, albeit with a slightly different strategic approach and a unique set of motivations. While Google's AI efforts are often framed around search dominance and technological leadership, and Microsoft's around enterprise solutions and cloud computing, Meta's AI strategy is inextricably linked to its ambitious, and arguably still nascent, pivot towards the metaverse. Meta, for years, has been leveraging AI extensively to power its core social media platforms – Facebook, Instagram, WhatsApp – using AI algorithms for content moderation, personalized newsfeeds, targeted advertising, and a vast array of other functionalities essential to its social media business model. Their AI research division is extensive and well-funded, contributing significantly to the advancement of AI in areas like computer vision, natural language processing, and recommendation systems. However, Meta's AI efforts, for much of its history, have been largely invisible to the broader public, primarily focused on internal applications and infrastructure for its social media empire, less overtly participating in the public AI hype cycle compared to companies like Google and OpenAI.

The metaverse pivot, however, has fundamentally reshaped Meta's AI strategy and its participation in the AI hype ecosystem. The metaverse, Meta's ambitious vision of a future dominated by immersive virtual and augmented reality experiences, is explicitly and inextricably linked to artificial intelligence, with AI positioned as the crucial enabling technology for realizing the full potential of the metaverse. Meta's metaverse vision is predicated on the widespread adoption of AI-powered avatars, AI-generated virtual worlds, AI-driven personalized experiences, and AI-augmented social interactions within immersive digital environments. AI, in Meta's metaverse narrative, becomes not just a useful tool but an essential prerequisite, the very foundation upon which the metaverse is built, and the key to unlocking its transformative potential. This strategic convergence of metaverse hype and AI hype has created a powerful new force in the tech landscape, a synergistic narrative that amplifies both the metaverse vision and the AI revolution, and positions Meta as a central player in both domains, attracting investment, media attention, and a renewed sense of technological dynamism to a company that had begun to face increasing skepticism about its long-term growth prospects and its societal impact.

Meta's open-source AI initiatives, particularly its release of LLaMA (Large Language Model Meta AI), further contribute to the AI hype cycle, albeit in a more nuanced and arguably more democratizing way than some of the more overtly commercial hype strategies employed by other tech giants. Meta's decision to open-source LLaMA, a powerful large language model that rivals models like GPT-4 in certain benchmarks, was framed as an effort to "democratize access" to advanced AI technology, empowering researchers, developers, and smaller companies to leverage cutting-edge AI models without being beholden to proprietary or commercially restricted platforms. This open-source approach, while seemingly altruistic and beneficial for the AI research community, also inadvertently fuels the AI hype cycle, further amplifying the buzz surrounding large language models and reinforcing the perception of their transformative potential. The hype surrounding LLaMA, as a powerful open-source alternative to closed-source models, contributes to the overall narrative of AI inevitability and widespread adoption, further solidifying the deep learning monoculture and further solidifying the deep learning monoculture and reinforcing the perception of LLMs as the dominant and inevitable path forward for artificial intelligence. Meta's open-source LLaMA initiative, therefore, while seemingly democratizing access to AI technology, also inadvertently democratizes and amplifies AI hype, contributing to the overall frenzy and potentially obscuring the limitations and risks associated with large language models and the broader deep learning paradigm. It allows Meta to participate in the AI hype cycle, to project an image of AI leadership and innovation, and to contribute to the narrative of AI inevitability, while simultaneously shifting some of the development costs and ethical scrutiny to the broader open-source community, a strategically savvy move that further complicates the already complex dynamics of the AI hype ecosystem.

Meta's broader AI hype strategy, therefore, is multifaceted and strategically nuanced, leveraging both the metaverse vision and open-source initiatives to amplify its message and participate in the AI frenzy. They are actively joining the "AI arms race," investing heavily in AI research and development, and seeking to position themselves as a major player beyond their traditional social media domain, driven by a desire to regain technological leadership, diversify their business beyond social media, and capitalize on the immense market opportunity and investor enthusiasm surrounding artificial intelligence. Meta's marketing and PR efforts increasingly emphasize AI, showcasing their AI research, metaverse vision, and open-source contributions, aiming to counter negative perceptions, attract talent and investment, and regain relevance in a rapidly evolving tech landscape increasingly dominated by AI narratives and hype cycles. Meta, therefore, represents another crucial player in the broader ecosystem of AI hype, contributing its considerable weight and influence to the overall frenzy and further amplifying the hype narratives, albeit with a unique strategic approach that intertwines AI hype with metaverse aspirations and a veneer of open-source democratization.

Beyond the tech giants, Venture Capital (VC) firms play a critical, and often underestimated, role in fueling the AI hype fire, acting as powerful engines of narrative creation, amplifying buzz, and driving the trillion-dollar dream with relentless financial force. VC investment in AI has exploded in recent years, with trillions of dollars pouring into AI startups and AI-focused research, creating a gold rush mentality and a frenzied investment landscape characterized by irrational exuberance and a potentially unsustainable hype bubble. VC firms, by their very nature, are incentivized to generate hype, to amplify buzz, and to create a sense of urgency and inevitability around emerging technologies like AI, particularly in a sector as speculative and attention-grabbing as artificial intelligence. Their business model hinges on identifying and funding companies with the potential for exponential growth, for disrupting entire industries, and for achieving astronomical valuations – the so-called "unicorn" status that signifies a billion-dollar valuation and the promise of even greater future returns. This inherent pressure to identify and cultivate unicorns, combined with the intensely competitive landscape of venture capital, creates a powerful incentive to over-promise, to exaggerate potential, and to actively participate in the hype cycle surrounding emerging technologies like AI.

VC funding models inherently incentivize hype, as VC firms typically operate on a "spray and pray" approach, investing in a large portfolio of startups with the expectation that only a small percentage will become wildly successful "unicorns," generating outsized returns that compensate for the losses from the many startups that inevitably fail. This model necessitates a focus on rapid growth, aggressive market expansion, and the creation of buzz and excitement to attract further investment and drive up valuations quickly. AI startups, particularly those promising to leverage large language models and generative AI to disrupt existing industries and create entirely new markets, are particularly attractive to VCs, as they fit the "unicorn" profile perfectly – high-risk, high-reward ventures with the potential for exponential growth and transformative impact, precisely the kind of companies that VCs are incentivized to identify, fund, and, crucially, hype. The VC funding cycle, therefore, becomes a powerful engine of AI hype, as VC firms actively seek out and amplify the hype surrounding their portfolio companies, exaggerating their potential, downplaying their limitations, and creating a self-fulfilling prophecy of AI dominance and trillion-dollar market opportunities, all in service of generating quick returns and maximizing their financial gains.

VC firms actively participate in amplifying AI hype through various channels, leveraging their media connections, industry influence, and "thought leadership" platforms to promote AI as a revolutionary technology, exaggerate its near-term potential, and create a sense of urgency around AI adoption and investment. VC-authored blog posts, articles, podcasts, and social media pronouncements frequently tout AI as the "biggest investment opportunity of our lifetime," the "next industrial revolution," and the key to unlocking untold wealth and technological progress in the 21st century. They often uncritically repeat tech company narratives, amplify exaggerated claims about AI capabilities, and promote overly optimistic visions of the AI future, further fueling the hype cycle and driving investor enthusiasm for the AI sector. VC firms also host and sponsor industry events, tech conferences, and investor summits, providing platforms for AI startups and tech leaders to showcase their technologies, disseminate hype narratives, and attract further investment, creating a self-reinforcing cycle of hype, investment, and market frenzy. This

VC-driven hype amplification, while undeniably effective in driving investment and fueling the AI gold rush, also contributes to a potentially distorted and unbalanced AI ecosystem, prioritizing hype and short-term market gains over genuine scientific progress, responsible innovation, and a more balanced and realistic assessment of AI's true capabilities and limitations.

The "fear of missing out" (FOMO) cycle within the VC community further exacerbates the AI hype frenzy, creating a competitive environment where VCs are driven by a pervasive anxiety of being "left behind" in the AI revolution, leading to increasingly irrational investment decisions and further inflation of the AI hype bubble. VC firms, acutely aware of the boom-and-bust cycles that characterize the tech industry and the potential for early-mover advantages to accrue to those who identify and invest in disruptive technologies early and aggressively, feel intense pressure to invest in AI startups, even if they have doubts about the technology's near-term viability, long-term potential, or the often-exaggerated hype surrounding it. The fear of missing out on the next Google, the next Facebook, or the next OpenAI, the fear of being sidelined in the AI revolution and missing out on the potential for astronomical returns, drives VCs to compete fiercely to invest in AI companies, often bidding up valuations to unsustainable levels and further fueling the hype and investor exuberance that characterize the current AI landscape. This VC-driven FOMO cycle creates a self-reinforcing dynamic, where each new massive funding round, each new AI "unicorn," and each new hyped AI breakthrough only serves to further amplify the fear of missing out, driving even more investment into the AI sector, further inflating valuations, and solidifying the perception of AI as the ultimate investment opportunity of the 21st century, regardless of the underlying realities of current AI capabilities and the potential risks of an unsustainable hype bubble.

Beyond the tech giants and venture capital, a broader ecosystem of actors and institutions further contributes to the AI hype machine, creating a self-perpetuating echo chamber of exaggeration and unrealistic expectations. AI consultants and self-proclaimed "futurists" play a significant role in amplifying hype, profiting handsomely by selling AI-related services and advice to businesses and organizations eager to embrace the AI revolution and avoid being "left behind." These consultants often exaggerate the capabilities and benefits of AI, promote unrealistic implementation timelines, and sell generic "AI strategies" that lack substance or real-world applicability, capitalizing on the anxieties and FOMO of businesses grappling with the complex and often-confusing world of artificial intelligence. They feed the hype machine by reinforcing exaggerated narratives, promoting technological solutionism, and creating a sense of urgency and inevitability around AI adoption, further fueling the demand for AI-related products, services, and, crucially, consulting expertise, regardless of its actual value or effectiveness. The proliferation of AI consultants and "futurists," therefore, represents another facet of the broader AI hype ecosystem, a self-serving industry that profits directly from the exaggeration and amplification of AI hype, further contributing to the overall frenzy and potentially misdirecting businesses and organizations seeking genuine guidance and responsible AI implementation strategies.

Even the seemingly virtuous domain of "AI ethics" is not entirely immune to the dynamics of the hype ecosystem, with some self-proclaimed "AI ethicists," inadvertently or deliberately, contributing to the hype cycle, albeit in a more nuanced and ethically packaged form. While many AI ethicists genuinely and commendably strive to promote responsible AI development and mitigate potential harms, some, particularly those closely affiliated with tech companies or VC firms, may inadvertently or deliberately contribute to hype by focusing on narrow ethical issues, promoting performative ethics, and ultimately legitimizing the underlying AI technology and its hype-driven development, rather than offering more fundamental critiques or challenging the dominant narratives. Corporate "AI ethics" initiatives, often underfunded, lacking real power, and primarily serving as PR tools, can also function as a form of "ethical washing" for AI hype, providing a veneer of ethical soundness to potentially problematic technologies and allowing companies to project an image of social responsibility while simultaneously continuing to aggressively promote and deploy hyped AI systems, potentially obscuring deeper ethical concerns and hindering more fundamental and critical discussions about the responsible future of artificial intelligence. Even the discourse around "AI ethics," therefore, while seemingly intended to counter hype and promote responsibility, can, in some instances, become co-opted and weaponized as a marketing tool, further complicating the already challenging task of discerning genuine progress from carefully crafted illusions in the age of AI overdrive.

And finally, the media, in its relentless pursuit of clicks, sensationalism, and novelty, often acts as a willing and even enthusiastic amplifier of AI hype, uncritically repeating tech company narratives, exaggerating technological claims, and prioritizing attention-grabbing headlines over in-depth analysis, critical investigation, and balanced perspectives. Mainstream media outlets, from traditional newspapers and television networks to online news platforms and social media channels, often lack in-house expertise in AI, relying heavily on tech company press releases, marketing materials, and soundbites from self-proclaimed "AI experts" who often have vested interests in promoting hype narratives. The media's inherent bias towards novelty, technological breakthrough narratives, and sensationalist stories, combined with the competitive pressures of the 24/7 news cycle and the click-driven economics of online media, creates a fertile ground for AI hype to flourish, often at the expense of balanced reporting, critical investigation, and a more nuanced public understanding of the true capabilities and limitations of current artificial intelligence technology. The media echo chamber, therefore, acts as a powerful amplifier of AI hype, further distorting public perception, influencing investor behavior, and contributing to the overall frenzy surrounding artificial intelligence, often at the expense of informed public discourse, responsible technological development, and a more balanced and realistic assessment of the true potential and very real perils of the AI revolution.

This broader ecosystem of AI hype, encompassing tech giants like Google and Meta, venture capital firms, consultants, some "AI ethicists," and the media itself, collectively creates a self-perpetuating hype cycle, a complex and powerful apparatus that transforms trillion-dollar dreams into perceived technological realities, fuels the AI frenzy, and amplifies the often-misleading narratives surrounding artificial intelligence in the age of overdrive. Dismantling this hype machine, exposing its mechanisms, and challenging its dominant narratives requires a multifaceted and sustained effort, demanding critical thinking, media literacy, and a willingness to question the prevailing assumptions, resist the seductive allure of hype, and seek out more balanced, realistic, and scientifically grounded perspectives, such as the indispensable voice of Gary Marcus, to navigate the complex, often bewildering, and potentially dangerous landscape of artificial intelligence in the 21st century. The Big Three may be the most visible architects of hype, but the broader ecosystem, this sprawling network of interconnected actors and institutions, provides the foundation, the fuel, and the amplification necessary to transform their individual gambits into a full-blown cultural earthquake, reshaping our economy, our media, our social interactions, and our very understanding of what it means to be human in an age increasingly defined, and perhaps dangerously distorted, by the seductive illusions of AI hype.

PART IV

A Path Forward

Chapter 11

The Neuro-Symbolic Bridge

The preceding chapters have meticulously dissected the pervasive and often misleading AI hype machine, exposing its mechanisms, dismantling its fairy tales, and highlighting the fundamental flaws inherent in the dominant deep learning paradigm. We have explored the brittleness, opacity, data dependency, and hallucination problems that plague current AI systems, and we have examined the roles played by various architects of hype – from tech CEOs and venture capitalists to media outlets and even some self-proclaimed "AI ethicists" – in perpetuating unrealistic expectations and driving the trillion-dollar dream. However, critique alone, however insightful and rigorously argued, is insufficient. To truly navigate the age of AI overdrive responsibly and constructively, we must move beyond simply dismantling illusions and actively chart a path forward, a more promising and genuinely beneficial trajectory for artificial intelligence. And it is precisely in this crucial endeavor of constructive vision-building that Gary Marcus's work truly shines, offering not just a critique of what is wrong with current AI, but a compelling and scientifically grounded blueprint for a better AI future, a future built upon the "Neuro-Symbolic Bridge."

Marcus's advocacy for neuro-symbolic AI is not a mere technical preference, not just a knee-jerk reaction against the deep learning monoculture. It is a deeply considered and rigorously argued position, rooted in his decades of expertise in neuroscience, cognitive science, and artificial intelligence, and informed by a profound understanding of both the capabilities and the inherent limitations of different AI paradigms. He recognizes that deep learning, while undeniably achieving remarkable feats in certain narrow domains, is fundamentally ill-equipped to deliver on the promise of truly general, robust, and human-like intelligence, and that a more fundamental shift in approach is necessary to overcome the deep flaws and limitations that plague current AI systems. The Neuro-Symbolic Bridge, in Marcus's vision, is not just a technical fix or an incremental improvement; it is a paradigm shift, a fundamental rethinking of AI architecture and learning mechanisms, a move beyond the statistical mimicry of deep learning and towards a more knowledge-rich, reasoning-capable, and more intelligent form of artificial intelligence, one that draws inspiration from the remarkable complexity and efficiency of the human brain and mind.

The imperative for a new paradigm, for a move beyond the deep learning monoculture, stems directly from the increasingly apparent and intractable limitations of purely data-driven, connectionist approaches to artificial intelligence. The inherent flaws of deep learning, meticulously documented and rigorously analyzed throughout this book, are not merely minor imperfections or temporary setbacks that can be easily overcome with more data, larger models, or incremental algorithmic tweaks. They are fundamental and systemic limitations, deeply ingrained in the very architecture and learning mechanisms of deep neural networks, and reflecting a more profound disconnect between the statistical nature of deep learning and the complex, multifaceted, and knowledge-rich nature of human intelligence. The brittleness and lack of generalization of deep learning models, their vulnerability to adversarial examples and out-of-distribution failure, expose a fundamental lack of robustness and adaptability, highlighting their reliance on superficial statistical correlations rather than genuine understanding of underlying principles and causal relationships. The black box nature of deep learning, its opacity and lack of explainability, raises serious ethical concerns about bias, fairness, accountability, and the trustworthiness of AI systems deployed in critical real-world applications, hindering our ability to debug, improve, and ethically govern these increasingly powerful technologies. The hallucination problem, the disconcerting tendency of large language models to confidently fabricate falsehoods and generate factually incorrect information, reveals a fundamental "truth deficit" in current AI, exposing its inability to discern fact from fiction and its reliance on statistical plausibility over factual accuracy and real-world grounding. And the insatiable data hunger of deep learning, its voracious appetite for massive, meticulously labeled datasets, limits its scalability, practicality, and data efficiency, contrasting sharply with the remarkable data efficiency and generalization abilities of human intelligence and suggesting that data alone, no matter how vast, is insufficient to achieve true understanding, reasoning, and general intelligence.

These limitations, taken together, paint a stark picture of a technological paradigm that, despite its undeniable successes in certain narrow domains, is fundamentally constrained, deeply flawed, and inadequate as the sole foundation for a future of truly intelligent, robust, and beneficial artificial intelligence. The deep learning monoculture, while driving rapid progress in specific applications and generating immense hype and investor enthusiasm, is, in Marcus's assessment, a technological cul-de-sac, a path that, if pursued exclusively and uncritically, will ultimately lead to diminishing returns, disillusionment, and a missed opportunity to explore more promising and genuinely transformative approaches to artificial intelligence. The limitations of deep learning are not simply engineering challenges to be overcome with better algorithms or more computational power; they are paradigm-level limitations, reflecting a fundamental mismatch between the statistical, data-driven nature of deep learning and the knowledge-rich, reasoning-based, and inherently robust nature of human intelligence. Overcoming these limitations, therefore, requires more than just incremental improvements or scaling up existing models; it necessitates a paradigm shift, a fundamental rethinking of AI architecture and learning mechanisms, a move beyond the deep learning monoculture and towards a more holistic, integrated, and scientifically grounded approach to artificial intelligence, an approach that Marcus eloquently articulates and rigorously defends in his vision of the Neuro-Symbolic Bridge.

The Neuro-Symbolic Bridge, as Gary Marcus envisions it, is not a mere technical compromise or a pragmatic blending of two distinct AI paradigms; it is a deliberate and principled synthesis, a carefully engineered fusion of connectionist and symbolic approaches, designed to create a unified framework that transcends the limitations of both individually and unlocks the potential for a truly more intelligent and human-like form of artificial intelligence. It is a recognition that neither neural networks nor symbolic AI, in isolation, can fully capture the complexity and richness of human cognition, and that true AI progress requires a hybrid approach, leveraging the complementary strengths of both paradigms and building a bridge between data-driven learning and knowledge-based reasoning, between statistical fluency and genuine semantic understanding, and between perceptual prowess and abstract thought. The Neuro-Symbolic Bridge is not just about adding symbolic components to neural networks, or vice versa; it is about creating deeply integrated architectures where neural networks and symbolic reasoning mechanisms work in concert, seamlessly exchanging information, mutually reinforcing each other's strengths, and collectively overcoming the limitations that neither paradigm can address on its own. It is a vision of AI synergy, a belief that the whole, in this case, is greater than the sum of its parts, and that by bridging the gap between connectionism and symbolism, we can unlock a new era of artificial intelligence, one that is not just more powerful and capable, but also more robust, reliable, explainable, and ultimately, more beneficial for humanity.

The core idea behind the Neuro-Symbolic Bridge is to strategically allocate cognitive tasks to the AI paradigm best suited to handle them, leveraging the strengths of neural networks for perception and pattern recognition and the strengths of symbolic AI for reasoning, knowledge representation, and abstract thought. Neural networks, with their proven ability to process raw sensory data and learn complex patterns from vast datasets, are ideally suited for handling perceptual tasks, such as image recognition, speech recognition, natural language understanding, and other tasks involving messy, real-world data and complex sensory inputs. Neuro-symbolic architectures leverage neural networks as their perceptual front-end, using them to extract meaningful features, identify patterns, and create rich representations of sensory information, effectively harnessing the data-driven learning capabilities of connectionism for the crucial tasks of perception and pattern recognition. These perceptual representations, generated by neural networks, then serve as input to the symbolic

AI components of the neuro-symbolic system, providing a foundation of grounded, data-driven information upon which symbolic reasoning and knowledge-based inference can be built.

Symbolic AI, with its strengths in reasoning, knowledge representation, and abstract thought, then takes over, leveraging the perceptual representations provided by neural networks to perform higher-level cognitive tasks, such as logical inference, deductive reasoning, common sense reasoning, planning, problem-solving, and knowledge-based decision-making. Symbolic AI modules within neuro-symbolic architectures utilize explicit knowledge representations, such as knowledge graphs, ontologies, and rule-based systems, to represent structured knowledge about the world, to reason logically with that knowledge, and to perform complex inferences and deductions, adding a layer of cognitive depth and reasoning capability that is fundamentally lacking in purely data-driven neural networks. This division of labor, with neural networks handling perception and pattern recognition and symbolic AI handling reasoning and knowledge representation, allows neuro-symbolic systems to leverage the complementary strengths of both paradigms, creating a synergistic hybrid that is more powerful and versatile than either approach in isolation. The Neuro-Symbolic Bridge, therefore, is not just about combining two different types of algorithms; it is about creating a division of cognitive labor, strategically allocating tasks to the AI paradigm best suited to handle them, and building a unified system that harnesses the full potential of both connectionism and symbolism to achieve a more robust, reliable, and genuinely intelligent form of artificial intelligence.

To illustrate the practical potential and architectural possibilities of the Neuro-Symbolic Bridge, it is helpful to consider concrete examples of neuro-symbolic architectures and research projects that are actively exploring and demonstrating the viability of this hybrid approach. Neural-Symbolic Integration Architectures (NeSy), for example, represent a class of neuro-symbolic systems that aim to tightly integrate neural networks with symbolic reasoning engines, creating systems that can seamlessly combine data-driven learning with symbolic inference within a unified computational framework. NeSy architectures typically involve neural networks learning to extract perceptual representations from raw data, and then feeding these representations into symbolic reasoning modules that perform logical inference, deductive reasoning, or other forms of symbolic computation, with the results of symbolic reasoning then potentially feeding back into the neural network for further learning or refinement. These architectures often utilize differentiable reasoning techniques, allowing for end-to-end training of the entire neuro-symbolic system using gradient-based optimization methods, enabling the system to learn both perceptual representations and symbolic reasoning rules from data in a unified and integrated manner. NeSy architectures represent a powerful approach to building neuro-symbolic AI, demonstrating the feasibility of tightly integrating neural and symbolic components and creating systems that can leverage the complementary strengths of both paradigms within a unified computational framework.

Knowledge-Infused Neural Networks represent another prominent class of neuro-symbolic architectures, focusing on incorporating explicit symbolic knowledge, often in the form of knowledge graphs, directly into neural network architectures, enhancing their learning, reasoning, and generalization capabilities. Knowledge-infused neural networks aim to overcome the data dependency and knowledge bottleneck of traditional deep learning models by providing them with access to structured knowledge, allowing them to learn more efficiently, reason more effectively, and generalize more robustly to novel situations. These architectures often involve incorporating knowledge graph embeddings, symbolic rules, or other forms of structured knowledge directly into the neural network's architecture, allowing the network to leverage this explicit knowledge during the learning and inference processes, enhancing its ability to understand relationships between concepts, reason about factual information, and make more knowledge-based decisions. Knowledge-infused neural networks represent a valuable approach to building neuro-symbolic AI, demonstrating the benefits of explicitly incorporating symbolic knowledge into neural network architectures and creating systems that are more knowledge-rich, reasoning-capable, and data-efficient than traditional deep learning models.

Differentiable Reasoning Models represent a further innovative direction within neuro-symbolic AI, focusing on making symbolic reasoning processes differentiable, allowing them to be seamlessly integrated into end-to-end learning systems and trained using gradient-based optimization methods, similar to neural networks. Differentiable reasoning models aim to bridge the gap between symbolic AI and neural networks by creating differentiable approximations of symbolic reasoning operations, such as logical inference, deductive reasoning, and rule-based reasoning, allowing these symbolic operations to be incorporated directly into neural network architectures and trained jointly with perceptual components in an end-to-end learning framework. These models often utilize techniques like neural program synthesis, neural theorem proving, and differentiable logic to create differentiable approximations of symbolic reasoning processes, enabling the creation of hybrid AI systems that can seamlessly combine data-driven learning with symbolic reasoning within a unified and trainable architecture. Differentiable reasoning models represent a cutting-edge approach to neuro-symbolic AI, demonstrating the potential to tightly integrate neural networks and symbolic reasoning mechanisms within a fully differentiable framework and creating systems that can learn both perceptual representations and symbolic reasoning rules directly from data in an end-to-end fashion.

These examples of neuro-symbolic architectures and research projects, while representing just a small fraction of the ongoing work in this rapidly evolving field, serve to illustrate the feasibility, diversity, and immense potential of the Neuro-Symbolic Bridge as a viable and increasingly compelling alternative to the deep learning monoculture. They demonstrate that it is indeed possible to combine the strengths of neural networks and symbolic AI, to create hybrid systems that overcome the limitations of each individually, and to build artificial intelligence that is not just statistically fluent but also possesses genuine understanding, robust reasoning capabilities, and a more human-like form of intelligence. The Neuro-Symbolic Bridge, therefore, is not just a theoretical concept or a distant aspiration; it is a tangible and increasingly well-defined research direction, actively being explored and developed by researchers worldwide, and offering a clear and scientifically grounded pathway towards a more responsible, realistic, and genuinely intelligent future for artificial intelligence, a future that begins with embracing hybrid approaches, moving beyond the limitations of deep learning, and building a bridge between connectionism and symbolism to unlock the full potential of artificial intelligence and realize its true promise for humanity.

Gary Marcus's Neuro-Symbolic Bridge is not just a technical blueprint for building more capable AI systems; it is also a manifesto for a more responsible and human-centered approach to artificial intelligence development, one that prioritizes robustness, reliability, explainability, and ethical considerations, moving beyond the hype-driven pursuit of algorithmic power and towards a more balanced and beneficial integration of AI into human society. Marcus's vision extends beyond the technical details of neuro-symbolic architectures, encompassing a broader set of values, principles, and ethical guidelines that should guide the development and deployment of artificial intelligence in a responsible and human-centered way. He emphasizes the importance of building AI systems that are not just intelligent but also trustworthy, reliable, and aligned with human values, advocating for a shift in focus from narrow performance metrics and benchmark scores to broader considerations of societal impact, ethical implications, and the long-term consequences of AI technology for humanity.

Robustness, in Marcus's vision, is not just a desirable technical feature but a fundamental ethical imperative, particularly for AI systems deployed in safety-critical applications or interacting with humans in complex and unpredictable real-world environments. He argues that AI systems must be demonstrably robust against adversarial attacks, out-of-distribution data, and unexpected environmental changes, ensuring that they operate reliably and predictably even in challenging and unforeseen circumstances.

Robustness is not just about achieving high accuracy on carefully curated benchmark datasets; it is about building AI systems that are resilient, adaptable, and dependable in the face of real-world complexity and uncertainty, minimizing the risk of errors, failures, and unintended consequences that could have serious and even harmful impacts on human lives. Neuro-symbolic AI, with its combination of data-driven learning and knowledge-based reasoning, offers a pathway towards achieving greater robustness, by grounding AI systems in structured knowledge and symbolic representations, making them less susceptible to superficial statistical correlations and more capable of generalizing reliably to novel situations and adapting to unexpected changes in their environment. Robustness, therefore, is not just a technical engineering challenge; it is a fundamental ethical responsibility, a prerequisite for building AI systems that can be safely and reliably deployed in the real world and entrusted with tasks that have significant consequences for human well-being and societal safety.

Explainability and transparency are also central to Marcus's vision of responsible AI, as he argues that AI systems, particularly those deployed in decision-making roles that affect human lives, must be fully explainable and transparent in their reasoning processes, allowing humans to understand why they make particular decisions, to identify and mitigate potential biases, and to ensure accountability and ethical oversight. The black box nature of deep learning, its inherent opacity and lack of interpretability, is, in Marcus's view, a fundamental ethical liability, undermining trust, hindering debugging and improvement, and making it virtually impossible to ensure fairness, accountability, and responsible governance of AI systems. Neuro-symbolic AI, with its integration of symbolic reasoning components and knowledge representations, offers a pathway towards achieving greater explainability and transparency, by making the reasoning processes of AI systems more auditable, interpretable, and understandable to humans. Explainability is not just about satisfying intellectual curiosity or making AI systems more user-friendly; it is a fundamental ethical requirement, a prerequisite for building AI systems that are accountable, trustworthy, and aligned with human values, allowing for meaningful human oversight, ethical scrutiny, and the establishment of clear lines of responsibility when AI systems make errors or cause harm.

Ultimately, Gary Marcus's vision for the Neuro-Symbolic Bridge and a more responsible AI future is a call to action, a challenge to the AI community, the tech industry, and policymakers to move beyond the hype-driven pursuit of algorithmic power and towards a more balanced, realistic, and human-centered approach to artificial intelligence. It is a call to embrace critical thinking, to question dominant narratives, to resist the seductive allure of hype and technological utopianism, and to demand evidence-based progress, ethical rigor, and a commitment to building AI systems that truly serve humanity, augmenting our intellect, enhancing our lives, and contributing to a better world for all. The Neuro-Symbolic Bridge is not just a technical blueprint; it is a roadmap for a more responsible and human-centered AI future, a pathway out of the hype cycle and towards a more sustainable, ethical, and genuinely intelligent trajectory for artificial intelligence, a future that begins with dismantling the illusions of hype and embracing the clear-eyed, scientifically grounded, and profoundly necessary vision championed by Gary Marcus, the pragmatic architect of a better, more human-centered, and more real AI future.

Chapter 12

The Emperor's New Algorithms

The AI revolution, or what is relentlessly presented to us as a revolution, has arrived. It's in our phones, our cars, our homes, our workplaces. It's shaping our news feeds, influencing our purchasing decisions, and even, in some cases, making life-altering judgments about our futures. The age of AI overdrive, as this book has termed it, is characterized by a dizzying pace of technological development, a relentless barrage of hype, and a pervasive sense of both utopian possibility and dystopian anxiety. Trillion-dollar dreams dance with algorithmic fairy tales, as tech companies, venture capitalists, and media outlets compete to capture our attention, shape our perceptions, and ultimately, control the narrative surrounding this transformative technology. But amidst the deafening roar of the hype machine, amidst the breathless pronouncements of imminent technological singularity and the seductive promises of sentient machines, a crucial question lingers: are we truly witnessing a revolution in intelligence, or are we, perhaps more accurately, experiencing a revolution in hype, a sophisticated and technologically amplified reinvention of age-old patterns of over-promising, under-delivering, and ultimately, misdirecting our resources, our attention, and our collective future?

This book has meticulously dissected the AI hype machine, exposing its mechanisms, dismantling its illusions, and highlighting the often-stark contrast between the seductive promises of artificial intelligence and the more complex and nuanced realities of its current capabilities and limitations. We have explored the economic incentives that drive the hype cycle, the cultural narratives that amplify its message, and the key figures – the "architects of hype" – who shape the dominant narratives and fuel the trillion-dollar dreams. We've seen how venture capital fuels the frenzy, how tech companies craft narratives of revolution and inevitability, how media outlets uncritically amplify hype, and how even the discourse around "AI ethics" can, in some instances, become co-opted and weaponized as a marketing tool. And throughout this journey, one voice has remained constant, a beacon of clarity, reason, and scientific rigor amidst the often-turbulent and frequently misleading waters of the AI discourse: Gary Marcus.

Marcus's contribution to the AI debate is multifaceted and profoundly important. He is not merely a critic, content to point out flaws and limitations; he is a constructive force, an active participant in the AI field, and a visionary architect of a better AI future. His work transcends simple debunking, offering not just a critique of what is wrong with current AI, but also a compelling and scientifically grounded vision of what AI could be, a blueprint for a more robust, reliable, and human-centered approach to artificial intelligence. To fully appreciate Marcus's significance, we must understand the core tenets of his critique, the depth of his intellectual engagement, and the long-term implications of his unwavering commitment to scientific truth and intellectual honesty in a field often characterized by hype, hyperbole, and uncritical enthusiasm.

At the heart of Marcus's intervention lies his unwavering commitment to intellectual rigor and evidence-based argumentation. In a landscape often saturated with anecdotal evidence, marketing spin, and speculative pronouncements about the future of AI, Marcus consistently grounds his critiques and his constructive proposals in solid scientific principles, drawing upon his decades of expertise in neuroscience, cognitive science, and computer science. He does not simply assert that deep learning is flawed or that AGI is not imminent; he meticulously demonstrates these points, citing relevant research, providing concrete examples, and employing rigorous logical reasoning to support his claims. His arguments are not based on intuition, gut feeling, or a reactionary resistance to technological progress; they are rooted in a deep understanding of the underlying science, the inherent limitations of current AI paradigms, and the fundamental complexities of human intelligence. This commitment to intellectual rigor and evidence-based analysis is what sets Marcus apart, lending his critiques a weight and credibility that is often lacking in the broader AI discourse. When Marcus speaks, he speaks with the authority of a scientist, a scholar, and an experienced practitioner, demanding that the AI community, the tech industry, and the broader public engage with the evidence, confront the limitations of current AI, and embrace a more realistic and scientifically grounded approach to artificial intelligence. He repeatedly and effectively challenges us to move beyond surface-level assessments of AI capabilities, to delve deeper into the underlying mechanisms, and to critically evaluate the claims being made on behalf of artificial intelligence, not based on marketing hype or technological utopianism, but on rigorous scientific evidence and a clear-eyed understanding of both the potential and the limitations of this transformative technology.

This commitment to intellectual rigor is inextricably linked to Marcus's remarkable ability to communicate complex ideas with exceptional clarity and accessibility. He is a master of translating intricate scientific concepts and nuanced technical arguments into language that is clear, concise, and readily understandable to non-experts, avoiding jargon, technical obscurity, and overly specialized terminology. He employs analogies, metaphors, and relatable everyday examples to illustrate complex points, making his critiques accessible and engaging even for readers with limited prior knowledge of artificial intelligence. His writing is direct, persuasive, and often infused with a wry humor that makes his arguments all the more compelling and memorable. This clarity of communication is not just a stylistic choice; it is a deliberate strategy, recognizing that countering the pervasive and often deliberately obfuscating nature of AI hype requires clear, direct, and widely understandable messaging. By communicating his ideas in a clear and accessible manner, Marcus empowers a broader public to engage critically with AI narratives, to question the hype, and to demand a more responsible and evidence-based approach to artificial intelligence development. He effectively democratizes the AI discourse, breaking down the barriers of technical jargon and allowing a wider audience to participate in the crucial conversations about the future of this transformative technology. He enables informed public debate, not by dumbing down the science, but by elevating the discourse, making complex ideas understandable without sacrificing intellectual rigor or scientific accuracy.

Perhaps most significantly, Marcus is not afraid to challenge the powerful, to speak truth to power, even when it is unpopular or inconvenient. He is a vocal and persistent critic of the dominant narratives in the AI field, directly confronting tech CEOs, influential researchers, and venture capitalists, holding them accountable for exaggerated claims, misleading marketing, and potentially harmful practices. He does not shy away from naming names, from directly critiquing specific companies and individuals, and from challenging the prevailing assumptions and economic incentives that drive the AI hype cycle. This intellectual courage, this unwavering commitment to intellectual honesty, even in the face of intense pressure and criticism, is what makes Marcus such a vital and indispensable voice in the AI discourse. He is not content with polite disagreements or subtle hints; he directly and forcefully exposes the flaws, limitations, and potential dangers of current AI approaches, demanding a more rigorous, responsible, and human-centered approach to artificial intelligence. He is the "skeptic-in-chief," the relentless questioner, the persistent challenger of hype and illusion, and it is precisely this unflinching directness and intellectual courage that makes his voice so crucial in navigating the turbulent waters of the AI revolution. He is not afraid to disrupt the echo chamber, to challenge the status quo, and to advocate for a fundamentally different path forward, even when that path runs counter to the prevailing narratives and the powerful economic forces that drive the AI hype machine.

However, to reduce Marcus to the role of "critic" or "skeptic" is to fundamentally misunderstand the nature of his contribution. He is not merely a naysayer, content to point out flaws and limitations; he is an active builder, a constructive force, and a visionary architect of a better AI future. His critiques are not driven by negativity or Luddism; they are motivated by a deep and abiding commitment to realizing the true potential of artificial intelligence, to building AI systems that are not just statistically impressive but genuinely intelligent, robust, reliable, and beneficial for humanity.

This constructive vision is most clearly articulated in his advocacy for the Neuro-Symbolic Bridge, a hybrid approach to AI that he champions as the most promising path towards overcoming the limitations of deep learning and achieving a more human-like form of artificial intelligence. The Neuro-Symbolic Bridge, as we have explored in detail, is not just a technical alternative to deep learning; it is a fundamental paradigm shift, a rethinking of AI architecture and learning mechanisms, a move towards a more knowledge-rich, reasoning-capable, and more intelligent form of artificial intelligence. It is a vision of AI synergy, a belief that by combining the strengths of neural networks and symbolic AI, we can create systems that are greater than the sum of their parts, overcoming the limitations of each paradigm individually and unlocking a new era of AI innovation, one that is both more powerful and more aligned with human intelligence and human values.

The Neuro-Symbolic Bridge, as envisioned by Marcus, addresses the core limitations of deep learning head-on. By incorporating symbolic reasoning and knowledge representation, neuro-symbolic AI systems can overcome the brittleness and lack of generalization that plague purely data-driven models. They can reason logically about the world, understand causal relationships, and adapt to novel situations with a degree of flexibility and robustness that is currently unattainable with deep learning. The integration of symbolic components also enhances explainability and transparency, making the decision-making processes of AI systems more understandable and auditable, addressing the ethical concerns surrounding the "black box" nature of deep learning. Furthermore, neuro-symbolic AI offers a pathway towards addressing the hallucination problem, by grounding AI systems in structured knowledge and enabling them to verify their claims against real-world facts and logical constraints, moving beyond the statistical mimicry of large language models and towards a more truthful and reliable form of artificial intelligence. And by leveraging explicit knowledge representations, neuro-symbolic AI can potentially achieve greater data efficiency, reducing the reliance on massive datasets and making AI development more sustainable and accessible. The Neuro-Symbolic Bridge, therefore, is not just a technical fix; it is a comprehensive and scientifically grounded approach to building AI that truly understands, reasons, and thinks in a more human-like way, paving the way for a future where AI systems are not just powerful tools, but also trustworthy partners, capable of augmenting human intelligence and collaborating with humans to solve complex problems and address societal challenges in a responsible and beneficial way.

Beyond the technical architecture of neuro-symbolic AI, Marcus's vision encompasses a broader set of values and principles that should guide the development and deployment of artificial intelligence in a responsible and human-centered way. He emphasizes that AI systems must be not just intelligent but also trustworthy, reliable, and designed for the benefit of all people. Robustness is a key principle: building AI systems that are resilient to unexpected inputs, changes in the environment, and deliberate attempts to fool them. This is not just about high accuracy on benchmarks; it's about creating systems that can be safely and reliably deployed in the real world. Explainability and transparency are equally critical, allowing humans to understand why an AI system made a particular decision, increasing trust and enabling accountability. Fairness, ensuring that AI systems do not perpetuate or amplify existing biases, is also paramount. And finally, he stresses the importance of human control, ensuring that humans remain in charge of AI systems and their deployment, preventing unintended consequences and ensuring that AI is used for beneficial purposes.

The question, then, is not whether Marcus's vision is valuable, insightful, or ethically sound – the evidence overwhelmingly demonstrates that it is – but whether it will be realized, whether his ideas will gain sufficient traction, his principles will be widely embraced, and his vision will ultimately shape the trajectory of artificial intelligence. The challenges are, undeniably, immense. The deep learning monoculture remains deeply entrenched, reinforced by billions of dollars in investment, a massive influx of talent, and a pervasive media narrative that continues to amplify hype and downplay limitations. The "AI arms race" continues to escalate, driving competitive pressures and incentivizing companies to prioritize speed and market dominance over responsible innovation and ethical considerations. And the broader ecosystem of hype, encompassing venture capitalists, consultants, and even some "AI ethicists," continues to churn out exaggerated claims and unrealistic promises, further distorting public perception and hindering a more balanced and informed discourse about the future of artificial intelligence. These challenges are substantial, representing powerful forces that resist change and perpetuate the status quo, making the path towards a more responsible and human-centered AI future a difficult and uphill battle. The inertia of the current trajectory is significant, and overcoming it will require a concerted and sustained effort, involving not just technological innovation but also cultural shifts, policy changes, and a fundamental reorientation of priorities within the AI field and the broader tech industry.

However, despite these formidable challenges, there are also reasons for cautious optimism, glimmers of hope that suggest the tide may be, slowly but perceptibly, turning. There is a growing awareness, both within the AI community and in the broader public, of the limitations of current AI, the dangers of unchecked hype, and the urgent need for a more responsible and realistic approach. The media narrative, while still often dominated by hype, is beginning to show signs of shifting, with increasing coverage of AI failures, hallucinations, ethical concerns, and the limitations of deep learning. Journalists are becoming more skeptical, more critical, and more willing to challenge the hype narratives and expose the gap between promise and reality. The public, increasingly exposed to the flaws and limitations of AI systems in their everyday lives, from chatbot miscommunications to self-driving car accidents, is also becoming more wary of AI hype and more demanding of transparency, accountability, and responsible innovation. The viral success of ChatGPT, while initially fueling the AI frenzy, has also inadvertently served to expose the limitations of large language models to a broad audience, revealing their propensity for errors, their lack of common sense, and their inability to consistently distinguish between truth and falsehood. This increased public awareness and skepticism represents a crucial shift, a potential turning point in the AI discourse, creating a more fertile ground for critical voices like Gary Marcus to be heard and heeded, and potentially paving the way for a more balanced and responsible approach to AI development and deployment.

Within the AI research community itself, there are also encouraging signs of a growing recognition of the limitations of the deep learning monoculture and a renewed interest in exploring alternative paradigms, such as neuro-symbolic AI, causal inference, and knowledge-based approaches. Funding agencies, while still heavily invested in deep learning, are beginning to show a greater willingness to support research beyond deep learning, recognizing the need for a more diverse and balanced AI research ecosystem. Researchers, increasingly aware of the brittleness, opacity, and hallucination problems of deep learning, are actively seeking new architectures, learning mechanisms, and hybrid approaches that can overcome these limitations and lead to more robust, reliable, and genuinely intelligent AI systems. The resurgence of interest in neuro-symbolic AI, championed by Gary Marcus and other leading researchers, is particularly promising, suggesting a potential paradigm shift within the AI field, a move away from the dominance of purely statistical methods and towards a more integrated and knowledge-rich approach to artificial intelligence. These trends, while still nascent and far from representing a complete transformation of the AI landscape, suggest that the tide may be turning, that the dominance of the deep learning monoculture may be weakening, and that a more diverse, balanced, and responsible AI future is still within reach, if we choose to embrace it.

The path towards realizing Marcus's vision, towards building a better AI future, is not a singular, monolithic endeavor; it is a multifaceted and collaborative effort, requiring a concerted and sustained commitment from all stakeholders in the AI ecosystem: researchers, developers, tech companies, policymakers, journalists, and the public at large. It requires a fundamental shift in mindset, a move away from the hype-driven pursuit of algorithmic power and towards a more responsible, realistic, and human-centered approach to artificial intelligence, one that prioritizes genuine understanding, robust reliability, ethical considerations, and long-term societal benefit over short-term market gains and technological utopianism. This shift requires a series of concrete actions, a multi-pronged strategy that addresses the technical, ethical, societal, and cultural dimensions of the AI revolution.

First and foremost, we must reclaim the AI narrative, shifting the public discourse away from hype and towards a more balanced, realistic, and evidence-based understanding of AI capabilities, limitations, and societal implications. This requires a concerted effort from journalists, educators, and public intellectuals to communicate complex AI concepts clearly and accessibly, to challenge hype narratives, to expose misleading claims, and to promote a more informed and critical public understanding of artificial intelligence. Journalists must move beyond sensationalism and clickbait headlines, embracing responsible reporting practices, seeking out diverse perspectives, and prioritizing in-depth analysis and critical investigation over uncritically repeating tech company talking points. Educators must incorporate AI literacy and critical thinking skills into curricula at all levels, empowering students to understand the underlying principles of AI, to evaluate AI claims critically, and to engage thoughtfully with the ethical and societal implications of this transformative technology. And public intellectuals, scientists, and ethicists must actively participate in the public discourse, challenging hype, amplifying critical voices, and promoting a more balanced and nuanced understanding of AI's potential and its limitations. Reclaiming the AI narrative is a crucial first step towards building a more responsible AI future, fostering a more informed public, and creating a more fertile ground for evidence-based policy-making and responsible innovation. This means actively promoting accurate information, dispelling myths, and fostering a culture of healthy skepticism around AI claims.

Secondly, we must actively support responsible AI research, prioritizing funding, recognition, and career opportunities for researchers working on neuro-symbolic AI, causal inference, knowledge-based systems, and other alternative approaches that promise to overcome the limitations of the deep learning monoculture. Funding agencies, both government and private, must shift their investment priorities, allocating a greater proportion of resources to research that addresses the fundamental challenges of AI, such as common sense reasoning, explainability, robustness, and ethical alignment, rather than simply scaling up existing deep learning models. Academic institutions must foster interdisciplinary collaboration, encouraging researchers from neuroscience, cognitive science, philosophy, and ethics to work alongside computer scientists and engineers, creating a more holistic and human-centered approach to AI research and development. And the tech industry must invest in long-term, fundamental research, moving beyond the short-term focus on product development and market share, and recognizing that genuine AI progress requires a commitment to scientific inquiry, exploration of alternative paradigms, and a willingness to challenge the dominant deep learning narrative. Supporting responsible AI research is not just about funding specific projects; it is about fostering a more diverse, balanced, and intellectually vibrant AI research ecosystem, one that is driven by scientific curiosity, ethical considerations, and a long-term vision of building AI that truly benefits humanity. This includes actively seeking out and supporting researchers who are pursuing approaches that go beyond the current dominant paradigms.

Thirdly, we must demand transparency and accountability from tech companies and policymakers, holding them responsible for the societal impact of AI and advocating for policies that promote responsible innovation, ethical oversight, and meaningful human control over artificial intelligence. Tech companies must move beyond superficial "ethics washing" and performative ethics, embracing genuine transparency in their AI development practices, disclosing the limitations of their systems, the sources of their training data, and the potential biases embedded within their algorithms. They must implement rigorous testing and validation procedures, ensuring that AI systems are robust, reliable, and safe before deploying them in real-world applications, particularly in high-stakes domains where errors and misjudgments can have serious consequences. And they must establish clear lines of responsibility for AI decision-making, ensuring that humans remain accountable for the actions of AI systems and that there are clear mechanisms for redress and remedy when AI systems cause harm. This requires a cultural shift within the tech industry, moving away from a focus on speed and profit maximization towards a more ethical and socially responsible approach to technology development.

Policymakers, in turn, must develop regulations and guidelines for AI development and deployment, focusing on transparency, accountability, and human oversight, ensuring that AI technology is developed and used in a way that aligns with fundamental human values and promotes the public good. Independent oversight bodies, with the expertise and authority to monitor AI systems, investigate potential harms, and enforce ethical standards, are crucial for ensuring that AI is governed responsibly and that its societal impact is carefully considered and managed. This includes developing clear legal frameworks for addressing AI-related harms, establishing standards for AI safety and reliability, and promoting international cooperation on AI governance. Policymakers must also address the potential economic and social consequences of AI-driven automation, ensuring that the benefits of AI are shared broadly and that workers are not unfairly displaced or disadvantaged by technological advancements.

The public, as informed citizens and consumers, must demand transparency and accountability from both tech companies and policymakers, holding them to a high standard of ethical conduct and advocating for policies that protect human rights, promote opportunity, and ensure that AI is used for the benefit of all, not just a privileged few. This requires becoming informed consumers of AI technology, understanding its capabilities and limitations, and questioning the hype and exaggerated claims that often surround it. It also requires actively participating in public discussions and debates about AI, supporting organizations and initiatives that advocate for responsible AI, and holding elected officials accountable for their policies and decisions related to artificial intelligence. An engaged and informed public is essential for ensuring that AI is developed and deployed in a way that reflects democratic values and serves the common good.

Finally, and perhaps most fundamentally, we must embrace a human-centered approach to AI development, prioritizing the design and deployment of AI systems that augment human capabilities, enhance human lives, and contribute to a more just and flourishing world for all. AI should be seen not as a replacement for human intelligence or human labor, but as a powerful tool that can empower individuals, enhance creativity, and address societal challenges in new and innovative ways. Human-AI collaboration, where AI systems work alongside humans, leveraging their complementary strengths and skills, should be the guiding principle for AI design and implementation, creating systems that are not just intelligent but also intuitive, user-friendly, and aligned with human needs and values. This requires designing AI systems that are not just technically proficient but also ethically sound, taking into account the potential impact of AI on human autonomy, dignity, and well-being. It means ensuring that AI systems are developed and used in a way that promotes opportunity, access, and fairness, preventing them from perpetuating or amplifying existing societal biases and inequalities.

The future of artificial intelligence is not predetermined; it is a future we are actively creating, a future that will be shaped by our choices, our values, and our willingness to confront the hype, embrace critical thinking, and demand a more responsible, realistic, and human-centered approach to this transformative technology. Gary Marcus, through his unwavering commitment to scientific truth, his intellectual courage, and his constructive vision for a better AI future, has provided us with a roadmap, a blueprint, and a powerful call to action. He has shown us the dangers of unchecked hype, the limitations of current AI approaches, and the urgent need for a paradigm shift towards a more robust, reliable, and ethically grounded form of artificial intelligence. He has offered us the Neuro-Symbolic Bridge, a concrete and scientifically sound alternative to the deep learning monoculture, and a vision of AI that is not just powerful but also understandable, trustworthy, and aligned with human values.

It is now up to us to heed his warnings, to embrace his vision, and to collectively build a future where artificial intelligence truly serves humanity, guided by reason, grounded in ethics, and dedicated to the betterment of all. The age of AI overdrive presents us with both immense opportunities and profound challenges. The path we choose will determine whether this technological revolution leads us towards a brighter and more human-centered future, or down a more precarious and potentially dystopian path. The choice, ultimately, is ours. Let us choose wisely. Let us choose the path of responsible innovation, of genuine understanding, and of a future where artificial intelligence truly serves humanity, informed by the clear and crucial insights of Gary Marcus. The time for complacency and passive acceptance of hype is over. The time for action, for critical engagement, and for demanding a better AI future is now. We must move beyond the simplistic narratives, the trillion-dollar dreams, and the algorithmic fairy tales, and embrace a more nuanced, rigorous, and human-centered approach to artificial intelligence. The future is not something that happens to us; it is something we create. Let us create an AI future worthy of human intelligence, human values, and human aspirations.

Acknowledgements

Big thanks to Gary Marcus for being a constant source of inspiration. Your boldness in challenging the AI hype is what sparked this whole project. You're an absolute legend.

Thanks to all the researchers and engineers whose work laid the foundation for today's advancements in artificial intelligence. Without your innovations, insights, and tireless contributions, AI wouldn't be anywhere near where it is today, and this conversation wouldn't be happening.

To my friends and family who endured endless discussions about the potential and the limitations of AI while I wrote this: thank you for tolerating my obsession and keeping me grounded.

And finally, a special thanks to the Paint.NET team for providing the excellent and accessible image editing software that made designing the cover a breeze.

Cover photo of Gary Marcus by Athena Vouloumanos, sourced from Wikimedia Commons

https://commons.wikimedia.org/wiki/File:Gary_Marcus.JPG. Used under the Creative Commons Attribution 4.0 International license.

www.ingramcontent.com/pod-product-compliance
Lightning Source LLC
LaVergne TN
LVHW051326050326
832903LV00031B/3395